For Mrs. Webb Everett

With sincere good wishes

David Alexander

May, 1966

A Sound of Horses

"...to hear a sound of chariots, and a sound of horses, even the sound of a great host ..."—II KINGS 7:6

THE WORLD OF RACING / FROM ECLIPSE TO KELSO

THE BOBBS-MERRILL COMPANY, INC.

A Sound of Horses

DAVID ALEXANDER

A Subsidiary of Howard W. Sams & Co., Inc., Publishers · Indianapolis · Kansas City · New York

The Challenge by Faye Moore, reproduced on the jacket, is one of 30 paintings by the artist in the permanent collection of the Detroit Race Course and is used with their permission.

This book is dedicated to a horse.
His name is Kelso,
and he's the greatest champion
the turf has ever known.

Contents

List of Illustrations

Foreword: The Morning Line

The Morning Line means the probable odds posted against entrants in the afternoon's races. In England this is called The Forecast, which may be a more felicitous term, since it connotes a kind of foreword to coming events.

This is a book about horse racing.

Horse racing is a peculiar institution and a gracious, exciting way of life. It is also a state of mind, like Greenwich Village, Christmas, and schizophrenia.

Fifty million Americans go to a hundred racetracks in twenty-seven different states every year and bet three and a half billion dollars on the horses. Horse racing, by actual turnstile count, is far and away the most popular spectator sport the world has ever known, yet its public image remains a rather unpleasant one. It is the image of the shifty character in a checkered suit chewing a fat cigar and talking out of the side of his mouth, convict style. This image persists despite the fact that the most devoted patrons of the sport in the United States include a former Secretary of the Treasury, a former Ambassador to the Court of St. James's, the owner of a large publishing empire, and the head of a great cultural foundation.

Racing is a little bit of everything, because it is a microcosm, a world in miniature, with good people and bad people, heroes and villains, great sportsmen and petty thieves. It is a world as supercharged with emotion as a melodrama by Dion Boucicault, filled with dizzying successes and dismal failures. The world of racing has all the components of the greater world except one. It is never, under any circumstances, a world of boredom.

It is a world that appeals to the most diverse human beings.

Not too long ago that pillar of respectability, wealth and conservatism, a gentleman, scholar and patron of the arts named Joseph E. Widener, owned the Hialeah racetrack in Florida. Up the road a piece was another racetrack called Tropical Park, which was owned and operated by Big Bill Dwyer, a bootlegger and henchman of Owney Madden, New York's boss mobster.

The most successful racetrack in the history of the world is Aqueduct and its proprietors never make a penny. Although Aqueduct and the other courses of the New York Racing Association contribute upward of seventy million dollars in taxes to the State of New York annually, they are operated on a nonprofit basis by a group of sportsmen, all members of the Jockey Club, who turn every cent of the tracks' net earnings into maintenance and improvement of their properties and into purses for horsemen.

At its foundation level, racing is supported entirely by immensely wealthy and socially prominent people, many of whom have led the list of money-winning owners several times and almost always have suffered staggering losses on their operations. On the other hand, a couple of penniless cowboys named Rex Ellsworth and Meshach Tenney decided to go into the racing business thirty years ago and to treat thoroughbreds in the same way they treated cow ponies, mules and other farm animals. Today they frequently win as much as a million in a year with their horses and tithe 10 per cent of their earnings to the Mormon Church, which both serve as missionaries.

It is said that it takes a million-dollar investment to win a $125,000 race—the Kentucky Derby. It usually does. John Galbreath paid two million dollars for the stallion Swaps who sired his 1963 Kentucky Derby winner Chateaugay.

However, back in the 1920s, an illiterate Oklahoma Indian named Hoots owned a cheap, nondescript thoroughbred mare, Useeit, and raced her at the leaky-roof half-milers of the West. On his deathbed the Indian dreamed Useeit produced a foal who won the Kentucky Derby. In his last delirium he made his wife Rosa promise to breed the mare to Black Toney, the most famous stallion in Kentucky. Useeit was mated with Black Toney and her foal, Black Gold, won the Kentucky Derby of 1924.

More recently Jack Price, a manufacturer of machinery in Cleveland, Ohio, became a turfman when he took an unfashionable mare named Joppy in payment of a three-hundred-dollar debt. Joppy was bred to an equally unfashionable Maryland stallion named Saggy and produced a foal named Carry Back, who not only won the Derby but went on to become one of the five horses who have won a million dollars on the racetracks.

On the other side of the coin we have the yearling sales at Saratoga in 1929, which came two months before the Wall Street

Crash. A young horse to be named New Broom brought what was then the all-time record price of seventy-five thousand dollars, but the only thing he swept clean was his owner. In three years of racing he never won and was placed only twice in the cheapest races, winning the magnificent sum of two hundred dollars during his entire turf career. They despaired of him even as a stud prospect when he was four years old and he eventually became the most expensive polo pony in the world. At the same horse auctions, a yearling to be named Broadway Limited was bid in for sixty-five thousand dollars, the second highest price paid for a young colt up to that time. As a three-year-old he dropped dead while running eleventh in a race in Chicago and that was about as close as he had ever been to the money.

Organized racing as we know it today was begun by a gentleman with a Mary Pickford hair-do who is usually pictured in the midst of a pack of poodles with tresses as curly as his own. He was Charles Stuart—occupation: king; avocation: jockey. Charles II managed to import an unrecorded number of Arab mares to England, even though the men who sold them risked decapitation, since it was a capital offense to export this *Kohlani* breed from Arab countries at the time. These horses, now known as the Royal Mares, formed one of the important sources from which the thoroughbred race horse of today finally developed. Charles II was such an enthusiastic horseman that he forced all his able-bodied courtiers, even the ladies, to become jockeys and ride against him in the contests he staged over Newmarket Heath, the first organized race meetings in the history of the world. Newmarket is still inhabited by men who devote themselves entirely to breeding, training and racing horses. They live out their lives in the brick lodges of the great heath and prefer the smell of horses in the adjoining stables to the fragrance of the rosebushes that bloom beside their doorways.

Most of them piously believe that King Canute himself bred the first English race horses on the exact spot where the Epsom Derby winner Psidium now stands at stud in Newmarket's Cheveley Park.

The entire history of horse racing is tinged with fascinating irony. The name of the sport's greatest hero is completely unknown, for instance. He was stud groom for a Yorkshire squire and horse breeder named John Hutton in the eighteenth century. If it hadn't been for this anonymous groom, there might well have been no line of horses called thoroughbred.

In 1732 one of Hutton's mares, known delightfully as "Sister to Old Country Wench," gave birth to a foal by the stallion Bartlett's Childers. The chestnut colt was so undersized and scrawny that the Yorkshire farmer wished to destroy it. The groom loved the little animal and pleaded for its life. Hutton relented and named the colt Squirt, for obvious reasons. Squirt later sired another small horse called Marske, who found his way into the great Cranbourne Lodge Stud of the Duke of Cumberland, the third son of England's second George.

During a total eclipse of the sun on All Fools' Day of 1764 Cumberland's mare Spiletta, who carried the blood of desert Arabians in her veins, produced a foal by Marske who was named Eclipse because of the natural phenomenon that was occurring at the time of his birth. Eclipse is the direct forebear of 90 per cent of the race horses on earth today.

An irony of racing in America is that it entered its period of greatest expansion in the 1930s at the depth of the Great Depression when all other businesses were going bankrupt.

There seems to be no doubt that aesthetic as well as practical motives were involved in the centuries of experimentation that finally produced the thoroughbred. Man had been tampering with natural processes for millennia before he split the atom.

5

In the case of the thoroughbred his tampering achieved a creature of surpassing grace, perfect balance and elegant form who also served the practical purpose of running faster over a racetrack than any other breed of horse. A whole school of sporting art developed around the thoroughbred, and modern painters of the stature of Dufy, Toulouse-Lautrec and Degas have found the racetrack an inexhaustible source of inspiration.

Apologists for the thoroughbred are fond of pointing out that he has improved the breed of work horses, cavalry mounts and mules, which is true, but of little importance. The thoroughbred is a perfect animal because he does exactly what he is supposed to do: he runs faster than any other horse. And because he does this, virtually the entire educational system of California is supported by taxes on racing, and the General Fund of New York's State Treasury gets as much from the tracks as it does from taxes on all state and national banks, trust companies and savings and loan associations combined.

Many dramatic events completely unrelated to whip-lashing finishes in great classics have occurred on racetracks. In 1913 a militant suffragette named Emily Davison threw herself beneath the hoofs of Amner, a horse owned by King George V, as the field thundered into the stretch in the Epsom Derby. Apparently she reasoned that this spectacular form of suicide would attract attention to the cause of Rights for Women.

Pancho Villa and his bandits used to cut their way through the lines of Mexican Army troops who were chasing them, and attend the races at the Juarez track. The outlaw and his merry men would spend a pleasant afternoon drinking American whiskey and betting the horses, then exit, shooting.

A Rhode Island governor named Robert Quinn completely wrecked what seemed to be a brilliant political future when he closed the Narragansett Park racetrack with bayoneted militia in 1937 because of a quarrel with the track's owner, a gaudy promoter named Walter O'Hara. There were stories at the time to the effect that Democratic boss Jim Farley was grooming Quinn as the vice-presidential nominee in 1944 and had warned him to forget his vendetta with the racetrack. Quinn refused. He was a forgotten man by the time of the 1944 convention which nominated Harry Truman for Vice-President of the United States.

During the German occupation of Paris in World War II, the Nazis placed anti-aircraft guns in the infield of the Longchamp racecourse in the Bois de Boulogne. One day, while races were being run, there was a British air raid, 170 spectators were killed and hundreds of others were injured. It took two hours to remove the dead and injured. Then racing was resumed.

The attitude toward racing in different countries of the world is a provocative field for study.

Racing is threaded into the warp and woof of English life, like the old school tie and afternoon tea.

In France, especially at Chantilly, where horses virtually race over the drawbridge of a baroque château, racing is more of an art form than a sport.

In Russia all race horses have the same owner—the State—and thoroughbreds are instruments of propaganda, like sputniks. The main stimulus for breeding thoroughbreds in the Soviet Union seems to be the possibility that a Russian horse can humble American, English, Irish, French, Italian, South American and other capitalist thoroughbreds in the annual Washington, D. C., International decided at the Laurel racetrack. No Russian had taken the event through 1965.

During World War II all the racetracks in Japan were razed and the steel girders of the stands were melted down and fashioned into bullets. Priceless race horses and breeding stock, tracing back to Matchem, Herod, and Eclipse, were butchered and canned as meat rations for the military.

At the El Comandante course in Puerto Rico racing is a dramatic performance staged by grandstand customers that far overshadows the events on the track. There are certain rigid and expected patterns of behavior from losers and winners that the crowd watches with a critical eye and applauds or hisses according to its evaluation of the performers' adherence to tradition.

A Micawberish gambler named E. Phocion Howard used to say that "All horse players die broke." This maxim is generally regarded as one of the eternal verities of racing. However, a five-dollar-a-day bricklayer namer Chicago O'Brien laid aside his trowel and did nothing but bet horses for the next thirty years. He was worth a million dollars when he died.

Despite this inspiring success story, there are so many compulsive and unfortunate horse bettors that they have formed an organization called Gamblers Anonymous to shake the monkey off their backs through the use of group therapy similar to that of Alcoholics Anonymous.

Horses are as varied in their natures as the people who own, train, groom, ride and bet on them.

The great gelding Exterminator used to bow politely to the crowds in recognition of the applause his winning performances received. He ran in the days of the tape barrier and when Starter Mars Cassidy had a bad actor at the post, he placed Exterminator next to him, because the bony gelding would lean against the fractious horse and hold him still. "Exterminator was the best assistant starter I ever had," Cassidy said.

In 1963 a zany horse named No Robbery showed the greatest speed potential of any thoroughbred since Man o' War, but he was a wild, free spirit who liked to win races running sideways. His running style was much like that of a crazy kid who pedals a bicycle downhill and keeps his hands off the handlebars. He would cavort from rail to rail, as if he were doing an uninhibited bacchanalian dance. He kicked up his heels for the sheer hell of it so often that he was constantly bucking his shins and had to be retired.

Harry Warner, the movie producer and California booster, had an unbounded admiration for a horse of his named Pageboy, although his thoroughbred's talents as a stakes performer were limited. Pageboy was loved by his owner solely because he preferred California oranges to heavy oats.

The great champion Kelso suffers frequent feelings of insecurity despite the affection his owner lavishes on him and the constant attentions of his trainer, groom, and exercise boy. He can be comforted in one way only when he is apprehensive. They feed him a chocolate sundae and he is reassured.

Jaipur, the three-year-old champion of 1962, was a superb runner and an affectionate horse so long as he was fat as a butterball. When they put him on a diet, he kicked down fences, bit his trainer and sulked in his races, and was finally sent to stud where he didn't have to count calories.

There is another axiom of racing that states "All men are equal on and under the turf." This seems to be basically true, despite the fence that divides the clubhouse from the grandstand.

The Broadway gangster Arnold Rothstein, whose murder is still a mystery, fixed a World Series and several championship fights, they say, but it is doubtful that he ever fixed a horse race or even tried to fix one. Rothstein, apparently, had one redeeming feature: he loved horses. He raced a string under the name of the Redstone Stable with no success whatsoever, and the bookies regarded him as one of the unluckiest bettors at the track. This odd quirk of character which made a horse lover out of an otherwise completely despicable human being was noted and studied by such men as August Belmont, the most formidable and respected turf figure of his time, and Herbert Bayard Swope, the brilliant journalist who was said to edit the New York *World* from Belmont Park. When pressure of public opinion finally forced Belmont to rule that Rothstein's presence at the track was in conflict with the best interests of the turf, he said, "I hated to do it. Horses were the only good thing in Rothstein's life."

The migratory gypsies of the turf, the smaller owners and trainers and jockeys and stablemen and camp followers who trail the horses from place to place as the seasons change, live entirely in a world of their own that has almost no tangible connection with any other world. They seldom are in one place long enough to establish legal residence and therefore hardly ever vote in any election.

The future to them is next Saturday when their "Big Horse" goes to the post. The past is the year that Man o' War won the Belmont Stakes. When they wish to check the economic state of the country, they consult the racing charts on the sports pages of their newspapers, not the stock-market reports on the financial pages. They are completely insular in character and their island is bounded by a paddock fence.

There was an incident at the Agua Caliente track, just over the Mexican border, on Sunday, December 7, 1941, that may serve as a case in point.

A horseman was looking over the day's entries. A wildly excited man rushed up to him and screamed, "The Japs are bombing Pearl Harbor! I just heard it on the radio!"

The horseman did not raise his eyes from the program he was scanning. "Oh, yeah?" he said. "Whaddya like in the first race?"

1

The Duke Held High the Lanthorn

Man has always suspected that such natural phenomena as bright new stars, thunderstorms and earthquakes portend great events. In eighteenth century England there was an eclipse of the sun . . .

At high noon of All Fools' Day in the year 1764 England was as tar black as it had been at midnight, for there was a total eclipse of the sun, and superstitious farmfolk knelt on hilltops shouting prayers as they waited the Coming and the Judgment. The Royal Duke was a beefy fellow with a fleshy nose that the port in his decanter had tinted royal purple to befit his station. He stood near a stone barn in the brood-mare paddock and held the lantern high, and his shadow was a black giant painted on the stable wall. His Hanoverian nose twitched and snorting sounds came out of it as he breathed the acid reek of manure and the musty smell of stored hay and the warm, sharp scent of the animals that were stirring and murmuring in the midday darkness of their box stalls.

Now there were wild, tremendous sounds of a great beast floundering, and insane, whinnying screams, and the piping squeal of a thing that had just been given life. If the praying people on the surrounding hills heard the bedlam near the barn, they must have thought the devil and not the Lord had come and was rendering judgment on the damned.

The mare, having given birth, stumbled to her feet, her suddenly deflated belly sagging like an empty sack, and dripping. In the lantern light her eyes were diamond bright with fear and her bay coat foamed with curdled sweat as she lurched toward the quivering creature that had been inside her body. The foal, too, had scrambled upright, although its eyes were still blinded by unopened lids. The spindly legs on which it teetered sprawled abruptly and it would have fallen if the stud groom had not grabbed it while the stableboy restrained the lunging mare, who was intent upon reaching this bloodstained thing that had issued from her womb.

From the dark barns the other horses set up a clamor of neighing and kicking, but they were drowned out by the voice of the Royal Duke, whose booming laughter shook his bloated frame and made the lantern tremble in his hand as the shadows became cavorting dervishes upon the walls and haylofts.

"Now here's a rum and sickly varmint for ye, men!" the Duke roared.

The hip-booted and leather-vested stud groom held the dwarfish foal in bare and heavy-muscled arms. "At least the mare threw a colt, yer Highness," he said. "And he's got the blood of the Darley and the Godolphin in him."

The Duke was a little drunk. He usually was, these days. Lighting his way with the lantern, he staggered off, still hooting with laughter. "A colt, ye call it!" he bellowed to the stud groom. "Then name him Eclipse after this confounded blasphemy the devil has brought down on us. Name him Eclipse and send him back to that clod Hutton and tell him to feed the runt to Harry Harpur's staghounds!"

There was another All Fools' Day two hundred years later in 1964, but now the April sun spread yellow butter on the state capitol in Albany, New York. The sober-seeming State Assemblyman did not roar with laughter as the bibulous Royal Duke had done two centuries before, but he permitted himself a smug, discreet smile of triumph. He had managed to force an appropriation through the legislature that would authorize a large sum to be drawn from the state's general fund to mend a highway in a New York town.

The events in the paddock of Cranbourne Chase, England, in 1764 and those in the state capitol of Albany, New York, in 1964 may seem to have little or no relation. They had a close connection in point of fact, although it is probable the Assemblyman who was gloating quietly did not perceive it. In the curious concatenation of occurrences that we call history, the colt born in the paddock in the eighteenth century was responsible for the repairs made to the highway in New York in the twentieth century.

On April 1, 1964, there were roughly forty thousand thoroughbred race horses in training in the United States. Thirty-six thousand of them were direct descendants in the male line of the puny foal born to darkness at noon in England in 1764. About twenty-four hundred others descended directly from an eighteenth century stallion named Matchem. The other sixteen hundred stemmed from King Herod, who was bred by the same Royal Duke who called his scrawny All Fools' Day foal a "varmint" and named him Eclipse. The number of horses in training in the United States that trace back to Matchem and King Herod, some four thousand in all, are barely sufficient for staging racing in one of the twenty-seven states where the sport is operated. There would simply be no flat racing as we know it today in America and throughout the world if the colt named Eclipse had not arrived on earth, or if the Royal Duke had carried out his threat to feed the runt to Sir Harry Harpur's staghounds, for the line of thoroughbreds would almost certainly have died out.

And it is the tax on thoroughbred racing that supplies much of the money for building and maintaining the highways of New York and enables Assemblymen like the sober-seeming statesman in question to obtain funds for mending roads and accomplishing other civic enterprises in their home towns, which is their way of mending something else—their political fences.

The Assemblyman and the Royal Duke represent the polar extremes of the peculiar institution called horse racing. The Assemblyman symbolizes all the worst and most dangerous aspects of the sport. The Duke stands for all that is good and fine and decent about the business of racing thoroughbreds. It is very odd that this should be so, for the Assemblyman is ridiculously miscast in the role of villain and the Royal Duke is a dubious hero indeed.

Our Assemblyman is a composite, of course, representative of the thousands of state legislators who control horse racing in all the states where it is legal. In every respect save one he must seem a meek and pallid villain, yet he controls the two hundred million tax dollars that annually tinkle into the tills of twenty-seven states as the proceeds of horse racing. It is this that makes him become a ravening spoiler insanely intent upon destroying the goose—or horse—that lays the golden eggs.

It is our Assemblyman and a thousand legislators like him throughout the country who hold absolute, dictatorial powers of life and death over horse racing and who seem to be milking it dry.

That is why a great many intelligent people honestly believe the sport was better when it was illegal and was controlled by horsemen instead of politicians.

It is logical to hold racing in New York, for instance, from the middle of April until the last of October. By fiat of the state legislature, racing is now held from the middle of March, when gales blow sleet-sharp rain over the course, to the middle of December, when the decorative swans in Aqueduct's infield lakes are skating on ice instead of floating on water. It is politicians who have forced a little track called Charles Town to operate in winter when blizzards howl through the West Virginia mountains in which it is located. It is often very cold during April at the Bowie track in Maryland, but legislative edict compels the course to run in February when it is even colder and the racing strip is furred by snowdrifts.

There are only 365 calendar days in a year, but there are more than four thousand racing days from one January to the next in the United States alone. Horses so often suffer sudden and complete breakdowns from too much racing that the premiums of insurance policies for thoroughbreds have skyrocketed beyond all reason in recent years. A horse may be a champion potentially worth a million in the stud when he goes to the post in a great turf classic. Two minutes later, when the race has been run, he has broken a fragile leg and he is fit for nothing but a bullet behind the ear or a veterinarian's lethal needle. The high mortality rate of modern race horses is almost entirely due to the demands of money-hungry politicians for longer and longer racing seasons to provide more and more tax revenue. The supply simply cannot keep up with the demand and the horses who fill the races are forced to run far too frequently. When they show great promise, instead of continuing on to more and more glorious feats on the tracks, they are hastily retired to stud rather than risk a fatal breakdown.

Therefore, even though the Assemblyman we envision may be pious and pure, patriotic and philanthropic, in the limited focus of horse racing, from which we are viewing him, he is the villain in our piece.

The horse descended from Eohippus, a terrier-sized creature only eleven inches high, who lived before the age of man. His fossilized remains have been found in Tertiary rocks in the state of Wyoming. Also, in South America, scientists have discovered perfect specimens of the Hippidion, a remote descendant of Eohippus and the direct ancestor of the horse we know today. Yet no North American or South American Indian ever saw a horse until the Spanish came and brought along their Andalusian and Saracen steeds.

It is reckoned that before man himself evolved, a great plague swept the Americas and only a few horse-creatures escaped over the land bridges to Asia, where men first encountered horses and turned them to human use. It may well be that the horse, in his shape of the thoroughbred, cannot survive another plague in America—the plague of the politicians.

If our villain seems ridiculous, our hero, the Royal Duke, is no less so, for in every area of his life save his relationship to horses he seems to have been a gross and brutal man.

His name was William Augustus and he was Duke of Cumberland, the third son of King George II. He was forty-three when his colt was foaled, and he had little more than a year on earth left to him. He had no hope at all of succeeding to his father's throne, since his nephew, George III, had planted his plump Hanoverian posterior in King Edward's wooden chair in Westminster Abbey four years before and had had the crown of England placed on his brow.

Cumberland was obese, boozy, goutish, liverish, lame, one-eyed and a man of generally unpleasant mien. Also, he was a soldier in disgrace. Despite his royal eminence, he had never found a woman who would marry him, even in the days when a certain military glamor attached to his name. Women found him repulsive, it would seem. Some of the fashionable ladies of the time, who carried fastidiousness to the extreme of bathing themselves all over as frequently as once a week, complained that he always reeked of the bottle and the stables. When he was disgraced and virtually banished to his horse haras at Cranbourne Chase, poor Cumberland was a ready butt of jokes. One of his former mistresses declared he smelt like a drunken horse and that his love-making was as coarse and clumsy as the assault one of his precious stallions might make upon a brood mare. The gossipy Lady Sarah Lennox, a tireless diarist of the day, invariably called him "the fat wretch."

From what meager records remain, Cumberland must appear at once an oafish extravert and yet a curiously pathetic fellow. A king's son bears a heavy cross and sometimes he stumbles beneath its weight. At the age of twenty-five he was captain-general of his father's armies. In 1746 he was sent to the moorlands of Inverness in Scotland to quell the ambitions of an upstart Stuart, Prince Charles Edward, known to his followers as "Bonnie Prince Charlie." In an hour-long battle on the bloody, no-quarter field of Culloden, Cumberland blasted forever the hopes of the House of Stuart to regain the throne of England.

When he returned to England he knew one brief hour of triumph and glory and it was all that he would ever know. The beloved flower, the English pink, was renamed Sweet William in his honor (and called Stinking Billy in Scotland). An official ode, with symbolic references to the Stuart rose, the French lily, and the Scotch thistle, was written to celebrate his return:

> *The lily, thistle and the rose,*
> *All droop and fade, all die away;*
> *Sweet William only rules the day.*

Handel composed *Judas Maccabaeus* in honor of the conqueror and today the work is ranked second only to the great *Messiah* itself among his oratorios.

But the smell of flowers and the sound of music did not last long. News of the sadistic reprisals his soldiers were wreaking on their defeated enemies reached London. His legions who had won the field at Culloden were now an unruly mob that swept through Scotland, raping, burning, pillaging. Cumberland returned to Scotland, but he seemed to encourage the lawless acts of his soldiers. Now even the Hanoverians, for whom he had won the shortest and most decisive battle in the history of English arms, turned against him and called him "Butcher" Cumberland, the name that he carried the rest of his short life.

His final, completely disastrous military adventure came in 1757 during the Seven Years' War when his father set him the hopeless task of defending his ancestral seat of Hanover with raffish and undisciplined mercenaries against the superb French forces of d'Estrées. He was routed as utterly as he himself had routed the Bonnie Prince on the moor of Culloden. Cumberland accepted terms of surrender so unconditional that they were degrading and fled back to England, where he was dealt his final blow when his father, the King, refused point-blank to honor the agreements he had signed and sent out other captains to replace him. "He has disgraced me and ruined himself," George II told his ministers.

Cumberland retired in disgrace, albeit with an ample pension of some £40,000 a year, to his stud at Cranbourne Lodge, the only place on earth he really loved, and was made Ranger of Windsor Forest. Oddly enough, he was more popular in defeat than he had been in victory when his reward had been the nickname "Butcher." He supported the public hero William Pitt, whom his father hated, and this made the great majority of Englishmen look more kindly on him. One wonders, however, if Cumberland espoused Pitt because of political convictions or out of spite for his father.

In any event, he withdrew from the world to a great extent and devoted himself almost entirely to his bottle and his horses. His closest friends were his stud groom and his stableboys and titled gamblers who won huge sums from him. His only serious studies were the pedigrees of the horses on his place and at the studs of lords and farmers not too far away. Speculations that had nothing at all to do with military campaigns or political issues consumed almost all his time. These concerned certain patterns that were beginning to appear in the mating of horses, sometimes through pure chance.

It seems to have occurred to Cumberland—and to a great many other Englishmen almost simultaneously—that certain qualities in horses could almost invariably be expected from the commingling of certain bloodlines. For one thing, the English race horses of the time were almost all incestuously bred. This did not result because of theory; it was a matter of sheer necessity, since there was an ever-increasing demand for race horses and relatively few stallions and mares to supply it. Now, it was noted, this incestuous breeding over several generations was resulting in faster and faster horses.

Cumberland was a phlegmatic Hanoverian, a man of little sensitivity or perception, but it is obvious he felt almost intuitively that some new force was stirring in the world, that some hitherto unknown form of living thing was beginning to take shape and substance. A man who devotes himself to horse breeding usually finds it a preoccupation that has the obsessive fascination of a game of chess played by masters. Exactly this was happening to the Royal Duke who had come home with his tail between his legs because of his inglorious defeat in battle.

In the spring of 1757, before he girded on his sword and left to meet his destiny on the now forgotten field of Hastenback, near the Pied Piper's town of Hamelin in Germany, Cumberland had bred one of his stallions to one of his mares. The stallion's name was Tartar, although you will discover other names for him in the ancient records. It is probable that he was originally called either Partner or Young Partner and that Cumberland, who exhibited a penchant for bravura at times, renamed him. The mare was a bay called Cypron, and it is evident from her pedigree that even before he went away to war Cumberland had given thought to the possible advantages of incest among horses.

Cypron's family tree would have pleased the more decadent of our Deep South novelists and playwrights who pattern their plots on the tragic legend of King Oedipus. In her sire's line, the Darley Arabian was her great-grandfather. In her dam's line the Darley Arabian was her great-great-grandfather. Tartar, to whom Cypron was bred, traced directly to the Byerly Turk through his sire and grandsire, horses quaintly named Croft's Partner and Sir Mostyn's Jigg.

Soon after the Duke returned to Cranbourne Lodge, Cypron presented him with her bay foal by Tartar. The Duke named the colt King Herod. (In our democratic times his name is usually shortened to Herod.) It was customary in the eighteenth century to keep horses on the farm until they were five years old, for they were not deemed mature enough for the racecourse before then. (Today we race horses as soon as they turn two and aid and abet the politicians in breaking them down.)

King Herod went to the races in 1763, the year before Eclipse was born. In Cumberland's lifetime he ran only five times, winning three of his starts. He was bought by Sir John Moore in the dispersal sale after Cumberland's death and there is a famous print still in existence that shows him running second to Bay Malton in a race over Newmarket Heath in 1767. He went to stud in 1770. His descendants won 497 races worth some two hundred thousand pounds, the equivalent of about a million dollars today. For nearly half a century after his death the line of King Herod was prepotent in the world of racing, but it is now disappearing rapidly and only about 4 per cent of modern thoroughbreds stem from it.

We must leave the Duke to his cogitations and his decanter and briefly survey the teeming world of English horses that existed when he came homing from the wars. It was a colorful world painted in bold strokes of bay and chestnut and brown and black, in gray and sorrel and strawberry roan.

Indeed, it must have seemed at times that all of eighteenth century England was one great horse fair waiting the brush of

Rosa Bonheur. Tun-girthed draft animals, descended from the English Great Horse who had borne knights in armor, grazed on the farmer's pastureland and already were taking the shape of the Shire, who would grow as monstrous as the Belgian; or the compact, knotty-muscled Suffolk Punch, the John Bull of the horse world; or, farther north in Scotland, the Clydesdale whose fur spilled down his fetlocks like a fall of lace at a gentleman's collar.

When the huntsman's horn coughed out its stuttering summons and the hounds gave tongue, lean-barreled horses plunged over gorselands and leaped thorn hedges in hot pursuit of a frenzied fox or a wild-eyed stag driven on by panic, for this was a lusty age when blood sports were the rage.

There was hardly a country lane that did not have its portly squire jogging on his cob at a pace called the canter because the Canterbury pilgrims taught it to their mounts, or a lady of the manor in velvet habit, sidesaddled on her palfrey. The cobbled streets of cities, the heathered country downs, the rutted paths of villages resounded to the cadenced clop of horses' hoofs.

Men spoke knowingly of the English breed of horse and the English race horse, but the English breed of race horse did not exist then any more than the English race had existed in the days when Picts and Scots, Angles and Saxons, Vikings and Normans had contended for survival in the isles. They finally became a breed of men by merging their blood together. When the strains of horses merged, the thoroughbreds evolved.

If there was a typical English horse, it must have been the cob, who was a little bit of everything, in both his antecedents and accomplishments. His name was not a compliment; "cobby" was slang for something rough-hewn, unrefined. Perhaps he had originally come from the Saracen horses that had been brought to the foggy islands for barter in the ships of those supersalesmen of ancient times, the Phoenicians. He was the farmer's work horse, the squire's mount, the cart horse, and very often the race horse. In size he was somewhere between a pony and a full-grown horse. He appeared reliable, but not handsome. Already he had been outbred to the aristocrats, the Turks and Barbs and Arabs, and something was emerging. It was too soon to tell just what, but it was something very interesting indeed to men like Cumberland who had an eye for a horse.

The hackney line had been established in Norfolk by a horse named Blaze, who had sired Cumberland's mare Cypron, the dam of King Herod. But this line was not named then, or even recognized, any more than the thoroughbred had been named and recognized.

Formerly, in the days before Charles II, the race horses of England had been the cob and hunter, the horses that squires rode and sometimes raced against their neighbors to "yon steeple," steeples being the highest and most visible landmarks of the countryside (thus "steeplechase"). Then Charles had brought the Arab mares to England and Arab stallions followed, and the Englishman thought he had found his perfect race horse in the Arabs and the Turks and the Barbs, but there simply weren't enough of them. A century before when the Stuart reign had been restored, racing was the Sport of Kings—or, more precisely, the sport of a king named Charles II. Now it was no longer limited to kings and lords or even the gentlemen farmers called squires. It was becoming the people's sport in the eighteenth century. Lowly farmers who could not sign their names were breeding horses and their horses were sometimes winning against the blooded stock of the aristocracy.

A new thing had arrived on the earth. People sensed the fact, reacted to it, but did not know quite what it was, nor did they put a name to it at once. Or rather, they called it by many names. Blooded Horse. English Runner. Hot Blood. And, worst misnomer of all, English Oriental. This new thing that breathed came first in the form of a horse named Matchem, as we reckon now. He was a son of Cade, who was by the great Godolphin Arabian, already a fabled creature. His dam, too, had the blood of orientals. She traced back to the Byerly Turk, and even farther to Place's White Turk and one of Charles II's own Royal Mares. She herself had no name, as happened often in those days. She was known variously as "Changeling's Dam" and "Sister to Miss Partner."

Since the time of the Restoration there had been an avid interest in Eastern things among Englishmen. As the Empire was expanded and the British East India Company became more powerful, fascination with the Middle East, the Far East, the Orient increased to the point of faddism, and it reached its most ridiculous and ultimate point in the early nineteenth century when the Prince Regent built his gaudy Chinese Pavilion at Brighton as a roistering place for the beaus and buckos of his circle.

The most fashionable ladies of the eighteenth century, of Cumberland's time, owned small, black boy-children. They called them their blackamoors and swathed their heads in turbans and draped their bodies in gorgeous oriental silks. The eighteenth century blackamoors played much the same role for stylish hostesses that dwarfs and jesters had played for ancient kings. Some of the more daring ladies even dressed in harem costumes themselves when they held their levees.

On the turf the imported oriental horses were viewed with the same awe that a farm yokel might regard a Bedouin chieftain in flowing robes who rode his charger into a village market place in Sussex.

These Eastern horses were desert Arabs and Turks (or Turkomans) and Barbs from the Barbary States. It was hard indeed for even the most astute horseman to distinguish a Turk or Barb from an Arabian. The Turks and Barbs supposedly had noses that were more Semitically hooked than those of the pure Arabians, but the difference ended there, for in all other points of conformation, even to the structure of the vertebrae, they were the same. If they weren't blood brothers of the Arab, they were his double cousins.

Not only were these imports from the East horses of devastatingly impressive appearance and fiery temperament, but heroic legends surrounded most of them. And even their names—the Lister Turk, the Byerly Turk, Place's White Turk, the Akaster Turk, the D'Arcy Yellow Turk, Curwen's Bay Barb, St. Victor's Barb, the Duke of Rutland's Black Barb, the Leedes Arabian, Bethell's Arabian, the Oglethorpe Arabian, Lord Oxford's Bloody-Shouldered Arabian, the Godolphin Arabian, the Darley Arabian—seemed to ring of far places and mighty deeds. The Lister Turk had been captured by the Duke of Berwyck's army at the siege of Buda. In both the sire's and dam's lines there are three crosses of his war-horse blood in the pedigree of Eclipse, the small and shivering foal that Cumberland greeted with gusts of bitter laughter.

The Byerly Turk, from whom King Herod descended, bore Colonel Byerly of Goldsborough Hall, Yorkshire, when he led his regiment at the Battle of the Boyne in Ireland. The Darley Arabian was a pure *Anazah Keheilan* from the rocky, windswept plateau of Nejd in Arabia, carrying royal blood that had been kept pure for three thousand years. His name was Ras el Fedowa, which may be translated as "The Headstrong One." He was purchased very secretly in Aleppo by Mr. Darley, Queen Anne's consul to the Levant, and virtually smuggled out of the country. Darley, it was said, lived in mortal fear the rest of his life that vengeful Arabs would murder him for sending this purebred stallion to an infidel land. The most romantic tale of all was that surrounding the Godolphin Arabian, now usually called a Barb. He had been presented to Louis XV of France by the Sultan of Morocco, and, according to the legend, an Englishman named Coke had found him some years later pulling a water cart over the streets of Paris, had verified his noble ancestry and bought him on behalf of Lord Godolphin.

The world of eighteenth century England was a place of sweaty reality and Arabian Nights fantasy. Its lords and squires stuffed themselves with food to the point of gluttony, drank to sprawling intoxication, were as licentious as the swains of Fanny Hill. They gambled as few men had ever gambled before—on cards and dice and horses—mainly horses. They were stubbornly heroic on the battlefield, skilled in politics, versed in the mannered artifices of the court, yet they often reeked of the stables. And always, it seemed, they dreamed a dream, like Zachariah of the Testaments, who was haunted by visions of "red horses, black horses and white horses." They wanted to bring a perfect creature to the earth, and largely through the fumbling efforts of the fat man of Cranbourne Lodge, they succeeded.

Matchem, the horse we call "the first thoroughbred" (with some inaccuracy, to be sure), had been foaled at the stud of John Holme, a Carlisle squire, in 1748. He had come nearer than any horse of his day to realizing the dreams of English breeders on the tracks and in the stud. But Cumberland, seeking something better, had reckoned that Matchem was too refined, too close to the orientals, and indeed he was drenched with Eastern blood. The Duke had consciously tried to achieve an animal of somewhat coarser quality when he bred King Herod, and he had been successful. But now he thought he had gone too far in the other direction, that his bay horse had too much of the cob and farm horse in him to make the perfect racer. King Herod had been beaten twice on the tracks, once by a more refined runner owned by Lord Sandwich, who virtually lived off his gambling gains from Cumberland.

In Eclipse, the Duke sought a proper balance of the steady, rugged qualities of the English horse and the fiery temperament and dazzling speed of Turks and Barbs and Arabs.

He had traded Hutton, the farmer-squire, an Arab filly for a sway-backed, undersized, mud-brown horse named Marske (often spelled "Marsk"). Marske carried the Darley's blood, but was as rough and cobby himself as any nag that bore a bumpkin down the lanes between the hedgerows. Hutton had wanted to send Marske's even smaller sire Squirt to the kennels of Sir Harry Harpur to be minced into dog food, and it was this incident to which the Duke had reference when he cursed Squirt's grandson Eclipse, who was born on all Fools' Day.

Cumberland owned the most beautiful mare of her time—or of any time, judging from the portraits that remain of her. She was called Spiletta (or Spilleta, in the various spellings of an unlettered age) and in the line of her sire Regulus she was a granddaughter of the cart horse that a sultan had presented to a king, the great Godolphin himself. In the line of her dam, Mother Western, she traced through such vaunted steeds as the Akaster Turk and Hautboy and Brimmer to one of Charles's precious Royal Mares. The great majority of her remoter ancestors had been bred in the wastes of singing sands called Arabia, although her less romantic English forebears bore such earthy names as Grey Robinson, Smith's Son of Snake, Bald Galloway and, most delightful of all, Sister to Old Country Wench.

Spiletta herself seemed pure Arab, though she was not. She was a bay, with the lustrous, dark-rimmed eyes of the true *Kohl-*

ani of the *El Khamseh* strain, then the most valuable animals on earth. She was slim of barrel, delicate of limb and haunch, and her small, patrician head was molded to a classically arching neck. The Duke tried her on the racecourse only once and she was beaten, but he loved her far more than he had ever loved a woman—or even another horse. When Cumberland bred his darling to the rough-hewn Marske, he literally mated beauty to the beast. The Royal Duke was above all else a gambler. At the time of this historic mating, he had lost such tremendous wagers at the racecourses (he was once reputed to have carried a hundred thousand pounds to Newmarket for a day of gambling) that his game warden no longer sought poachers in Windsor Great Park. Instead he stood at the gates of Cranbourne Lodge with loaded musket at the ready to stave off the dunning usurers from London whom the Duke called "greeks, sharks and blacklegs."

The Duke had reason to be fond of Marske, despite his common look. Marske was the first of Cumberland's horses to win a sweepstakes over the Round Course at Newmarket and on that day the Duke's winnings were colossal enough to bankrupt Lord Gower, whose runner, Shock, was beaten by the ugly, swayback horse. Furthermore, Cumberland wanted Darley blood and his ugly duckling was the Darley's grandson. And the compact, homely Marske had those qualities of ruggedness and endurance that the Duke believed Matchem lacked because of his overrefined breeding. Oddly enough, up until the moment of mating him with his finest mare, Cumberland had used Marske mostly as a pony sire who served the mares of neighboring farmers for half a guinea, plus a few shillings for the groom who officiated.

On the day of the great eclipse, when Cumberland saw the scrawny foal skittering to its feet in a slippery mess of afterbirth, he was convinced his gamble had failed like so many other exploits of his ill-starred life. At birth Eclipse seemed as small as his grandsire, whose very name of Squirt had been a mockery.

In the years since his defeat at Hastenback, the Duke had spent long hours at his desk in Cranbourne Lodge, his decanter beside him, a quill clutched in his sausage-sized fingers, keeping scrupulous records of his studs and mares and race horses, studying their breeding and performances, attempting to find some mystic formula, some exquisite balance of bloodlines that would bring to earth a perfect creature. If the records he kept still existed, they might afford a kinder measure of the man than we possess, for in these experiments he was as selflessly devoted as a fanatic. In Eclipse and King Herod he bred horses whose lines produced ninety-four out of every hundred thoroughbreds on earth today, yet not a single scribble of his stud records remains. Poor Cumberland was despised, even by his family. The records went to Princess Amelia, his niece, upon his death and she was so contemptuous of her royal relative that she promptly burned them all.

The bitterest irony of all is that today only the most sophisticated students of racing history even associate the name of Eclipse with that of the man who bred him. Far oftener Eclipse is linked to a charming scoundrel, a picaresque Irish rogue named Dennis O'Kelly, who bought him and raced him after the Duke had died. In two hundred years there have been only two biographies of Cumberland. They come in thick volumes and deal at length with the Duke's military campaigns and his politickings, but give no space at all to his one great accomplishment of establishing the dynasty of thoroughbreds.

Cumberland himself died exactly nineteen months after Eclipse's birth, believing that all his experiments in the breeding of horseflesh, especially the climactic one of giving life to Eclipse, had been dismal failures. Today, although the man he defeated at Culloden, the Bonnie Prince, remains a shining legend, the Duke is virtually forgotten. Yet there might never have been a sport called thoroughbred racing had Cumberland not lived, and the New York legislator might never have mended his road without him.

Besides breeding two of the three fountainhead sires of the thoroughbred line, Cumberland spent vast sums of money in supporting racing at Ascot, Newmarket and elsewhere. He was the guiding influence in establishing the Jockey Club, which he founded in 1750 with other racing noblemen, between drinks at a Pall Mall tavern called the Star and Garter. The Jockey Club was no misnomer. Several of its members rode their own horses in races. During his latter years, Cumberland was deprived of this pleasure. He weighed three hundred pounds. He limped painfully from a war wound. He was further crippled by gout. He lost the sight of one eye, partly because of another war wound, partly because of soaring blood pressure, doubtless brought on by his feats at the table and with the bottle and by the tensions he suffered through his prodigious gambling.

The racing silks that all jockeys wear today were Cumberland's idea. His own silks—royal purple—were the first ever registered on the turf. Many of the basic rules of racing that are universally followed two centuries after Cumberland's death were suggested by him and adopted by the Jockey Club he formed.

Actually, the Royal Duke lived long enough to suspect that Eclipse was something more than a mouse in eternity, had he only had eyes for the self-willed, vicious-tempered foal that galloped in the paddocks of Cranbourne. Eclipse was in the seventh month of his yearling season when Cumberland died, and since his weanling days he had grown enormously. At full maturity he would stand fifteen hands, two inches, a small horse by present-day standards, but fine size for a race horse of his time.

As a yearling he was not prepossessing, however. In appearance he never would be. He was a chestnut with brownish strands in mane and tail. His head was small, blunt and exceptionally ugly, a fact best brought out by Sartorius' portrait of him at full gallop. This painting has been damned as a work of art and called "primitive" but it has many virtues. It depicts the Eclipse that contemporaries, including the astute John Lawrence, described. It reveals his unsightly head, his blazed face and the deep stocking of his off-hind leg plainly. And it shows the peculiar, sprawling action of his hind legs, which he threw very wide and which, it was said, helped make his stride the longest of any horse up to his time. It was a quirk of stride that many of his best sons, including the peculiarly named Pot-8-0s, inherited. Sixty years later his descendant Touchstone also had the sprawling gait.

During the last two centuries a few turf scriveners have attempted to compensate for the contumely Cumberland suffered in his lifetime by fabricating romantic stories concerning him, but they give us a myth and not a man. The prettiest concerns his death. According to this oft-told tale, he died at his beloved Cranbourne and at the end he called for his stud groom instead of his doctor. "Saddle the bay mare," he is supposed to have said. "There's a long ride ahead."

The bay mare, of course, was his beloved Spiletta, but Cumberland said no such pretty words as he was dying, nor did he die at Cranbourne, as he might have wished, within smelling distance of his stables.

The Duke's health, precarious for years, had been failing badly all during 1765. In October of the previous year, he collapsed at Newmarket from the excitement of seeing King Herod beat Antinous and from winning a large wager on his horse. He most probably suffered a stroke, but his contemporaries were contemptuous even of the poor man's illnesses and said "he was seized by a foaming fit and scrabbled on the gorse." The following summer he at least received a compliment. His surgeon praised his courage because he "held the tallow steady while I lanced his leg-sore, which had suppurated."

It was during this summer of 1765 that the sick man emerged briefly (and with a fortitude that does him credit) from his self-imposed retirement from public life and politics. His nephew, George III, faced by a chaotic political situation, urged Cumberland to use his influence and form a new ministry under his sporting crony and fellow member of the Jockey Club, Lord Rockingham. Pitt, remembering favors the Royal Duke had bestowed upon him in the past, supported him. Cumberland opened his town mansion on Upper Grosvenor Street in London, where he met with Rockingham and his own closest friend, Lord Albemarle, and other powerful figures of the day.

Cumberland's biographer, Sir Evan Charteris, filled two thick volumes with the life and works and bitter disappointments of his subject. He is painstakingly scrupulous in locating exactly each stand of trees, each hill, each country road on the fields of France and Flanders and Germany and Scotland where Cumberland waged his battles. He does not tell us where Cumberland died. He merely tells us that William Augustus, Duke of Cumberland, died on October 31, 1765. No where nor how nor what-he-said. He merely died, period, paragraph, end of story.

We must turn to Albemarle's journals and to his *Life of Rockingham* for the true circumstances of Cumberland's death. Eclipse was born on All Fools' Day and Cumberland died on

Allhallow Eve. Albemarle relates that Halloween of 1765 was chill and foggy. Mist hovered over the London streets like wispy witches celebrating their foul sabbath. There was a cabinet council at Cumberland's house on Upper Grosvenor Street that day and Albemarle had arrived early. He and Cumberland awaited Rockingham and the others.

"We took our port before the fire and spoke of politicks and horses. His Highness seemed in highest spirits and said he planned a levee soon. The fit struck him of a sudden and he fell into my arms. He said no word, but gurgled like a baby, and he died."

He said no word. He did not call for the lovely mare he treasured above all else on earth, as legend has it. Even at the end Fate denied him the dignity due a prince. He had been the only Englishman except Marlborough to hold the rank of captain-general. He had won the shortest and bloodiest battle in English history at Culloden. But that victory was forgotten when his comic-opera command of mercenaries was slaughtered by the French near the nursery-tale town of Hamelin. In espousing Pitt, he had changed the course of British foreign policy. Yet his contemporaries regarded him as a fat clown who disdained the glories of the expanding Empire and preferred to spend his days pottering doltishly about his manure-reeking stables, or else they looked upon him as a foolish gambler, constantly dazed by the bottle.

He had given breath to the most enduring and beloved breed of animals man had ever known when his mating of Marske with Spiletta begot the foal called Eclipse, but he had greeted this accomplishment with railing laughter, for he thought that he had failed.

Finally he died, ingloriously, in a manner that did not befit a prince of the blood, with spilled port streaming over the weskit that girthed his bloated body. He merely gurgled like a baby, and he died. Irony pursued him to the end.

The dispersal sale of Cumberland's stables, which included two of the three founders of the thoroughbred line, was nothing more than a country livestock auction. King Herod had started five times and won three races and Sir John Moore, a member of Cumberland's Jockey Club and a heavy gambler who sometimes bet as much as five thousand pounds on a horse, bid him in. The price is in dispute, like most records of the times, but seems to have been in the neighborhood of one thousand pounds. When the weedy, mean-tempered Eclipse was brought on the block, he tried to savage the auctioneer and kicked his groom. His price has been reported variously as forty-five pounds, seventy guineas, seventy-five guineas and eighty guineas. Those prices are very low indeed by today's standards, even though money in 1765 had many times the purchasing power it has today. Still, any of the prices named would have been good for an untried yearling at the time.

Eclipse was bought by William Wildman, gent., who owned him only briefly and who lives on in turf history mainly because the great George Stubbs included him in the most famous portrait of Eclipse, "Eclipse with Mr. Wildman and His Sons." Stubbs glorifies and romanticizes Eclipse far more than Sartorius does. Mr. Wildman appears as a pleasantly paunchy and decently clothed little man who seems very proud of both his horse and his offspring. The fact that Wildman bought Eclipse and raced him for a season shows that the middle-class merchant was already becoming an important figure in a sport that had previously been the exclusive province of the aristocracy. We know little of Wildman except that he was a London meat dealer who had a stall in Leadenhall Market, and even this scanty information is hard to come by, since he is often confused with a squire named Wildman who never owned a race horse. The fact that Wildman was in the meat business set the wags to wagging, of course. It was predicted that the late Duke's friends would soon be served the late Duke's yearling in the form of steaks and cutlets.

This grisly idea of butchering race horses permeates the whole saga of Eclipse and his forebears and has some basis in fact, since horsemeat was the standard diet for hounds and the culls of the breeding farms frequently became dog food. Cumberland had jested bitterly about condemning Eclipse to being turned into dog food, and had he had a few more drinks on the day the foal arrived, he might well have done just that. Now a meat dealer actually had possession of the colt who was to found a dynasty.

Wildman found Eclipse to be so wild and vicious that he doubted he ever could be broken to the saddle, much less disciplined to racing, and this lent some credence to the tales that a descendant of the fabled Darley Arabian, bred by a Royal Duke, would soon become a carcass hanging from a hook in a Leadenhall Market butchershop. The poor as well as dogs ate horsemeat in the eighteenth century. Even at the lowest figure quoted as the price he brought at auction—forty-five pounds—Eclipse would have been a very expensive piece of meat indeed.

In the years between the sale in 1765 and 1769, when Eclipse went to the races, the thoroughbred line as we know it today was again in serious danger. The standard practice then, as now, with horses that are headstrong and vicious or undersized was to geld them. Often the geldings became great race horses, just as they have in modern times in such cases as those of Exterminator, Armed, and Kelso. There is little doubt that many racing men advised the meat dealer turned turfman to do just this.

However, at the time he purchased Eclipse, Wildman already owned a few nondescript race horses, most of whom had only the barest trace of oriental blood. He wanted the blood of the Darley for breeding purposes and Eclipse had it.

There were many peculiar professions in the eighteenth century, among them that of "roughrider." The roughrider made his living by breaking balky horses. Wildman engaged the services of a very tough roughrider who was also a felon. His name has come down to us as both George Elton and George Ellers, depending upon which contemporary account you read. Never has any great race horse been given the treatment that George gave Eclipse. He not only rode him all day over the roughest woodland paths, but also took him out for most of the night. One wonders just how he explained these nocturnal forays to the highly respectable Mr. Wildman. Actually George was a poacher and he was making Eclipse his partner in crime. And again the barely borning thoroughbred line stood in peril of extinction before it really began. Gamekeepers of the great estates showed no hesitancy at all in shooting down poachers and they were just as likely to shoot any horse a poacher rode.

Almost any thoroughbred of the present time who was subjected to three years of such treatment would break down completely. Even if he bore up physically, his spirit would be broken and he would be no good at all for racing. Eclipse bore up and his spirit was never broken. The artists who depicted him in action show him running with his head far down, the bit in his teeth, ample indication that he is a self-willed horse, running on his own, and that his rider has little or no control over him.

In April of 1769, when Eclipse was a fully matured five-year-old, large in size for his time and extremely rangy, Wildman finally took him to the races at Epsom Downs. The plump little butcher-become-turfman had acquired the services of a good

jockey, John Oakley, who was not afraid of the wildly uninhibited descendant of the Darley. The records are not clear, but
it would seem that Oakley rode Eclipse in all but three of his
races. He was ridden once by Fitzpatrick, once by Merriott, and
once by John Whiting. In his old age, when he was a shriveled,
toothless mummy of a man, John Singleton, one of the best and
most eccentric of the turf's early jockeys, claimed he had ridden
Eclipse. The records that exist dispute him.

Oakley was an ideal rider for a horse like Eclipse because he
was an intelligent man and he did exactly what intelligent
jockeys do today when they ride unruly but enormously talented
horses. Oakley let Eclipse run his own race and merely exerted
mild restraint when it seemed his mount was about to run right
off the course. In 1963 the highly capable Johnny Rotz did this
same thing with the brilliant but utterly mad No Robbery from
the Greentree Stable.

It was at Epsom that the gaudiest of all the characters surrounding Eclipse came on stage. In the half-world of gambling,
boozing and wenching in which he existed most of his life he
was called "The Count," a name he had been given in Fleet
Prison, where he served time for debt, because of his jaunty
pretensions, his high-handed manners and his engaging suavity.
His name was Captain Dennis O'Kelly and he was the first of a
long succession of merry rascals who have decorated and enliv-
ened the wonderful world of racing far more than they have
harmed it. Captain O'Kelly may very well have been the racetracks' first tout, and certainly he was the most talented and
most persuasive con man who ever existed. The Irishman seems
far more of a gay adventurer than a black villain.

For two centuries it has been said that the great caricaturist
Rowlandson depicted O'Kelly when he drew the hook-nosed,
jut-lipped, villainous, Fagin-like figure who is speaking to a

jockey in his famous sketch "Tricks of the Turf." Figures in Rowlandson's Newmarket sketches, "The Start" and "The Betting Post," resemble the same monster he caricatured in "Tricks of the Turf" and are also reputed to be his conception of "The Count."

Oddly enough, O'Kelly, one of the vainest men who ever lived, never seems to have had his portrait painted. The only authentic likeness of him that exists is a cameo that was made for a curious reason. It is a funeral ring. During the late eighteenth and early nineteenth centuries, there was a ghoulish fad of presenting these funeral rings, with miniature death masks of the deceased as the setting, to relatives and friends of the departed. O'Kelly's funeral ring is an exceptionally fine one. It was made by Lochee, a famous artisan who later designed basaltware for Josiah Wedgwood. The cameo shows a man who is going jowly, but is still handsome. His features are pleasant and Lochee has caught the slightly cynical yet good-humored look of a man born with the gift of laughter. It could possibly be this face that Rowlandson contorted in caricature, but it is doubtful that O'Kelly ever was the evil being who emerges from the sketches, although he was certainly amoral in a rather delightful way and often guilty of sharp practice.

O'Kelly began life in a cart-horse capacity, between the shafts of a sedan chair, carrying fashionable ladies about the streets of London. He was a fellow who always had his eye on the main chance, and he did not neglect the fringe benefits of even so lowly a profession. When he became famous as the owner of Eclipse, he encouraged the pamphleteers who abounded in his time to write bawdy stories of his adventures. He got his start in life when a noble lady noticed that the youth between the shafts of her chair was "a well-grown, saucy fellow with straight, clean limbs who might fit better between softer shafts." She promptly sent her maid to arrange a rendezvous. O'Kelly seduced her (or vice versa), and she became his patroness. According to the hacks who were his most numerous biographers, O'Kelly had such a fatal attraction for noblewomen that he could not hire a bed at an inn without finding a scantily attired and incognito gentlewoman between the sheets when he took his candle up to bed. Each of them gave him "costly presents" for his favors and he was relatively affluent even in the first sweet bloom of youth, having advanced rapidly from the estate of cart horse to that of stud horse.

He used his stud fees for gambling and proved so skillful at cards and dice that, because the gentlemen from whom he won large sums claimed he was a blackguard and cheat, he was banned from White's, today an exclusive London club, which began as a gambling room and bookmaking parlor.

The gentlemen seldom made such accusations to his face, however. O'Kelly, in many respects, was an odd combination of Restoration rake and modern Madison Avenue account executive. He fully realized the value of personal publicity and a public image. He used his gambling winnings to buy a captaincy in the Westminster company of an unstylish and very unwarlike Middlesex militia, in which his fellow captains were respectively an alehouse proprietor and a tailor. The rank gave him prestige, and stories soon began to circulate in London that he was a fearsome swordsman. Actually, he never took a fencing lesson or fought a duel, but the best swordsmen in England hesitated to challenge him even though he cheated and cuckolded them. When Eclipse began winning under his red jacket and black cap, O'Kelly bought himself a lieutenant-colonelcy in the same militia, which doubtless made him even more feared as a duelist who talked a good fight.

Gamblers could meet the most prominent men of the eighteenth century because virtually every leading figure of the time was a gambler himself. In 1768 O'Kelly met Charles James Fox, a twenty-year-old nobleman who had come straight from Hertford College, Oxford, to occupy the Midhurst seat in Parliament, which his indulgent father, Lord Holland, a famous rake and gambler himself, had bought for him. Young Fox was a brilliant statesman and an erratic human being who drank and gambled as much as any figure of his time. He founded the scandalous Hellfire Club, where roistering lords celebrated Black Masses during sexual orgies with London doxies. He already owned a large stable of race horses. A fellow of O'Kelly's kidney must have delighted Fox, who was completely cynical about the virtues of humanity even though he was a leading liberal, a staunch defender of the underprivileged and a champion of the American colonists who were about to revolt against his king.

It was Fox who suggested to the Count that the racetracks offered a neglected business opportunity to an ambitious and industrious man.

Fox pointed out that gamblers of the time really had little line on the form of horses other than those they had seen run. The Jockey Club had begun to compile records, but they were so long in the compiling that they were of little help to bettors. Fox suggested that a group of observant fellows should watch the races at all the tracks and compare notes on the horses they had seen. He said titled gamblers would back them in the enterprise. Thus was the famous (or infamous) "O'Kelly Gang" formed, and thus did touting as a business come into being—at the behest of a great statesman.

The derivation of the word "tout" is of interest in itself. It had not come into general use in O'Kelly's time. The touts who followed him attracted attention to themselves by blowing tin horns. They were called "tooters," which was shortened to "toots" and finally corrupted to "touts." The term "tinhorn gambler" derives from the same source.

O'Kelly himself may not have been the Fagin-like figure of Rowlandson's caricatures, but his gang of sharp-eyed youths closely resembled the alliance of adolescent felons who worked under the direction of Dickens' villain. O'Kelly evaluated their reports, suggested wagers to the lords who sponsored his enterprise and took a cut of the profits. In 1769, when he first encountered Eclipse, he owned a few race horses himself.

The alliance of the prim and fussy little Mr. Wildman and the bravura-style adventurer known as Captain O'Kelly was one of the most ludicrous human combinations of all time. Wildman seems to have been completely bedazzled by the dashing Irishman. He must have been, for he let O'Kelly talk him out of the most remarkable animal the world has known.

O'Kelly has been described as a cheat and charlatan, but most Irishmen, like most Kentuckians, have an eye for a horse regardless of their morals. The Count seems to have recognized the potential of Eclipse upon sight and he immediately went out of his way to ingratiate himself with the horse's owner. Eclipse was entered in a fifty-guinea plate on May 3, and he needed training over the up-hill-and-down-dale course at Epsom. Since he had never started and was a horse of uncertain temper, he also needed a workmate. This offered the Count the opportunity for cultivating the acquaintance of Mr. William Wildman. He suggested a horse from his own stable as Eclipse's workmate and the offer was eagerly accepted.

Even though O'Kelly's gang had been in operation less than a year by this spring of 1769, the success of their betting operations had been so notorious that rival gangs of touts were proliferating throughout England. O'Kelly did his best to keep the ugly duckling's first serious trial a secret, and he almost succeeded. Eclipse and his workmate went on the downs when it was barely light enough to distinguish a horse from a bush. The rival touts were still sleeping off their wine, but somehow the news of the sensational trial leaked out. An old woman who lived in a thatched cottage at Epsom, almost on the racecourse, was about her chores at dawn, and she saw the horses. The touts found her and plied her with gin and she told them that "a horse with a white leg had run off from another horse at a monstrous rate, like he would run right off the edge of the earth." As a result, Eclipse was held at 4 to 1 *on,* or 1 to 4 by American reckoning, in his very first start, and this would be the longest odds ever laid against him. Later he would be 1 to 20 and in many of his starts he was 1 to 100. No other horse in the entire history of the turf has ever been held consistently at such unbettably short odds. Man o' War is the only horse in U.S. turf history ever held at 1 to 100 and he was held at those odds only once, when he faced a single opponent, a horse named Yellow Hand, in the Stuyvesant Handicap at Jamaica in 1920.

Fortunately the canny O'Kelly had managed to obtain better odds at the great gambling center called Medley's Coffee Rooms a few days before the race. There were five starters, including Eclipse, in the event, which was run in four-mile heats. Eclipse ran off with the first heat, although he apparently did not "distance" his field, since records show that Mr. Fortescue's highly regarded Gower was placed second and Mr. Castle's Chance third. There was a peculiar rule at the time that if a horse won by two hundred yards he "distanced" his rivals and the others were simply regarded as "unplaced." In every single race in which he met competition after this first effort, Eclipse won by at least a furlong.

The story is often told that O'Kelly's most famous bet on Eclipse was made in 1770 at Newmarket with the running of the

King's Plate. This story is erroneous. The bet was made, according to the best contemporary accounts and according to O'Kelly's only reliable biographer, Theodore Andrea Cook, on the very first day Eclipse went to the post. In the second heat the odds were 20 to 1 *on* for Eclipse; O'Kelly, finding them unreasonable, offered to wager he could name the exact placing of every horse in the race. He found plenty of takers for this wager, of course, and scribbled on a piece of paper *"Eclipse first, the rest nowhere."* Eclipse distanced his field by well over an eighth of a mile in the second heat, and O'Kelly won the bet, since the others were unplaced under the rules. The phrase "Eclipse first, the rest nowhere" is one of the most famous in racing.

Eclipse went to Ascot and on May 29 won another fifty-guinea event just as easily. After this race O'Kelly managed to buy a half interest in the horse for 650 guineas. Eclipse won all of his other races that season at Winchester, Salisbury, Canterbury, Lewes and Litchfield, and at the end of the year the persuasive O'Kelly contrived to buy the horse outright for another 1,100 guineas. This was, of course, one of the great bargains of all time, yet it is a bit hard on O'Kelly to say he cheated little Mr. Wildman in view of the purses Eclipse won. The nearest approximation we can make in dollars for the price O'Kelly paid Wildman is about $8,750. Eclipse's total winnings on the turf were only 2,149 guineas, or $10,745.

At Newmarket's Spring Meeting of 1770, Eclipse, running under O'Kelly's black cap and red jacket for the first time, met the only serious competition he had ever known or ever was to know. Mr. Wentworth's Bucephalus, named for Alexander the Great's war horse, stayed abreast of him for three and a half miles of the first four-mile heat. At that point, half a mile from the finish, Bucephalus collapsed completely. Eclipse simply broke his heart, and Bucephalus was never able to go to the post again. Oddly enough, Bucephalus was by Regulus, the sire of Eclipse's dam, and might be reckoned as his opponent's uncle, although both were six years old at the time.

Eclipse carried eight stone, or 112 pounds, in his first race. The highest weight he ever carried was the crushing burden of twelve stone, 168 pounds. He carried that weight several times.

Eclipse's record may not be the greatest in racing, but like everything else about him it was the most peculiar. He started eighteen times, was never defeated, won all but the first heat of his first race by an eighth of a mile or more, met only one horse who challenged him seriously, yet he scored only nine victories altogether. He went to the post nine times in 1769 and nine times in 1770, but three times during his first year of racing and six times during his final year, he simply walked over the course to collect the purse, since there were no opponents willing to try him. In view of the fact that Eclipse almost missed getting born, was almost destroyed after birth, and seemed to be so wild and unmanageable that he could never be brought to the track, the record of eighteen starts, no defeats and but nine victories is only a minor curiosity.

There was even a Shakespeare controversy over Eclipse long after he died. It did not involve Sir Francis Bacon or Christopher Marlowe, but a horse named Shakespeare. It was based on a completely unfounded story to the effect that Shakespeare had covered Spiletta before Marske covered her. The story was told by a garrulous groom of O'Kelly's who could not possibly have been privy to the Duke of Cumberland's stud records at the time he bred Marske and Spiletta in the spring of 1763. Thanks to the incendiary activities of the Princess Amelia, Cumberland's records were not available to dispute the claim, which was given some credence by John Lawrence, who had seen Eclipse and was the most enlightened commentator on horses of his time. Lawrence thought Eclipse traced to Shakespeare instead of Marske because of his coat color, a theory completely exploded by veterinary research a hundred years later.

Although Shakespeare, like Marske, traced to the Darley, he was far more finely bred, for Shakespeare went back to Hobgoblin and Aleppo instead of Squirt and Bartlett's Childers and was even more refined than Matchem himself, and Cumberland was seeking a more balanced horse. The clinching argument, in lieu of Cumberland's incinerated stud records, is an entry in the journal of John Hutton during the summer of 1764: "I am informed the Duke of Cumberland has a colt at Cranbourne from Spilleta [sic] by the brown horse Marsk [sic] I traded for the Arab filly."

The relationship of the sprightly rogue O'Kelly to the immortal animal Eclipse is perhaps the most interesting facet of the extraordinary story of the horse that founded a dynasty, and it is an ennobling relationship of man to horse that has been repeated again and again over the past two centuries. Theodore Andrea Cook, whose scarce book *Eclipse and O'Kelly* was published in a limited edition of only one hundred copies in 1907, is the Count's most admiring and sympathetic biographer. Cook points out that O'Kelly barely won Eclipse out in purses and that he could not possibly have won real money betting on him, since he had to bet a hundred pounds to win a pound in most of the nine starts where his horse faced competition. He stresses the fact that if O'Kelly had been the unmitigated villain pictured by Rowlandson and other contemporaries, he could easily have won a comfortable fortune by "stopping" or pulling Eclipse and betting on another horse at tremendous odds. He never did this. You may recall from our foreword that Arnold Rothstein, a latter-day villain, raced his Redstone Stable horses with apparent honesty and that he won few bets on the turf.

This has happened time and again when a man, regardless of his immorality in other fields, has fallen in love with a horse.

Finally, of course, O'Kelly profited vastly as the owner of Eclipse. He sent him to stud in 1771.

Eclipse stood at O'Kelly's Clay Hill Stud in Epsom for nineteen years and his sons and daughters won 344 races. His stud fees were very low by today's standards when a champion race horse can easily command $5,000 for service to a mare. His fee over the years varied between 20 guineas (about $100) and 50 guineas (about $250). Even so, O'Kelly took in 25,000 guineas, or about $125,000, in stud fees alone, in addition to winning an enormous amount in purses and bets with the sons and daughters of Eclipse he raced himself.

More than a century ago somebody made a typographical error and reported that Eclipse's sons and daughters won £518,047 in prizes. They didn't, because there simply wasn't that much money to be won in the late eighteenth century. The oft-repeated typographical error is a transposition. The direct descendants of Eclipse won £158,047 on the turf in a racing period of just under twenty-five years. His son Young Eclipse won the second running of the Epsom Derby in 1781 under O'Kelly's silks. Another son, Saltram, won the fourth Derby for a Mr. Parker in 1783, and the next year Sergeant, by Eclipse, won the fifth Derby under O'Kelly's red jacket. Thus Eclipse's direct descendants won three of the first five Derbies. The first was won by Diomed, who traced to Cumberland's other stallion, King Herod, through his sire Florizel. The third was won by Assassin, a son of Sweetbriar who traced to Eclipse's despised grandsire, the runt, Squirt. So the Duke of Cumberland, the ancestors of Eclipse, and Eclipse himself provided the winners of the first five Epsom Derbies, the famed "blue ribbon of the turf." By 1900 the male line of Eclipse accounted for well over

80 per cent of thoroughbreds on earth and today that figure has risen to 90 per cent. Even fifty years ago Eclipse's line completely dominated the great classic races. There were thirty-four runners named for the Epsom Derby of 1906. Two traced to Matchem. Two traced to King Herod. All the others traced to Eclipse in the male line.

Since the hard facts of Eclipse's history are in themselves sheer romance, there seems little need for the myths, legends and outrageous falsehoods that have confused historians for two centuries.

There is no doubt whatsoever concerning the birthplace of Eclipse. Contemporary accounts agree, and Prince Christian of Schleswig-Holstein, one of the successors to Cumberland as Ranger of Windsor Forest, set a memorial tablet on the exact spot on March 7, 1879. The paddock was near Cranbourne Tower at Cumberland's Cranbourne Lodge estate in Cranbourne Chase, Berkshire. Yet various historians have argued that the colt was born in at least five other places. He was born "under Sir Francis Doyle's thorntree" at Mickelham, near Dorking. He was born in Berkshire, but at East Ilsey instead of Cranbourne Chase. He was foaled "at the Duke of Cumberland's stud in Sussex," a place that never existed at any time. He was born at Cumberland Farm at Plaistow, Essex, and there's an Eclipse Road there to prove the fact, only Cumberland Farm never belonged to Cumberland, but was the property of the Coopers Company. And, finally, he was born on the Isle of Dogs (perhaps this theory is engendered by the fact that both Eclipse and Squirt just missed becoming meat for Sir Harry's staghounds).

Soon after Eclipse died of an acute attack of colic on February 27, 1789, just a month and a day before his twenty-fifth birthday, there were no fewer than six "fully authenticated" skeletons of the great horse in existence. Even today museums and private owners possess nine "authenticated" hoofs of Eclipse. The "genuine" hairs from Eclipse's mane and tail are so numerous that every flagellant of the *Penitente* sect in Mexico could be shirted with them. Actually, hairs from the mane and tail were plaited into the Newmarket Challenge Whip, one of the most coveted trophies in racing. If all the "certified" pieces of Eclipse's hide were sewn together, they would make a chestnut carpet for Buckingham Palace. During the nineteenth century, racing plates "worn by Eclipse" were peddled as sporting relics in the same way that bones of the Apostles were peddled as religious relics in the Middle Ages. A nineteenth century English eccentric kept a large stone on his desk as a paperweight and insisted it was one of Eclipse's mummified testicles. An English foxhunter once owned a whip that he swore was made of Eclipse's sex organ. (The most treasured souvenirs of U.S. GIs in World War II were swagger sticks taken from Italian officers, which were supposed to be made from the sex organs of bulls.)

The legend of Eclipse might have died, of course, despite his unbeaten record on the turf, had he not been the most prepotent sire of any species of animal the world has ever known. Yet even the ebullient, optimistic and resourceful Dennis O'Kelly doubted he could ever mate his rambunctious stallion. No jockey had ever mastered the self-willed horse, or had ever tried to, since it was only necessary to let him have his own way in order to win. It was feared, however, that he was too much of a savage to be bred. Apparently there was no need for such apprehensions. Once Eclipse was exposed to the gentler sex he became as readily domesticated as any other obstreperous male.

A nineteenth century turf scribe who chose to call himself Jack Silverspur, writing in a sporting journal during the Regency period, is our authority: " 'Twas said the mighty runner and matchless sire Eclipse was most courtly for a beast. He ap-

48

proach'd the mares he serv'd as if he purpos'd wooing them, as elegant in mien as our gallants who beseech their ladies."

Here we may pause to pity the Royal Duke who bred the courtly beast. The ladies poor Cumberland beseeched had only unkind words for his bestiality as a bedmate.

William Augustus, Duke of Cumberland, held his lanthorn high on a Day of Fools when the world was dark at noon, and he saw only a dwarfish creature with spindly legs, still blooded by the womb. He did not see the wonderful, enchanted world that was being born with the chestnut colt named Eclipse.

The Book of Kings tells us that the Israelites were delivered when the Syrians heard a warning from Heaven—"a sound of horses."

In the eighteenth century there was a sound of horses in this blessed plot, this earth, this realm, this England, too.

It would echo down the ages and throughout the world.

2

Incident in a Barber's Chair

The curtain will be lowered to denote the passage of 165 years. When it rises, glamorous stars of motion pictures appear on stage.

Thoroughbred racing began with the birth of Eclipse on April 1, 1764. Modern American commercial racing, which is becoming more and more the pattern for the world and which helps to support more than half the states of the Union, began in a barber's chair in San Francisco on Black Tuesday, October 29, 1929.

In the 1920s it was the sybaritic custom of Dr. Charles Strub, a former painless dentist and professional baseball player who

was now one of the most successful stock-market speculators of
the West, to visit the barbershop of San Francisco's St. Francis
Hotel each day promptly at noon and have himself shaved by a
barber whose chair was always reserved for him at that hour. Dr.
Strub had reason to believe that the chair was lucky. One day,
a few months before, he had called his broker from the barbershop and instructed him to buy a certain block of stock on margin just before he sat down for his shave. While the barber
was slapping lilac lotion on his fresh-scraped face, a portable
phone was brought to the barber's chair. It was Dr. Strub's
broker calling. He informed his customer that the stock had
soared upward immediately after his order had been executed
and that he had earned a profit of $65,000 on his investment in
the brief time he was being shaved.

On this later day in October, 1929, while the good doctor relaxed in his chair, his face meringued like a Viennese pastry,
the portable phone was carried to him again, and again it was
his broker calling. This time the news was not good. This time
the news was downright disastrous, in fact. It was a few minutes
after noon Pacific time in San Francisco, and it was a few minutes after 3:00 P.M. Eastern Standard time in New York. Seconds
before Dr. Strub received the call from his broker, a loud bell
on the floor of the New York Stock Exchange had signaled the
end of the wildest five hours of panic-stricken selling in the history of finance. For five years the nation had been growing fatter
and fatter and richer and richer during an unprecedented era
of paper prosperity. In five hours the nation had gone flat broke
and the paper profits had been blown away forever by the great
hurricane called the Wall Street Crash.

Dr. Strub was worth several millions on paper when he said
"Hello" into the mouthpiece of the barbershop phone on that
Black Tuesday. He not only was broke, but was more than a

million dollars in debt when he said "Good-bye." He had been a blue-sky market plunger and he couldn't possibly raise the enormous sums his broker required to cover his margins. Even had he been able to do so, he would have been throwing good money after bad, as things turned out.

For moments after his broker hung up, Dr. Strub sat there, the phone still in his hand, staring straight ahead and looking rather foolish with the frothy icing of lather drying on his face. Then he spoke aloud—to his barber, perhaps, or to no one in particular—and his remark has become a classic among philosophic gamblers.

"You know," he said, "I always did enjoy my wife's cooking more than anybody else's."

Later, Dr. Strub would often say that the idea of Santa Anita Park, the most elaborate turf enterprise up to its time and still one of the great racetracks of the world, came to him while he was being shaved. Charley Strub was never a man to brood over disaster or whine about defeat. He considered that kind of emotional catharsis a waste of time. When Doc Strub lost a bet, he dug up some fresh money and made another one.

Santa Anita was Strub's biggest gamble, just as breeding Eclipse had been Cumberland's.

It is in this respect that two otherwise dissimilar men—the Duke who gave us our race horse and the dentist who gave us our racetrack—resemble each other closely. Both were essentially gamblers, and both possessed the gambler's daring. They were unorthodox men who did not hesitate to back a longshot. While other Englishmen attempted to breed a horse that was as exact a duplicate of his oriental ancestors as possible and belittled the English bloodstock they were forced to use because of the shortage of Eastern stallions and mares, Cumberland considered the virtues that might be inherent in the despised native cob. Cumberland owned full-bred Arabs and Barbs and other horses with a far greater infusion of oriental blood than Marske. Certainly he owned handsomer and more refined stallions, for Marske, with his short coupling, his swayed back, his muddy color and his blunt and ugly head was a caricature of the homely English farm horse, even though he traced directly to the Darley. Yet it was Marske whom Cumberland chose as a mate for his loveliest and most refined mare, Spiletta, granddaughter of the Godolphin and remote descendant not only of Hautboy but of one of Charles II's Royal Mares. The mating was a calculated risk that paid off enormously in the end, for it established the line of thoroughbreds we know today.

It was five years between the shave the barber gave Doc Strub in 1929 and the beribboned present Doc Strub gave the turf when Santa Anita opened on Christmas Day of 1934. They were five of the leanest and most Spartan years America had known since Continental soldiers froze at Valley Forge. The Great Depression had followed the Crash and men were starving. Austerity was not just a political maxim: it was a necessary way of life for most Americans. In view of this, the logic of the gambling dentist in building a luxurious racetrack in a time of poverty seems as zany as that of a young queen who stood on a balcony one day and asked her minister why the populace was rioting outside the palace.

"Because they have no bread to eat, Madame," she was told.

"Then let them eat cake," the queen replied.

The doctor prescribed cake for the depressed Americans of the 1930s and they liked it so much they ate it to the last crumb.

The Santa Anita that finally evolved from Doc Strub's meditations in a barber's chair was far and away the most commodious racetrack ever built anywhere, exceeding in lavishness even that dowager queen of the turf, old Belmont Park in New

York. It would serve as a model for all the great tracks that followed it throughout the nation. It would be studied when English racing finally moved out of the eighteenth century in 1961 and the Queen Elizabeth grandstand was constructed at Royal Ascot. It would be the first track in the United States to play to crowds that numbered up to eighty thousand persons, to see regular million-dollar betting days, to offer a race worth one hundred thousand dollars in added money. For several years, almost alone, it would support the educational system and the wildlife conservation program of California. And the sound of its tinkling tills would set tax-hungry legislators throughout the land to salivating like Pavlov's dogs. Modern racing, the gigantic and sometimes downright frightening enterprise we know today, began at Santa Anita Park in the mountain-shadowed town of Arcadia, California, on Christmas 1934.

Although Doc Strub enjoyed such indulgences as barbershop shaves, good home cooking and aged bourbon whiskey, sybaritism was foreign to his nature. He was a big man physically, built in the classic, rawboned mold of the Western American; big-handed, big-footed, jut-elbowed and awkward in his movements. His face, when it was relaxed, was not unhandsome, but he was a tense, hard-driving man and he found relaxation difficult. Usually his face was hard, uncompromising. He had just entered middle life in 1929, but his cheeks were already crosshatched by the red-and-purple hen tracks of the high blood pressure that would eventually prove fatal. His eyes were pale and cold. The fanciful who endured his steady gaze might think of the fabled gun-slingers of the American West. Strub looked tough—and he was.

He was born in Hollister, at the northern end of the Pacheco Pass, in California's lumber and mining and wine-grape country. He was graduated from the school of dentistry at the University of California in Berkeley, where he captained the baseball team. Like many tough-bodied and tough-minded men, Strub was revolted by unnecessary human suffering. The crude dentists of the time had caused him hours of untold agony in his childhood, and he had specialized at Berkeley in the study of the new pain-killing drugs, not only laughing gas, but the primitive local anesthetics, in relation to dentistry. He devoutly believed that a man who could pull an abscessed tooth painlessly was a benefactor of humanity.

He chose the fateful year of 1906 to hang out his shingle and await his patients. He had not pulled a tooth when the great earthquake and fire hit San Francisco and virtually destroyed the city. The street on which his office was located was razed completely. The youthful dentist had invested the whole of his scanty capital in a reclining chair, bottles of laughing gas and a formidable display of forceps and probes, all of which were destroyed when the earth cracked open.

For days and weeks San Francisco was a ghost town. Displaced persons roamed the streets by day and slept in parks at night. The communications systems of the city were completely disrupted and its citizens were virtually cut off from the outside world.

The San Francisco *Bulletin* had managed to continue publication. One day Strub bought a copy of the paper and read an item in Hy Bagley's sports column to the effect that a man named Charles Graham wanted to get in touch with him. Graham had been a Latin instructor and baseball coach at Strub's university and he now owned an interest in the Sacramento baseball club of the Coast League. Strub saw Graham and became a professional ballplayer with Sacramento. Athletes have always been greatly honored in lusty San Francisco and Strub discovered that his name and face were ample collateral for bank loans.

He borrowed as much as possible, set up his second office on the busiest corner of town and advertised his painless dentistry with the largest sign in the rebuilding city. Perhaps the earthquake had shaken loose the teeth of many citizens. In any event, Strub became prosperous within a matter of months and rich within a few years. He expanded his business to six dental parlors in various parts of the city and supervised the tooth pullers in all of them. He was never a man to let money molder in bank vaults. He gambled in real estate. He financed a large part of the rebuilding of the business district of the blasted metropolis. He extended his operations to the southern part of the state where the Los Angeles of the time was little more than seven villages in search of a city, and obtained huge real estate holdings.

In 1918 Graham and a partner named George Putnam came to San Francisco and signed an agreement to take over the local Coast League ball team called the Seals. They posed for sports-page pictures in the office of the San Francisco *Chronicle,* after which Putnam remarked, "Now, Charley, all we need is money."

Strub's main dental office, with its gaudy sign hymning the pure pleasure to be derived from painless dentistry, was right across the street. Graham pointed to it. "That's where we get it," he said.

Strub drove a hard bargain (he made himself president), but he financed them. The success of minor-league ball clubs in those days, as now, depended entirely upon the slave trade. Strub was the greatest flesh peddler of all time. He sold ballplayers to the major leagues for sums that were unheard of before his day. In one season his sale of Seals players alone to the

American and National Leagues totaled almost twice as much
as the sales of players from all the clubs of the American Association, the International League, and the Eastern League combined. Once, in a package deal, he sold his whole outfield down
the river for $150,000. In no time at all he'd made himself an-
other million. He made only one bad deal, but that came in
1933, the year before Santa Anita opened and the most pen-
urious time Strub had ever known. He was living on credit when
he sold Joe Di Maggio to the Yankees for a mere $25,000. Later
Strub, who was generally regarded as a grim and humorless
man, would say, "Of course I never dreamed he'd become the
husband of Marilyn Monroe."

The era of wonderful fiscal nonsense that began with the
Coolidge era of 1924 and continued for half a decade was a perfect ambience for Strub. These were the years when the big-time
gamblers became folk heroes. They did not gamble on the
steamboats, like Canada Bill Jones and George Devol, or on the
racetracks, like Chicago O'Brien and Pittsburgh Phil. They
gambled on the floor of the New York Stock Exchange. Oddly
enough, during this period of easy money, when the etiquette
of the roulette table became the mores of an entire nation, there
was virtually no expansion of horse racing, except for the construction of Arlington Park in Chicago, a precursor of the modern racing plants, which opened in 1927.

Through stock-market speculation, Strub had pyramided his
considerable fortune made by the honest sweat of tooth pulling,
slave trading and real estate investment into multimillions—on
paper—at the time he sat down for his shave. When he rose from
the barber's chair he was shorn of both beard and money and
was deeply in debt. His advisers—his bankers, his lawyers, his
broker and his best friends—urged him to declare himself a
bankrupt without delay. He was a stubborn man, as stubborn

in his way as the Duke who had formed his squares at Culloden and bred a lovely mare to a grotesque stallion. Before the breeze from San Francisco Bay had blown the fragrance of lilac lotion from his jowls, he was absorbed with a new idea. While he was in the barber's chair, Strub had heard a knell of doom, but he had also heard a sound of horses.

Since the first decade of the twentieth century, when California racing had been outlawed and the old Emeryville track on the East Bay of San Francisco had closed its gates forever, there had been sporadic agitation for the revival of the thoroughbred sport in the state. Such titans of the turf as the fabulous Ben Ali Haggin, Lucky Baldwin, Theodore Winters, and Leland Stanford had owned great studs and bred great champions in California during the nineteenth century. Even in 1929 one track was still operating in California, although the legal status of its betting system was dubious at best. This was Tanforan, in the little town of San Bruno on the peninsula outside San Francisco. It was owned and operated by John Marchbank, a bushy-haired, crippled man who also owned a big gambling house at the top of one of San Francisco's highest hills.

The betting system of Tanforan was euphemistically known as "options," and it was essentially the forbidden pari-mutuel system wearing false whiskers and smoked glasses. The theory was that "options" were not against the law because bettors bought an option to purchase shares in a horse and participated in his winnings. Marchbank, whose posh gambling palace had operated for years without a single raid, had enormous political influence and was probably the only man in the state who could get away with such arrant nonsense. In 1923 he had rebuilt the shabby old Tanforan course, which had originally been constructed in 1889. He also bred horses and raced them at his own track and in the East. He had used his influence to try to pass a racing law, but there had been little public interest, for in the 1920s no racetrack could compete with the great gambling casino called Wall Street.

There were at least two other promoters and gambling men in California who had been haunted by the distant sound of horses long before Doc Strub sat down for his shave on a day of disaster. One was Norman Church, who bred thoroughbreds in Southern California. The other was the beloved Bill Kyne of San Francisco, one of the most colorful figures the racetracks ever knew. Church was a rich, bellicose, table-pounding extravert who had tried for years to promote the cause of racing in his native state by bellowing loudly. Kyne was a poor man who would never get rich because he had a seemingly irresistible compulsion to gamble away or give away all the money that he made. Kyne just loved horses and horse racing, and profit was a secondary consideration with him. He had opened numerous racetracks throughout the West, but the man with the star on his shirt had closed many of them after only a few days of operation.

Strub heard the clatter of hoofbeats very late, but he heard it far more clearly than the other Californians, or other racetrack promoters throughout the nation. It was Strub, and Strub alone, seemingly, who sensed almost intuitively and at once the remarkable effect that the Wall Street Crash, which took fifty billion dollars out of the American economy in five short hours, would have on the sport of racing, moribund in most of the states of the Union at the time. Five thousand banks failed before the sands ran out for President Hoover, great industries went bankrupt and two out of every seven Americans—fourteen million in all—were unemployed. It was natural to suppose that the harassed public of the time could not afford a luxury like horse racing on the lavish scale that Strub conceived it.

Strub had a devious mind, however, and his uncanny faculty of guessing right had made him several fortunes.

He was convinced, seemingly against all logic, that the greatest depression the country had ever known would also be the period of greatest expansion for horse racing, and he was absolutely right. His theory was based on both psychological and practical factors. Ever since a wizened little New Englander named Coolidge had become the official resident of the White House, Americans had been conditioned to uninhibited gambling under the misleading name of national prosperity. They could no longer afford to gamble in the yellow-chip game called Wall Street. Some of them still *could* afford to gamble two dollars at the betting windows of racetracks.

The growth of racing in America had been restricted all during the early twentieth century by the Reform lobby, one of the strongest political forces in the land. The cynical captains of finance who really ran the country at the time were perfectly willing for the Reformers to ban gambling on horse racing as long as they did not attempt to restrict the gambling activities of the Stock Exchange.

Strub knew that only a prosperous nation can afford the Reformer. He predicted that in depression the ban on racetrack gambling in many states, including California, would disappear with the ban on the sale of spirituous liquors, which had been the Reformers' great achievement. This prediction was based on the cold logic that was a part of Doc Strub's nature. With fifty billion dollars gone from the national economy as surely as if that much currency had been set afire, the state treasuries would be desperate for tax revenue. State legislators could not levy further taxes on businesses that were bankrupt or on unemployed citizens whose banks had failed. Doc Strub gave them something to tax.

He gave them the great, overblown, commercial modern American racetrack. It is still moot whether he did the sport a service or disservice.

But Dr. Charles Strub founded modern racing when he opened Santa Anita Park in 1934 just as surely as the Duke of Cumberland founded the thoroughbred line when he bred Marske to Spiletta. The racing we have in America today resembles the racing we had before the Wall Street Crash in the same manner that an IBM computer resembles an abacus.

When Wall Street crashed in 1929, racetracks were operating in twelve states but were legal in only five. There were some twenty-five courses in the country, if you stretched a point and included many fairgrounds-type tracks that operated only a few days a year. In 1965 thoroughbred racing was legal in twenty-eight states and operative in twenty-seven. There were some hundred racetracks in the country, at least seventy of which had a pretense to major status. In the decade of the Great Depression, from 1929 through 1939, seventeen states passed racing laws. In the relatively prosperous period since 1939 only six other states have legalized horse racing with pari-mutuel betting.

There are no valid statistics in existence that reveal the amounts the tracks paid in taxes before Santa Anita opened in 1934. The amounts were too inconsequential to record, it would seem. *The Statistical Reports* issued by the National Association of Racing Commissioners indicate that in 1934 the existing tracks paid the states $6,024,193. Thirty years later, in 1964, the taxes paid by racing would run over $225,000,000.

And it all began in a barber's chair in San Francisco.

On the day that Wall Street crashed, racing was legal in Kentucky, Maryland, Ohio, Illinois, and Louisiana. It was conducted in Florida, Nebraska, Utah, Nevada, and West Virginia under the pari-mutuel system upon the assumption that there was no law that specifically prohibited such wagering. This was a precarious business indeed, since state, county or local officers might step in at any given moment and padlock the premises. In 1929 Bill Kyne opened a meeting in Reno where there was wide-open gambling on cards, dice, roulette and slot machines. The Nevada law forbade "lotteries," strangely enough, but Kyne argued that picking winners was a game of skill, like poker, not a game of chance, like a lottery. He had guaranteed shipping money to all the horsemen who came to Reno in case the meeting was closed. The sheriff had a different interpretation of the anti-lottery law and padlocked Kyne's track. Kyne stood in a hotel lobby for hours, peeling shipping money from a hog-fat roll and passing it to the stranded horsemen. When the last man was paid off, Kyne himself had to look up a friend and borrow his own railroad fare back to San Francisco.

At Tanforan, the one track in California that was operating in 1929, the "options" system was used, as we have seen.

It was in New York, the cradle of American racing, however, that the most peculiar system of all prevailed. New York tracks had operated under the bookmaking system all during the nineteenth and early twentieth centuries, but under the administration of Governor Charles Evans Hughes in 1911 the Percy-Gray Laws, which made bookmaking a criminal offense, were passed and the racetracks were closed. New York was the racing center of America and it seemed doubtful that the breeding industry, the foundation of the sport, could exist without the tracks of the Empire State. It was freely predicted that the sport of thoroughbred racing was finished in the United States.

In 1913 the New York tracks reopened and conducted so-called "oral" betting, the strangest legal fiction that ever existed, for a period of twenty-seven years.

Bookmaking was banned, but there was no law against betting

with a friend. The bookmakers, notoriously gregarious fellows, became everybody's friends. There was a pious pretense that no money was passed, that all bets were on credit, and that there was no written notation of such wagers. It was all, supposedly, word-of-mouth or "oral" agreements between friends. Naturally cash was passed and notations of the bets were made and the "oral" aspects of the system were pure fantasy. It was not until 1937, however, that the bookies were allowed to post slates with odds marked on them. Up to then they had simply penciled the odds on their programs.

The most important functionary of such a betting system was the arbiter of the ring, who settled disputes between bettor and bookie. This post went to a white-haired, judicious-looking gentleman named John Cavanagh, a famous turf figure of his time. Each book was taxed to pay Cavanagh's retainer fee, which was fifty thousand dollars a year. Technically the books were paying him to supply them with note pads, pencils and paper drinking cups. In the phone book, Cavanagh's occupation was listed as "Stationer."

There is no doubt whatsoever that the bookmakers also subscribed to another and more secret fund for paying off the police and civic officials who could have knocked the tenuous underpinnings of the "oral" system flying at any moment during the twenty-seven years it was in operation. It would seem almost certain that the bookmakers of New York saved racing in the state and that, in saving it, they preserved the sport throughout the country. Without them twenty-seven states would receive $225,000,000 a year less than they receive today in taxes. The bookies' reward for this considerable accomplishment was gall and wormwood. In 1940 a pari-mutuel law was passed by the state legislature and the bookmakers of New York were out of business forever.

It is probable that Bill Kyne did more than any other single man to pass a racing law in California and if he received the short end of the stick when dates were finally allotted to the tracks, he had no one but himself to blame. Strub was a maverick in the political field, although he later became an expert in his dealings with governors and legislators at Sacramento. He believed that the passage of a racing law was inevitable in any case and was more intent upon obtaining financial backers and property on which to build a track than he was upon getting a law passed. Church, who planned a track in Southern California, offended many politicians by his high-handed tactics and bombast and he was left out in the cold when dates and licenses were issued. Marchbank, the crippled gambler, worked quietly and effectively. He was a deft manipulator, but he shunned the footlights and labored behind the scenes.

The chain of mountains that splits the state of California in half is far more than an awe-inspiring topographical feature. It is a division of two peoples and two cultures that are as vastly disparate as those of the Nordic and Mediterranean countries. The tradition of the north, and of San Francisco particularly, is the lusty one of the Forty-niners, the placer miners, the lumbermen and the early railroaders, even that of the wildly bawdy Barbary Coast. There was once a softer, less hectic Spanish tradition in the south but that disappeared long ago and exists only in the synthetic "Mission" architecture of some of the early-day movie stars' mansions. If Southern California and Los Angeles have a culture, it is as transparently contrived as the scrims that grips push onto movie sets. It is the make-believe culture of the motion pictures (and today of television) created by physically beautiful people of meager talent and fatuous minds.

Both Strub and Kyne belonged to the north. They both were rugged, self-made men in the great tradition of San Francisco, which had produced and nurtured more determined individualists and outright eccentrics than any city in the country. Both were sublimely confident that it was the liberal, openhanded northerners who would be most likely to bet their money on a bobtailed nag, and they could hardly have been more wrong. As Bill Kyne once expressed it, "I thought those actors down south spent all their money getting their hair marcelled."

It was force of circumstance, or sheer blind luck perhaps, that sent the reluctant doctor south. He had taken an option on property in an exclusive suburban district of San Francisco, near a swanky golf course and country club. The rich and socially prominent residents of the district and members of the club were horrified at the prospect of having a racetrack within niblick shot of their rolling greensward, and Strub looked elsewhere. He took a tentative option on a tract in the shoddy purlieus of an impoverished area called Butchertown, but he decided almost immediately that in a time of depression this was no place for the luxurious racecourse he wished to build.

The deciding factor came in 1933 when the racing bill was passed. Kyne had worked tirelessly for the measure and had spent his entire personal capital of about seventy-five thousand dollars in promoting it. The legislature offered him his choice of sites. He had already chosen the north and had leased a stretch of salt-lick land on the peninsula just outside the little San Francisco suburb of San Mateo. He had even chosen a name for it—Bay Meadows. Marchbank, of course, would continue at the same old stand—Tanforan. Strub had to get dates for a third track in the San Francisco area or move south. He moved south, reluctantly. There was another strong reason for his move to the Los Angeles area. Church was a political "out" and would not be given dates. Hal Roach, who produced the "Our Gang" comedies and other slapstick features for the movies, had two hundred acres of ground in a singularly appropriate location, a part of the old Rancho El Santa Anita that in the nineteenth century had belonged to a fabulous peacock fancier and horse breeder named Lucky Baldwin. All he lacked at the time the bill was passed was money. Some four hundred of his friends and business associates had guaranteed to invest five thousand dollars each to build a two-million-dollar racetrack, but when it came to getting up the cash, not one of them had come through.

Strub, who was living entirely on credit and had been doing so ever since the day of his fateful shave, had the cash. *He* planned a three-million-dollar racetrack, and some of the most substantial men of California had guaranteed him backing. When he called on them to honor their agreement, every one of them came through. They never had reason to regret the fact. Their investment in Santa Anita made each of them a millionaire within a few years.

Strub, who had the money, teamed up with Roach, who had the ground. Santa Anita was off and running. Possibly because they were fascinated with his grandiose plans, the politicos issued Strub the first license for a California racetrack. Kyne got the second and actually opened his modest Bay Meadows plant, which could seat no more than ten thousand persons, before Santa Anita, in November of 1934. When Kyne, who was never more than a length or two ahead of his creditors for the rest of his life, was chided about his poor judgment in choosing San Francisco instead of Los Angeles, he would grin and say, "I'm not sorry. The way I operate, I like to know all my customers by their first names, and I couldn't remember more than ten thousand first names."

Kyne's November meeting was moderately successful, mainly because San Franciscans had been conditioned to betting on races at Tanforan. He had good reason to believe that he had chosen wisely in remaining loyal to the north when Santa Anita opened in the south the following month. Santa Anita was triple the size of Bay Meadows and had been built at about five times the cost. (It cost three million dollars then, would cost about twenty-five million for the same plant today.) On the first day the public bet slightly under ninety thousand dollars and Bill Kyne must have chuckled over those actors down south who spent all their money getting their hair prettily waved. Strub had been patient for five years, and he was not unduly disturbed. He said Southern Californians had to become "educated" to racing and that it might take two years for them to come out in profitable numbers.

His associates were not so philosophic. Roach was bitterly disappointed. Strub's backers were frantic. The banks considered Strub's racetrack a poor risk. On the third day of the meeting they refused even to advance him the money for his "bankroll," meaning enough money to make change at the admission booths and betting windows. The legend of the time, and Doc Strub himself never denied it, was to the effect that at ten o'clock on the morning of the third day the bankroll arrived in an armored truck from a mysterious source, and that Strub had borrowed it from a Los Angeles bookmaker. The much maligned bookies had saved racing in New York and it is possible that one of them saved racing in California, for the track could not have opened for the third day of sport without the bankroll.

Although Roach was given the title of president, he was never more than a figurehead at Santa Anita. He did contribute one invaluable asset to Santa Anita in the person of Fred Purner, a handsome, prematurely white-haired man with thick black eyebrows. Purner, who would remain with Santa Anita as public relations director for more than a quarter of a century, was press agent for the Hal Roach Studios. Before publicizing one-reel slapstick comedies he had served a strange apprenticeship. He had sold grave lots in Hollywood's fabulous status-symbol cemetery, Forest Lawn.

Purner had not been hired because he had any knowledge of horses or horse racing. He knew nothing at all about either at the time. Roach was a penny saver and he had simply required his studio press agent to double in brass at the track.

On the fourth day of the meeting Strub called Purner before him. As Purner later related the incident, Strub glared at him with his steady, gun-fighter's eyes and pointed a finger as if he were taking dead aim with a Colt revolver.

"You're a movie press agent," he said. "You're supposed to know a lot of movie stars. Get them out here. The big ones. Get them out here tomorrow."

Purner was a popular and persuasive man. Somehow or other he got the motion picture people out to Santa Anita. The movie crowd set the behavior pattern for the public in the Los Angeles district. The success or failure of any business enterprise was almost solely dependent upon their patronage. Strub saw that pictures were taken of the movie notables at the track and Purner saw that the pictures got in the papers. The public began coming to Santa Anita in droves, not to see the horses or to see the most beautiful and lavishly appointed racing plant the world had ever known, but to see the movie stars. Very soon Santa Anita, which had begun with a betting handle of under ninety thousand, was enjoying million-dollar betting days.

The movie people not only attracted crowds to the track, they bought horses in training, yearlings and breeding stock from Kentucky, Maryland and other thoroughbred centers throughout the country, and even from England, Australia and South America. They founded the modern thoroughbred breeding industry of the state which still prospers. Some of them would even establish other racetracks. Bing Crosby, Pat O'Brien, Walter Connolly and half a dozen other actors opened a track called DelMar near San Diego for a lark, and movie money originally financed Santa Anita's main competitor, Hollywood Park, on the far side of Hollywood.

Louis B. Mayer, the last of the great movie moguls, imported more foreign horses to America for more money in less time than any other man in history. He had discovered that losing money on a racing stable and breeding farm had distinct tax advantages, and his pay from M-G-M of six hundred thousand dollars a year made him the highest-salaried man in the world at the time of the Great Depression.

The perpendicular pronoun has not intruded itself into this chronicle up to this point. It enters now, as erectly vertical as a Guardsman on parade.

I did not know Cumberland, partly because I do not move in the circles of Royal Dukes and partly because I arrived on earth two centuries too late. I did know Strub well, and even worked for him for a while, and I found this complex man an utterly fascinating human being. He is worthy of far more detailed study than ever has been given him, for he, far more than any other man, was responsible for the gigantic enterprise of modern racing. Its virtues, and they are many, must be credited to him. Its shortcomings, and they, too, are manifold, must be laid to him.

Doc Strub was never beloved, even by his closest associates, and he never seemed to give a damn. He was cold, hard, unsentimental, undiplomatic, intolerant of fools and human weakness. He built a racetrack that would lure more customers and more money than any other course on earth until modern Aqueduct reared its steel bones on the Long Island flatlands a quarter of a century later. In one respect this painless dentist with no antecedents whatsoever in the ancient sport of racing achieved far more than the gentlemen and sportsmen of the New York Racing Association, all Jockey Club members steeped in the finest traditions of the turf, achieved when they constructed Aqueduct in 1959. Strub built something beautiful. Aqueduct is huge and efficient in the way a supermarket or an automobile assembly plant is huge and efficient. It is not, on any count, a thing of beauty.

I have always suspected that the lords and squires of Cumberland's time were seeking something more than an animal with which they could win purses and bets when they evolved the mutant we call the thoroughbred. I think, unconsciously perhaps, these lusty fellows were after beauty in both form and function when they devised their breeding patterns, and that they attained it in the thoroughbred. It has often been said by his detractors that Doc Strub's only motive was money. He achieved that aim, certainly, but he also achieved beauty when he created Santa Anita.

I first saw Santa Anita in December, 1936, two years after its founding. Life, like delirium tremens and abstract-expressionist painting, can afford some startling visual experiences. I recall a day in Paris when my metabolism had not yet adjusted to European time. I awakened as dawn was breaking over the Seine and wandered out on a Left Bank balcony and caught my breath with wonder at the spectacle. The Paris dawn does not come up like Kipling's thunder; it spills down, like pastel colors from an upset paintpot. Suddenly, from far across the river in Montmartre, an alabaster balloon, shaped like a Christmas pudding, rose through the rainbow mists, and it was the holy place called Sacré Coeur, suspended for one miraculous moment between heaven and the city's ancient chimney pots. There was another time when a ship was sailing through a slate-gray northern sea at dusk and the copper domes of Copenhagen, richly weathered to an unearthly patina, came floating through the watery twilight. There is a special color to the air of Denmark at dusk, a color that is neither quite green nor quite blue, that fades into grays as soft as kitten fur and glows with rosy sunset-pink. It is the color of Royal Copenhagen porcelain.

And there was a third visual experience when Santa Anita burst suddenly into view as the highway curved abruptly on that day in 1936. The ranging stands with their frieze of racing thoroughbreds and their palm-frond ironwork were the peculiar color of Denmark's old city, neither quite blue nor quite green, and snow-capped Old Baldy, the highest peak of the Sierra Madres, rose in the background for all the world like the rounded cathedral dome on Montmartre's sacred hill. Stately rows of coconut palms stood like absurdly attenuated parasols to shade the track, and the wind from the mountains ruffled the green feathers of Australian pines. Old Lucky Baldwin, who had bred such great horses as El Rio Rey and Rey El Santa Anita on these vast acres, had fancied peacocks and they had roamed at will over his thousand acres. This year Strub's gardeners had turned the acres of the infield into an enormous peacock made of millions of colorful blossoms. The total effect was breath-taking, and a painless dentist, whose motive, they said, was money, had brought it into being.

My first encounter with Doc Strub himself was a somewhat ruder experience. I was standing on a catwalk at Santa Anita, waiting for the press-box elevator. The elevator door flew open, slammed into a three-hundred-dollar pair of Zeiss binoculars that were suspended from my neck, and knocked them out of calibration. Doc Strub had pushed the door, and he stood there now, staring at me, not angrily or apologetically, but merely with cold appraisal.

"You stand too close to doors," he said. "It's dangerous." Then he strode away.

Later we met more formally. If he remembered our first encounter, he never mentioned it. We shared a taste for good Kentucky bourbon, and sometimes when he was relaxed and mellow he would recall how he had sat in the barber's chair that day and had learned he was a pauper instead of a millionaire and how, almost immediately, he had decided to build a racetrack and pay his debts and make another fortune. Sometimes he would pull back the window curtains and look out at the vast expanse of Santa Anita. They said he had no sentiment in his nature, but he had left an old, vine-grown stone building standing on the racetrack property. It had been Lucky Baldwin's winehouse. "I like to look at it," Strub would say, as if that were explanation enough.

Sometimes as he gazed out at his plant he would say, "It's a good racetrack, isn't it? It's been good for everybody. We've made money. The state has made money. The horsemen have made money. And the public has enjoyed it."

Strub was one of the first men to think of the racetrack as a part and parcel of community life. As the profits of the Los Angeles Turf Club, Santa Anita's corporate title, became more and more enormous, he formed a subsidiary foundation. Santa Anita purchased the Lake Arrowhead resort, and Strub donated hundreds of mile-high acres in the Great Bear area to the Boy Scouts of America as a campsite. His son Bob, who became president of Santa Anita after the doctor died, was a Scout bedecked with Merit Badges at the time.

Strub's compulsive urge to publicize Santa Anita as a great

public institution and a boon to California may well have resulted finally in one of the greatest evils of modern racing—political control of the sport. Even the good doctor, who was certainly one of the wisest men who ever graced the racing scene in any important capacity, could hardly have foreseen the ultimate result of such a public relations policy, and he should not be blamed too much, for his motives were as pure as those of Galahad. His insistence upon stressing the benefits that the Southern California community as a whole derived from Santa Anita was engendered by the peculiar problems he faced in a time of economic panic.

In the first place, most of the sportswriters from Southern California papers who were assigned to cover his meetings had never before written of racing. They knew almost nothing of horses and horsemen and the technical aspects of the sport. What impressed them was the fabulous sums of money that were being pushed into the yawning maw of the tote machine, and money, money, money—not horses, horses, horses—was the theme of virtually every story that they wrote.

The frantic Purner tried desperately to distract them. He conducted them to the exclusive Turf Club and pointed out the glamorous personalities of the films. Never before had so many famous stars of the screen been squeezed together in so small an area. He delivered little lectures in which he urged the newspapermen not to pose as financial experts but to fulfill their assignments as sportswriters. It did no good at all. As the years went by the greatest stables, greatest trainers, greatest jockeys of America came to Santa Anita, but dollar signs always made the headlines. Strub saw the danger of this at once. The times were parlous and no city in America was without its bread lines. This public image of Santa Anita as a place where the movie stars with overblown incomes engaged in Thorstein Veblen's parlor game of conspicuous waste had to be counteracted, and Strub did his best to counteract it.

Also, Strub was from liberal, sophisticated, highly civilized San Francisco and he was appalled to discover the vast number of lunatic-fringe reform movements in the southern part of the state where food faddists and freak religious cultists abounded. All of these weird people had votes and they could demand a referendum on racing at any time. If Santa Anita was pictured as a sea-green gambling hell instead of a place of public entertainment, it might be closed down forever by an outraged public.

The interest of the newspapermen in the flood of money was entirely legitimate, of course. Santa Anita at that time differed from other racetracks in only two respects: it was the largest and most luxuriously appointed course in the world with the most glamorous patrons, and its betting totals were unprecedented in the records of racing.

The betting totals could not be concealed. They flashed in neon lights on the infield totalisator board, in ever-mounting sums, every ninety seconds. These betting totals were at once an illuminated testimonial to the complete success of the man who had seen a racetrack instead of a castle in the air as he daydreamed in a barber's chair—and they were an ever-present danger. Since the newspapers and the public insisted upon seeing Santa Anita in terms of betting totals, Strub decided to make a virtue of the tremendous gambling at his track.

In publicity releases and paid advertisements he emphasized the huge taxes paid by the track and the fact that California's educational system and its enlightened wildlife conservation program were virtually supported by the gamblers of Santa Anita. He hinted darkly at the added taxes that must be levied if this source of revenue were not available and at the increased unemployment that would result from the closing of the track.

This publicity campaign achieved its purpose. There was no referendum and racing was accepted as a vital part of the state's economic structure. The doctor did not foresee the boomerang result of such publicity, however.

Not only in California but throughout the nation, legislators began to drool. Tracks in unlikely locations without proper financing were licensed. Racing seasons were extended to the ridiculous point where there were ten times the number of racing days that there were calendar days. Night racing was inaugurated to lure the bottom dollars of the working stiff who could not go to the tracks in the daytime. Such freak betting systems as the Twin Double were introduced to increase the betting totals—and the revenue to states. Legislators throughout the country, and especially in New York, pressed for off-track betting that would extend public gambling from the racetrack enclosure to business and residential neighborhoods. In 1964 New Hampshire legalized the first lottery of the twentieth century in America, and decided the winners by the result of a horse race at Rockingham Park. Rockingham expected fifty thousand persons for the race. Only seventeen thousand came, the smallest Saturday crowd of the season, and the track lost a hundred thousand dollars on the operation that enriched the state.

By the 1960s the politicians had taken over racing completely and they were operating one of the most complex businesses on earth not for the benefit of the horsemen or the horses or the public or even the track owners. They were operating it as a state-sponsored numbers game for tax revenue.

This, too, had its remote beginning when a painless dentist sat down in a barber's chair in 1929.

In the 1930s the long shadow of the politician did not darken the festive, sun-drenched scene of Santa Anita. If the looming shade was there, it was not noticed. Every day at the palm-fringed track beside the tall Sierra Madres was a joyous carnival, the Ascot scene from *My Fair Lady*, a brave parade of the beautiful and rich, with hoofbeats drumming the quickstep as the big tote tinkled to the tune of money.

Santa Anita was a lush oasis of bright blossoms and birds of plumage and natives decked out in gorgeous silks. Santa Anita glittered like some incredible mirage in the bleak desert of depression.

Bing Crosby, who just a few years before had been an unemployed Rhythm Boy splitting two-dollar bets with anyone who had a buck in the back-East bookie shops, had entered Seventh Heaven. Now he had a barn full of horses of his own on the backstretch and he was betting big, so big, in fact, that a special credit window had been installed in the Turf Club to accommodate him and other high-rollers. He wore the most outrageously gaudy sports jackets in the history of haberdashery to the track, and the bartender poured him bubbly from his special bottle after every race.

It was the era of the bust on Wall Street and the era of the bust in Hollywood, but in Hollywood the bust was more corporeal. The sunshine of Santa Anita danced on the bottled-blonde hair of Miss Lana Turner, who had made the homely sweater the most fashionable of feminine garments for those young women who could fill it properly. The sweaters Miss Turner wore to Santa Anita were always sequined.

Pat O'Brien, who had earned a modest fortune out of enacting the role of a professional Irishman, had a peculiar handicapping system. He bet on horses with Irish names or horses of Irish descent or horses whose jockeys' silks were emerald green.

Miss Betty Grable, who would become the pin-up queen of a thousand barracks and wardrooms just a few years later, could not afford the prices of the Turf Club. She and her husband, a big, awkward-looking fellow named Jackie Coogan who had been "The Kid" in the famous Chaplin film, scanned the program in the clubhouse, far below the dizzy heights where glamor dwelt, and grew very nervous when they hazarded two dollars on a horse, for their income at the time was limited.

Up above them, in the gilded precints of The Club, Charlie Chaplin, a man of untold wealth, grew nervous, too, when he bet two dollars to show on a favorite. Legend had it that he was a thrifty man who forced his consort of the time, Miss Paulette Goddard, to buy her dresses off the bargain racks. At Santa Anita he enacted the role that legend assigned to him as convincingly as he played the little tramp in films. When a race was in progress and his two bucks were riding, he would squeeze his eyes tight shut and ask, "Where is he, Paulette? Where is he now?"

The dark and menacing George Raft stalked about on built-up heels, always accompanied by a man called Killer Gray, who was supposed to be his bodyguard, but was actually paid a handsome stipend to serve uncomplainingly as the butt of outrageous jokes.

Jimmy Durante had a constant companion, too, a man named Bernie Rich, who was his personal turf adviser. Rich was a good handicapper and a form player, but Durante would often steal off from him and bet a hundred or so on a longshot that he fancied, a habit that infuriated his paid adviser.

Miss Louella Parsons, the dowager queen of gossip columnists, fluttered among these birds of plumage like a mother hen, gushing, cooing and scribbling notes for posterity on what they wore and what they said and who was getting divorced. Once a Hearst editor with a sense of humor assigned Miss Parsons to write a story of the running of the Santa Anita Derby from the woman's viewpoint. She sent in the name of the wrong winner and the wrong second horse and called the race the Kentucky Derby, but she had the name of the third horse absolutely right.

Oliver Hardy, the corpulent comedian, bet big and took his betting very seriously. He always wore a ridiculously small peaked cap on top of his large, round head and affected an old black raincoat that beat the breeze like buzzard wings. He liked to promenade back and forth, back and forth on the Turf Club bridge while he was engrossed in his *Racing Form* and each time he reached the grandstand end, a teen-aged bobby-soxer would beg him for his autograph. One day he signed her book. He signed SHIRLEY TEMPLE in a large black scrawl.

Mickey Rooney, who was still playing a slightly overaged Andy Hardy at the time, worked his way to the Turf Club gradually. He began his journey half a mile away at a bar for stable help located at the far end of the commoners' quarters called the grandstand. He would order whiskey and stand there belligerently, a politician's fat cigar clamped between his teeth, waiting to be recognized. If no one recognized him, he would growl and ask the nearest stable hand, "Hey, Bud! You know who I am?"

On a day when there was a race fit for a king or when one of the King's own horses was engaged, the Great Man would make his Grand Entrance. No trumpeter heralded his approach with brazen horn, but there was a kind of silent fanfare when he arrived, like a breeze that stirs tall meadow grass. The big, black hearse that served Louis B. Mayer as limousine would pull up at the Turf Club gate. Santa Anita's exquisitely tailored lackeys, mostly handsome youths who had come to Hollywood in search of stardom in the films, would snap to tremulous attention and doors would open and stars whose incomes were only a million or so a year would be shoved aside from the waiting elevator. The portly little man moved with a flat-footed pomposity, the dark balls of his eyes staring straight ahead through rimless lenses. A respectful three paces behind him, his fluttering entourage would follow, led by his press agent, Howard Strickling, and including more anonymous little men with worried looks and brief cases.

Even before he became visible, the glamor set in the Turf Club's empyreal heights would sense his presence in the way birds sense the approach of a marauding cat. Powder puffs would dab at noses surreptitiously, lipstick would reshape prettily pouting lips and all conversation would suddenly be hushed. Mickey Rooney would have reached The Club by now. He would hastily stamp his cigar underfoot, for Uncle Louis did not approve of Andy Hardy's smoking in a public place. He would stuff his mouth with Sen-Sen and fix his face in the impish grin of Uncle Louis's All-American Boy.

Mayer was the most powerful, most feared and most hated man in Hollywood, where many men were powerful and anyone of any importance at all was feared and hated. Soon after California racing was revived at Santa Anita, he became Hollywood's answer to those entrenched aristocrats of the Jockey Club back East and to the horsemen of Kentucky's Blue Grass who bred most of the thoroughbreds that raced in America. Uncle Louis was a horseman now and his horses were the biggest single deduction on the tax forms his auditors filled out.

He spent a lot of money on a lot of horses, but only one of them—the stallion Alibhai who left a lasting impress on our breeding patterns and is the grandsire of Kelso—amounted to very much. In Hollywood, however, Uncle Louis was the Duke of Cumberland, Lord Derby and all the Belmonts and Whitneys and Wideners and Vanderbilts in one roly-poly package. His press agent, Strickling, had summoned from the East (at handsome fees) men he deemed to be experts to advise the Little King about the bloodstock that he purchased and to publicize his purchases when they were made.

The drums rolled loudest when Mayer brought the champion stallion of Australia, Beau Pere, a fabled son of the English sire Son-in-Law, to America in 1940. The price was not made public, but there were hints that he had paid a quarter of a million for the horse, a sum unheard of then. A more accurate gauge might be the value set on him at Customs—one hundred thousand dollars. For a while it seemed that Beau Pere would live up to advance notices, for he contended with Kentucky's great Bull Lea as a leading sire of two-year-olds, but his produce seldom raced on after their first year on the tracks and the best horse Beau Pere ever got was a filly named Honeymoon.

Mayer spoke sagely of thoroughbreds as if he had grown up in a box stall or was regurgitating all the volumes of the Stud Book. Beau Pere stood at Mayer's farm near Perris, California, a sun-baked, shadeless oven where yearlings grew butterball-fat from inaction because of heat and stood about all summer as lathered with sweat as runners who had just set track records. Beau Pere was a giant of a horse, standing seventeen hands and weighing around fifteen hundred pounds in stud, and it was hard for even an unpracticed eye to mistake him. One day Mayer conducted a party on a tour of his breeding farm and paused at Beau Pere's paddock. He expatiated upon the points of the horse grazing in the paddock at the time, despite the timid nudges of farm workers. Beau Pere happened to be snoozing out of sight in the shade of his stall at the moment. The horse in the paddock was a stable pony, worth perhaps two hundred dollars.

Uncle Louis wreaked a poetic—even a motion-picture—vengeance upon the hardboots of Kentucky, however. These lean and market-hungry gentlemen had descended upon Southern California soon after the opening of Santa Anita because they had heard that bedazzled motion picture people wanted to breed and own thoroughbreds. They had discovered, to their disappointment, that the glitter set expected to pay rock-bottom, depression prices for the stock they bought, and the thoroughbred market was one of the few enterprises upon which the economic panic had had no great effect. In time, as frantic legislators throughout the country passed racing bills, the thoroughbred market would actually boom *because* of the depression. The hardboots made the best of a bad bargain and sold the culls of their farms to the starry-eyed innocents for the prices they were willing to pay. That inferior stock which arrived in California in the early 1930s is still a detriment to the state's stud farms.

When Uncle Louis started throwing his millions around, he refused to patronize the hardboots. He spent his money in England and Australia and South America. In 1947 he sold Beau Pere to a Kentucky syndicate for a whopping hundred thousand dollars, despite the stallion's advancing age, and his vengeance was complete. Beau Pere was injured during the trip and a month later developed an inflammation of the colon and died. For some inexplicable reason, neither Mayer nor the Kentuckians had a nickel's worth of insurance on the horse.

By 1949 Mayer had decided it was unprofitable to receive a salary, even with horses for tax deductions. He took studio stock instead and paid a capital gains rate to the government. He had no further use for thoroughbreds and sold all his holdings for $4,500,000 at a great dispersal and by private treaty. By that time the highest-salaried man in the world was another movie mogul, Nick Skouras. The second highest-salaried man in the world was Doc Strub of Santa Anita, who received $450,000 a year as vice-president and managing director of the track. He had no horses to claim as dependents and he told me once that the government allowed him to keep only about $50,000 of his earnings. He owned stock in the track, however. He had paid all his debts to the last cent and was again a millionaire.

The second most powerful man in Hollywood in the 1930s, and therefore the second most feared and hated, was Harry Cohn of Columbia pictures. Cohn had also heard a sound of horses. His horse holdings were by no means as pretentious as those of Mayer, but for a while at least they were about the most important things in his life. Unlike Mayer, he really studied thoroughbreds and became a very knowledgeable horseman. He would often come out to the track at dawn to see his horses work and spent a great deal of time in the stables. He was a Gray Eminence in the Hollywood power game, lacking Uncle Louis's flamboyance and desire for personal publicity. He raced under the name of Jobella Stable. Even such brilliant literary lights as Louella found it difficult to interview him, but any sports reporter who wanted to talk horses with Cohn would be invited to the studio and would most likely converse with the Great Man while he and the movie mogul sipped highballs in Cohn's private sauna bath.

Another Hollywood producer who heard a sound of horses at the time was virtually an invisible man. Harry Warner, eldest of the Warner Brothers, was a very small man who insisted upon wearing a very large Stetson and there were times in the Turf Club when he seemed to be one of the madder creations of Hieronymus Bosch—a ten-gallon hat propelled by stumpy legs.

Warner's farm at Calabasas was also a work of pure surrealism. In its pre-horse days it had doubled in citrus and celluloid, serving as both an orange-grower's grove and a location for outdoor motion picture sets. When Warner constructed stables of precious hardwoods (each equipped with a built-in hot-squat that would electrocute flies upon contact), they abutted upon the streets of Western frontier towns, the casbahs of exotic oriental cities and plantation manor houses of the Old South. Warner's bloodstock was as cheap as Mayer's was expensive. His principal stallion was a nondescript beast named Baltimore Boy who had been a selling plater. Warner had seen him finish a race on three legs and had decided that this was the stuff of a Grade B movie script and that it was his sacred duty to see that such courage was transmitted to posterity. Baltimore Boy never got a horse worth the saddle on his back, of course.

However ingenuous and foolish some of them may seem, the movie people made Santa Anita and in making Santa Anita, they made modern racing. On the level that they approached the sport, their empathy with the tense little dramas on the track was almost absolute. The little dramas lasted for only a minute or two and their own careers seldom lasted beyond the first flush of physical beauty. The races that lasted a minute or two had all the intense, concentrated quality of the movies they made, which lasted an hour or two. The thoroughbred's most striking quality was his physical beauty, and that was their most striking quality, too. And in a horse race almost anything could happen, as it could in Hollywood. A young girl named Lana had been sitting there in her sweater one day sipping a soda and a talent scout had seen her and lightning had struck and now she was one of the Great Ladies. Often an unknown young horse would come charging from nowhere in a race and lightning would strike and he would win a rich purse and become a champion.

Seabiscuit was a truly great race horse, but the movie people loved him because of his humble beginnings and because he was a cripple. They loved a cheap selling plater named Malicious almost as much because he was a stretch-runner who would seem hopelessly beaten early, then come flying down the stretch to win by a narrow margin, as if he were the star of a movie melodrama.

Strub had the movie people to thank for his success, but his own approach was different. The Old Breed of the East, the Establishment of American racing, had begun by regarding him as a cheeky interloper, but long before he died in 1958 they had come to respect him highly and receive him as an equal. In his latter years, he made as deep a study of racing as he had once made of pain-killing drugs and the stock exchange. He studied far more than the financial aspects of the sport. He studied its history and its traditions and he tried to honor them at Santa Anita. He brought sporting art, some of the finest in the world, to Santa Anita's public rooms. He memorialized such heroes of Santa Anita as Seabiscuit and Jockey George Woolf with marble monuments. He visited the ancient courses of Europe, where racing was much the same as it had been in the eighteenth century. He was one of the few men not directly connected with the New York turf ever honored by the coveted award of the New York Turf Writers' Association. He was received in the closed aristocratic circles of the turf hierarchy in France. He was admitted to the sacrosanct precincts of the English Jockey Club at Newmarket. And quite often he was received by Queen Elizabeth II herself when he visited England.

Strub made mistakes, of course, but even his mistakes were the result of his dedication to the cause of racing, for whatever the motives of the painless dentist had been originally, the sport soon beguiled him and absorbed him completely, just as it had beguiled and absorbed the Irish adventurer named Dennis O'Kelly. His overemphasis on the tribute that racing pays the state was a mistake, as we see it now, but it was a measure that saved California racing at the time. He almost made an even greater mistake in the late 1930s.

Although he himself was the founder of highly commercialized modern racing, he was disturbed by the forms it was taking at many tracks, particularly at Narragansett in Rhode Island, under less responsible promoters. He wished to found an association of the leading racetracks of the country to adopt a code of ethical practices and to inaugurate a national protective bureau to keep undesirables from the tracks. He dictated a letter to J. Edgar Hoover, asking in effect if he would consider heading such an association at an annual salary of a hundred thousand dollars. This was 1939 and there was war in Europe. Members of Nazi bunds were wearing swastikas and parading on the flatlands of New Jersey. German espionage and sabotage in the United States was an acute and frightening problem. And to the public at large Hoover, director of the FBI, was a national hero and a reassuring symbol in a time of peril. Had it ever become known that a sport which depended for its existence on gambling had tried to hire Hoover's services away from the national interest, an outraged public might well have banned racing entirely. Fortunately, Strub's press agent, Purner, and others of his staff, persuaded him it would be ill-advised to mail the letter he had written.

The organization that Strub conceived was formed in 1942 in Chicago and still exists without benefit of Hoover's services. At the time the Thoroughbred Racing Associations was founded, Santa Anita itself was closed. It had been shut down two weeks before its scheduled opening in December, 1941, by order of the Army's Fourth Interceptor Command, which feared crowds at the track might invite air raids from the Japs. Santa Anita was an Army ordnance depot in 1942, but Strub was present to urge the formation of the association at the Chicago meeting. Today most of the leading tracks of the country belong to the TRA, and its Protective Bureau is made up largely of former FBI agents, although Hoover is not among them.

Strub's obtuseness in wishing to make such an offer to Hoover is an interesting commentary on the man. Certainly he was not lacking in patriotism. He was cited time and again for his contributions to national defense during the war. Yet, as late as 1939, he simply could not imagine that anything was more important than horse racing. That has been the attitude of a great many men and some of their names have been among the most illustrious on history's pages.

Despite the public relations *gaffes* he committed in the matters of publicizing tax payments and his desire to lure Hoover into racing on the eve of war, Strub's instincts were almost always right. Long before a racing bill was passed in California he announced that the track he had dreamed of in a barber's chair would offer a race worth a hundred thousand dollars in added money, wherever it might be located. This announcement created nationwide publicity for Santa Anita years before the track came into being or even had a name or a plot of ground to build upon. The hundred-thousand-dollar prize was exactly twice that of the richest added-money race ever offered in the United States. The race became the Santa Anita Handicap, which is still decided annually. Except for it, Santa Anita might have been completely disregarded by the newspapers of the East when it first opened in 1934. Santa Anita at that time was known outside California almost solely because it was the home of the richest horse race in the world.

By the middle 1960s there were some three dozen races with an added value of a hundred thousand dollars or more in the United States, but the Santa Anita Handicap was the first one. The first running not only attracted national publicity but brought many of the greatest stables of the East to Santa Anita Park. It was won by an unlikely horse, a former steeplechaser of Irish breeding with the Spanish name of Azucar.

The idea of an annual hundred-thousand-dollar added race—meaning a race in which the track management puts up the

entire hundred-thousand-dollar prize instead of collecting it
from horsemen in the form of fees—was not original with Strub,
however. The first hundred-thousand-dollar added race in the
history of the world had been run during the 1920s at a track
just 150 miles from Santa Anita, but the track was outside the
United States, in a Mexican village where peons slept beneath
their sombreros on dusty streets and stray curs had the starved
and humpbacked look of coyotes. This was Tia Juana, as grotesque a setting as could possibly be conceived for the richest
race the Sport of Kings had ever offered.

The race was the Coffroth Handicap and the gaudy promoter
of the Tia Juana racetrack had established it as a monument to
himself. The track's owner was Sunny Jim Coffroth, a legendary
figure of the sports world, who had promoted the fights or managed the fortunes of all the heavyweight champions from Ruby
Robert Fitzsimmons through Jack Dempsey. The race was established in 1917, but was not then a hundred-thousand-dollar
stakes. It was given that value in 1926 and had only four runnings for such a prize.

The first hundred-thousand-dollar race was won by a turfman
named W. T. (Fatty) Anderson, a fellow as immense in physique as the Duke of Cumberland himself, who sent a fine horse
named Carlaris to the post. The last Coffroth came in 1929, the
year of the Wall Street Crash and Doc Strub's fateful shave. It
was won by Golden Prince, whose training for the race was as
curious as the setting for the great event. Golden Prince did not
work over the racetrack. His owner and trainer, Harry Unna,
conditioned him at a seaside resort just outside San Diego. Instead of working over the racetrack, Golden Prince swam in the
ocean every morning.

The Tia Juana track, where the race that set the monetary
pattern for the great classics of today was run, had a casino called

the International Club as its clubhouse and gamblers who could not find enough action on the races were able to play roulette, cards and dice games. Just outside the gates of the racecourse, wooden shanties and adobe huts had hastily been set up by the distinguished lawyers of Tia Juana who offered racegoers Mexican divorces at bargain rates. The most modern building in Tia Juana stood on a hill that overlooked the track. It had a red roof and an electric sign that blinked on and off twenty-four hours a day. It was called the Molino Rojo and it was a house of prostitution.

Kyne had been contemptuous of the sporting blood of the Hollywood set. Strub had been loath to build his magnificent racetrack within the precincts of the movie capital. But Coffroth had foreseen that the motion picture crowd was anxious to gamble its easy money. At Tia Juana a man could get drunk at a dozen bars, bet the horses, gamble on any game he chose, pick up an instant divorce just outside the gate and find all the commercial sex he needed just up the hill. The movie people found Tia Juana so attractive that they would motor 150 miles for the Sunday racing at Coffroth's course—and for other sports.

Coffroth was forced out of business when other gamblers, headed by Baron Long, built a more lavish racetrack called Agua Caliente at the other end of town. I never knew Sunny Jim in his heyday, but I got to know him well after he had retired into a curious ivory tower of his own devising just before America entered World War II.

He was one of the most completely zany and completely fascinating men I ever knew. Coffroth's ivory tower was a wooden house of no great architectural distinction on Homer Avenue in San Diego, near the Marine Barracks. Its exterior was the Hansel and Gretel gingerbread design of the Teddy Roosevelt era. Inside was madness with a sense of humor. Coffroth's hall tree was a totem pole he had brought back from Alaska during the Gold Rush because he said one of the more hideous faces of the carving reminded him of a business partner who had cheated him of money. His furniture was of all periods and the rooms were so cluttered that it was difficult even to move about, especially after a few glasses of the vintage champagne spiked with Napoleon brandy which he served his guests. On his walls a bawdy caricature by Milt Gross and a bathing beauty calendar flanked a priceless *kakemono* from the Kensington Museum, and yellowing photographs of forgotten prize fighters nudged misty Turner watercolors.

During his last years, Coffroth, who had decided he was an invalid without confirmation of doctor's diagnosis, never left the house. His only wardrobe was dozens of suits of silk pajamas and numerous silk dressing gowns. He lived alone except for a Negro servitor named Billy. He rose each day at four in the afternoon and breakfasted on tea and toast and brandy-spiked champagne in the area he called his "backyard," which was twenty-seven city lots planted almost solid with gorgeous dahlias. His street door stood open all night. Guests were never invited, but guests arrived almost every evening and all of them were welcome, for Coffroth had a lively interest in all sorts and conditions of people from the cop on the beat to the former champions of the ring, the great turfmen and the aging stars of the silent movies who visited him.

He did not retire until the sun was up. When his guests left, he read. He had thousands of books. Few dealt with sports. He considered himself an authority on Shakespeare. And for some queer reason he devoured weighty tomes on military strategy. One night he told me of the race he had named for himself and made the richest in the world and how he had chosen the trophy for it. The trophy was as distinctive as the famed Whip of England, made of the plaited hairs of Eclipse's tail and mane.

He had been in New York and he had wined and dined too well and he was seeking fresh air. He took one of those hansom cabs that stand in front of the Hotel Plaza as a lure for nostalgic tourists. He began to grieve over the sad condition of the spavined nag that pulled his hack and to reflect upon the fact that, even in the case of thoroughbreds, horses did all the work and people got all the money. The horse-drawn cab was moving down Fifth Avenue at the time. It was very late at night and there was little traffic. Coffroth looked up and saw the formidable bulk of Tiffany's to his left. He ordered the driver to take him back to his hotel at once. He knew the manager of Tiffany's well and he called him at this unearthly hour and gave him exact specifications for the trophy to be awarded the winner of the hundred-thousand-dollar Coffroth Handicap. It was to be a solid silver water bucket, an exact duplicate of the galvanized tin buckets that hang on the walls of every racing stable.

"The horse that won it could use that trophy," Coffroth said.

That was the last time I would ever see Sunny Jim, for ailments that were not of his imagining would kill him a short while later. He had been in a strange mood all evening and I imagined that he had had too much to drink. He had insisted upon speaking of military strategy and quoting Clausewitz. He kept saying, over and over, "Our peril does not come from the West. It comes from the East, and it approaches rapidly."

It is easy now to fancy that this strange old man who foresaw the colossal structure that racing would become and offered its first hundred-thousand-dollar prize was born with a caul signifying prescience.

The next day was Sunday and I journeyed over the border to attend the races at Agua Caliente. On the way I passed the decaying ruins of Coffroth's old Tia Juana course, now an abode of Mexican squatters and their squalling brood, where mangy curs scavenged in the stalls once occupied by thoroughbreds. I thought of Coffroth and the odd, cryptic warning he had kept repeating the night before.

As soon as I entered the track I heard the news. It was December 7, 1941. The Japs were bombing Pearl Harbor.

If the huge, unwieldy, money-stuffed business of modern racing had to evolve, it is fortunate indeed that it was Charles Strub and not Walter O'Hara who was most influential in determining its shape. Strub may have accented money too much for the sake of expediency, but he never once lost sight of the simple fact that racing is essentially a sport. O'Hara could never see the horses for the gamblers.

His enemies, and they were numerous indeed, called O'Hara "The Junk Dealer." He was a young-man-on-the-make, not quite thirty, when Wall Street crashed and he began at once to take full advantage of the opportunities that depression offered by buying up bankrupt New England textile mills at bargain prices and selling their machinery and equipment piecemeal for an enormous profit. He was a millionaire in his early thirties. When the New England states climbed on the bandwagon and passed racing bills, he opened Narragansett Park in the grubby town of Pawtucket, Rhode Island, a rather slumlike extension of Providence, in the incredibly short period of sixty days. He opened his first meeting in August, 1934, some five months before Santa Anita had its Christmas Day inaugural. The physical aspects of the track set the pattern for the big-hunk-of-concrete school of architecture that would be followed too often throughout the country as depression-driven legislators passed parimutuel bills and tracks proliferated like mushrooms.

Two weeks before his opening, O'Hara chartered an airplane, stocked it with cases of booze, hired a pretty hostess to mix the air-borne highballs and flew a group of New York's leading sportswriters to Rhode Island to inspect his plant, which even at that late hour was far from complete, although workmen labored on it twenty-four hours a day, seven days a week. Enormous arc lights flooded the place when darkness fell and riveting machines made the night hideous with sound.

After the inspection, O'Hara tendered the visiting writers a banquet at the Providence Biltmore Hotel and he made a remarkable speech. He was an extremely heavy drinker and most of the writers at the dinner put his remarks down to one too many, but this was not the case. In the four dizzy years that he operated Narragansett, he amply proved he meant every word he said that night.

He opened his remarks with the flat statement, "I don't give a God-damn about the improvement of the breed of horses. I'm here to improve the breed of the two-dollar bettor. I want every God-damned cent he's got, and I intend to get it at Narragansett."

Today's legislators who feed at racing's pork barrel do not put it so crudely, of course, for euphemism is the language of politics. But the statement O'Hara made in 1934 seems to govern their actions almost everywhere.

Doc Strub always worked on the principle that he was staging one of the biggest shows on earth and that, entirely aside from its gambling aspects, it was well worth the price of admission. A pass to Santa Anita then was as rare as a U.S. passport to Communist China is today. The horsemen, the employees, the press got in free, but everybody else paid. Strub believed that people who couldn't afford to pay their way through the gate, couldn't afford to play the races and didn't belong at the track.

O'Hara issued passes to Narragansett by the tens of thousands. Bartenders handed out a sheaf of complimentary tickets to the course with every drink. Tobacco dealers passed them out with cigarettes. Newsdealers supplied them with the morning paper. From one end to the other, New England was papered with passes to Narragansett Park. Gate receipts were peanuts to O'Hara. He wanted everybody there so everybody would bet and he could take his cut from every dollar in the tote machine.

O'Hara had the town of Pawtucket in his pocket. Mayor Tom McCoy (who looked so much like a *Last Hurrah* politician it was hard to believe he was exactly that) and Police Chief Leonard Mills spent more time at the track during Narragansett meetings than they spent in their offices. Many racegoers thought these civic officials were O'Hara's employees. The force of guards at the track was always augmented by Pawtucket cops, all of them big fellows whose dark uniforms and Sam Browne harness for their guns made them look rather like Himmler's Gestapo.

O'Hara built himself a private penthouse on top of the Narragansett clubhouse. Here he had his private office, a large bar with a bartender in constant attendance, a lounge for visiting notables and sleeping quarters for himself and his wife, Cle. He seldom left Narragansett during the meetings. He was suspicious of everybody and he was especially suspicious of the horsemen who raced at his track. Often he would rise from his penthouse bed in the middle of the night and pay a surprise visit to the stable area to see if the horsemen were burning down his barns. He had a large green light placed outside the penthouse that was visible from every starting point of the racetrack. His starters could not send the fields off until O'Hara punched a button and gave them the green light. The ceremonial of the post parade had usually lasted about ten minutes at most tracks. At Narragansett it was a funeral procession that went on for a minimum of half an hour and sometimes for forty-five minutes. O'Hara would not turn on the green light until every last dollar was bet in the mutuels. The mutuels department would signal him when there were no more bettors waiting and he would punch the button. This meant, of course, that many nervous horses were beaten before they ever went into the starting gate.

O'Hara gambled heavily on the races himself. Trainers who gave him tips on horses that won were likely to enjoy special privileges at Narragansett and were assured of stalls for the next season. Trainers who gave him tips on horses that lost or who refused to enact the role of private touts for the racetrack's owner would be treated shabbily and would often be denied stalls at a later date for no reason except O'Hara's capriciousness. He had had enough sense to hire capable racing officials, but he was not above hinting that they should make groundless rulings against horsemen he disliked for purely personal reasons. Usually they refused, and sometimes he fired them for refusing. O'Hara raced horses himself under the name of the Araho Stable and he would hint broadly to his racing secretary that he should card races whose conditions suited the Araho horses.

O'Hara had a long-standing feud with the Metcalf family who published the Providence *Journal* and *Bulletin,* papers that fought his racetrack and his highhanded management from the first. One day he needled his trainer, a tough little man named Bobby Curran, into attacking the *Journal's* turf reporter, John Aborn, when he entered the track. Aborn was bruised and cut and thereafter the *Journal* sent him to the track accompanied by bodyguards.

O'Hara bought a paper of his own called the Pawtucket *Star* in order to have a public forum in which to assail the Metcalfs and anyone else he disliked. This paper would prove his nemesis. In 1937 he bought another moribund newspaper property, the Providence *Tribune,* merged his Pawtucket paper with it under the name of the Providence *Star-Tribune* and virtually wrote his own death warrant when he began publishing irresponsible editorials attacking the leading citizens of the state.

The Racing Board steward at Narragansett, who was appointed by the state, was a Providence liquor store owner named James Doorley (not to be confused with Judge James Dooley who brought sanity to the management of Narragansett after O'Hara's time ran out). O'Hara hated Doorley for some purely personal reason, possibly because he had not appointed him himself. One day during the course of racing, O'Hara, who had been drinking heavily, stormed into the stewards' stand, directly in front of the grandstand, and protested some trivial ruling Doorley had made. He vilified Doorley with profanity and obscenities that only Walter O'Hara could use and, to the delight of the crowd, seemed on the point of attacking him physically. Doorley cited O'Hara for contempt of the State Racing Board and the case was referred to Governor Robert Quinn, another of O'Hara's political foes. Quinn immediately served notice upon Narragansett that he would close racing unless O'Hara was removed from office.

In 1937 Franklin Delano Roosevelt was considered a permanent feature of the political landscape of the United States, and he was known to be interested in the political future of Robert Quinn. It was said that the national party planned to make Quinn a U.S. senator, then to run him as Roosevelt's vice-presidential candidate when the election of 1944 came around. This could have happened, of course, and Robert Quinn instead of Harry Truman might have dropped the atomic bomb on Hiroshima. It didn't happen because an egocentric Irishman cussed out a Providence liquor dealer over the procedure he had dictated for posting photo-finish pictures at the Narragansett racetrack. When Quinn demanded O'Hara's resignation, there were writs and counterwrits and injunctions and counterinjunctions, and Jim Farley and the other Democratic bosses warned the governor to back off from the fight or give up all political ambition. Quinn refused to back off.

On the night of September 7, 1937, I was having a modest measure of bourbon in the oak and leather Falstaff Room of the Providence Biltmore when an ancient, bandy-legged waiter named Mac came to the table. "The Crazy Man wants you on the phone," he said. Old Mac always called Walter O'Hara "The Crazy Man." I picked up the phone that had been placed in the bar for the convenience of bibulous guests and heard O'Hara cackling. O'Hara always cackled when he was amused by some mischievous act of his own. He said he was putting out a midnight extra of his *Star-Tribune* and that he wanted to read me a front-page statement he had made regarding Quinn's charges. The statement comprised the most extraordinary editorial ever published in an American newspaper. It began: "Governor Quinn is a God-damned liar."

A special messenger from the newspaper office brought the extra over to the Falstaff Room an hour or so later. It contained far more dynamite than the editorial. Its lead story, a libelous attack on Quinn, had been written by O'Hara. It had an eight-column, double-decked headline in 48-point type that read:

GOV. QUINN WILL LAND
IN BUTLER'S, O'HARA SAYS

Butler's was a Rhode Island sanitarium largely devoted to the treatment of alcoholics. O'Hara had designed his headline cunningly. When the paper was folded on the newsstands, the public read only the first half:

GOV. QUINN
IN BUTLER'S

The governor immediately issued warrants for the arrest of Walter O'Hara. He had dug up two old New England blue laws that had never been invoked in modern times. Walter O'Hara was charged with felonies of criminal libel and blasphemy.

O'Hara said he would not accept the warrants and would not submit to arrest. He virtually barricaded himself in his penthouse at Narragansett. The Pawtucket police said they would not serve the warrants or arrest him. They were, in fact, acting as his bodyguards. They surrounded O'Hara's penthouse in the way Storm Troopers surrounded Hitler's Chancellery. Quinn said the State Police would serve the warrants and arrest O'Hara. He said he would call out the militia if necessary.

Newspapermen from all parts of the country, including such leading columnists as Heywood Broun, converged on Narragansett, not to see the horses run but to see the first test of city and state police powers in the history of the nation. (That test actually occurred at Phoenix City, Alabama, twenty years later when State Police and the National Guard arrested city officials and policeman along with mobsters in putting down a long reign of lawlessness.)

Shortly before the scheduled close of the Narragansett meeting on September 18, the Day of the Showdown arrived. O'Hara had been admitting a strange group of people into the penthouse all afternoon. It was said the State Police would arrive momentarily and shoot it out with the Pawtucket cops if necessary. It was also rumored that O'Hara's bail would be set at one hundred thousand dollars.

Only two newspapermen were admitted to the penthouse. One was Jack Conway, sports editor of the Boston *American*. For some strange reason, I was the other one. In the tarrying crowds that waited for a gun battle were dozens of other reporters from all parts of the land.

Up in the penthouse, O'Hara was maudlin drunk. He was enjoying himself immensely and thought it was a great joke that so tense a situation had arisen. He said he had no intention of resisting arrest. He was asked why he didn't inform the reporters outside of the fact. He looked out of the window and guffawed.

"To hell with the bastards," he said. "Let 'em stand there. It ain't raining, is it?"

Mrs. O'Hara was the only woman present. Mayor McCoy was there. So was Police Chief Mills. Old Jack Letendre, who served on Narragansett's board of directors, was slumped down in a chair, silent and scowling. A few years later he would be murdered by the Mafia in front of his Woonsocket home because he had opened a gambling house in Dade County, Florida, without the Syndicate's permission. O'Hara was a notorious hypochondriac and he had his personal physician at his side. The person most incongruously present was a Catholic priest. O'Hara was a Catholic, but he never went to church.

Twice O'Hara imagined he was suffering a heart attack and the physician had to feel his pulse and reassure him. Once he pillowed his head on the breast of the priest and cried, "I'm going to jail, Father! I'm going to jail!"

A little Irish politician from Woonsocket was very drunk. He had brought along ten thousand dollars in cash toward O'Hara's bail. He had the money in a paper bag. He kept falling out of his chair and the money kept spilling over the floor.

Finally a large young man in civilian clothes entered. He accepted O'Hara's offer of a drink and they left together. He was the State Police who arrested Walter O'Hara. Bail was set so low that there was no need to use the coarse money in the little politician's paper bag.

By October, when the Narragansett fall meeting was scheduled, O'Hara still refused to resign. The governor posted the state militia, with guns and bayonets, at the track and kept the meeting closed. O'Hara had been advised that if he took entries for a meeting that wasn't operating he would gain some legal point. Those mimeographed entry sheets of October, 1937, are now among the rarest curiosa of racing. The few horsemen at Narragansett made a game of entering champions of the past who had retired or had long been dead. Man o' War and Exterminator were entered every day. So were Eclipse, Herod, and Matchem. Quite often the names of the Byerly Turk, the Godolphin Barb, and the Darley Arabian appeared on the entry sheets.

O'Hara avoided a jail term by making an abject public apology to the governor. His directors deposed him as head of Narragansett and bought him out. In 1938 he formed something called the Square Deal Party and ran for Governor of Rhode Island. He received fourteen thousand votes, mostly from Pawtucket. He had been a millionaire twice by the time he was forty, but now he was broke again. He took to selling parking meters. His wife divorced him and he remarried almost immediately.

One day, three and a half years after the Battle of Narragansett, Walter O'Hara, who had been drinking, climbed in his car alone. He was driving down a tree-lined road from Providence to Taunton, Massachusetts, when his car overturned. They measured the skid marks later and said he was driving very fast. When the State Police picked him up there was still breath in his body. He was dead on arrival at the hospital in Taunton.

At the end, ironically enough, Walter O'Hara was in the hands of his old enemies, the State Police, again.

This time there was no one who could bail him out.

3

All the Jockeys Had Curly Hair

Landmarks are mileposts on the long road called Time, and they seem vital to man's sense of security as he makes his weary journey. If they do not exist in the form of a tree or a hill or a crumbling castle, man manufactures them, and calls them monuments. Lacking a monument, he may accept some existing feature of the landscape as a landmark, for he must have an object to point out as he says, "Here it all began."

If you watch the races from the highest perch in the huge grandstand of Aqueduct's "Big A" and the day is crystal clear and your binoculars are very powerful and you scan the far horizon north by west, you see two tiny balls suspended in the air like captive balloons. From the old grandstand of Belmont Park, which was condemned as unsafe for human habitation in 1963, the balls were clearly visible to the naked eye and took on shape

100

and substance. They are water towers, erected fairly recently for a purely utilitarian purpose, but they serve the function of landmarks almost perfectly for they define the outer limits of the first racecourse in America.

It was known once as Salisbury Plain and later was called Hempstead Heath. It extended in breadth for four miles, almost the exact distance between the water towers. America's first racetrack was established just a century before Eclipse was foaled at Cranbourne Chase, for racing of a sort predates the thoroughbred in every country where it is held. In fact, in 1963 when a scholarly gentleman named Dr. Mordecai Margalioth unearthed a long-lost fragment of the *Sefar ha-Razim,* or *Hebrew Book of Secrets,* used by a Gnostic sect of the second century, he discovered it to be a magic incantantion for ensuring the winner of a horse race. Perhaps Captain Dennis O'Kelly wasn't the world's first tout after all. A Jewish Gnostic may have antedated him in the profession by sixteen hundred years.

During the frugal Dutch era of wooden-legged old Peter Stuyvesant such frivolities as horse racing in New York would have been considered manifestations of the Devil himself. In 1664, when the Dutch inhabitants of the colony numbered only sixteen hundred peace-loving citizens who seldom fired a blunderbuss in anger, a swaggering, sword-clanking, curly-haired English Cavalier named Richard Niccols arrived with a large force of Restoration swashbucklers behind him. He took over the territory and proclaimed himself Governor in the name of His Majesty Charles II, who had regained the throne of England for the Stuarts four years before. Just about the first order of business for the invading Cavaliers seems to have been the clearing of a tract of land in the section now known as Nassau County in order to build a racetrack. They called it New Market, inevitably, since it was modeled after the Round Course in

England, where Charles II, the jockey-king, had conducted the first organized race meetings in history.

Unfortunately, no records of the races that were run between the water towers exist. We do know that Governor Niccols, following the custom set by his king, offered plates and trophies to the curly-haired gentlemen jockeys whose horses won. But we do not have the name of a single horse that raced at America's New Market. We can assume a great deal, however, for we know something about the races that King Charles was running in England at the time and we have some record of the kind of horses that contested them. Charles's own favorite mount was a mixed breed, with oriental blood, named Woodcock, not greatly different from the rudimentary thoroughbred that evolved a century later. Charles was so distraught when a gentleman of his bedchamber defeated Woodcock (King Charles up) on a horse inelegantly named Flatfoot that he took to bed with a migraine and refused to attend to State business for several days. The King, of course, had brought the Royal Mares to England and we know specifically of four who played a major part in the genesis of the thoroughbred. They were the D'Arcy Grey Royal Mare, D'Arcy's Royal Mare, the Sedbury Royal Mare and the Why Not Royal Mare. The horses that the Cavaliers brought to America were undoubtedly of the same type that were racing in England. They would have been the mixed breed called the English horse, with as much infusion of Arab and Turkish and Barbary blood as their owners could afford.

Whether any of the Cavaliers' horses that raced over Hempstead Heath had a part in founding the thoroughbred line in the United States will never be known. A century or so ago fanciers of the native-bred Morgan horse, one of the most useful and lovable animals that ever drew breath, liked to claim that the founder of the line, Justin Morgan, whose antecedents are unknown, had royal Arab heritage and was a descendant of horses owned by Niccols' Cavaliers. Veterinary research seems to have established that the Morgan horse has no Arab blood, however. In Colonial America Arabs were so rare and so highly valued that fairly scrupulous records of them were kept. There is one early American Arab, however, whose story is so romantic that it is a bit dubious. This is a stallion known variously as Ranger or Lindsay's Arabian, a handsome gray, who figures in American thoroughbred pedigrees and whose most famous offspring was a race horse named Magnolia who belonged to a gentleman farmer named George Washington. Judging from the naïve admissions in his own handwritten diaries, George was not only the Father of His Country, but the Father of His Country's Horse Players. He complains bitterly in his journals over sums he lost betting on Magnolia, which he misspells "Magnolio," as he misspelt so many words. He is especially concerned over a bet he lost on the colt to an architect and political philosopher of nearby Monticello named Thomas Jefferson. Washington traded Magnolia for a parcel of "Kentucke land" to his old comrade-in-arms, Light Horse Harry Lee, father of Robert E. Lee. After the Civil War there was speculation that Marse Robert's famed war horse, Traveller, may have descended from Ranger. Such stories were based solely on the fact that both Traveller and Ranger were grays and that Ranger's son Magnolia had belonged to General Lee's father. Ranger was reputed to have sired the matched gray mounts of a whole troop of Continental cavalry during the Revolution.

The prettiest tale about Ranger is open to doubt for no other reason than the fact that it repeats one of the most recurrent legends about horses throughout the ages. Since antiquity, there has been an almost mystical connection between horses and the sea. Ranger supposedly swam ashore from a shipwreck and landed in Connecticut. Poseidon, the Greek God of the Sea, was also Lord of Steeds in mythology. The ancient Greeks believed horses came out of the sea, possibly because they were not native to the isles and arrived in ships originally, or because of the arched, spray-maned horse-forms of waves rushing to the shore. In any event, horses were still coming out of the sea as late as 1904, when the New Zealand-bred steeplechaser, Moifaa, allegedly swam ashore from a wreck in the Irish Channel to win the Grand National of Aintree. This story is widely believed, and there is no truth at all in it. Maybe it arises from the fact that Moifaa's sire was Natator.

Some chroniclers hold that Ranger did not come out of the sea, but descended from one of the Arab-type horses ridden by the curly-haired jockeys of Hempstead Heath. In the cases of both English and American thoroughbreds, you reach a certain point in time and pedigree when all that went before is pure speculation, and usually the most romantic tale is the one that is accepted, for romance, not all of it contrived by any means, is the very breath of racing.

The Cavaliers with curly hair who raced between the water towers are nameless, forgotten men who rode nameless, forgotten horses, but the territory they staked out as racing country has remained racing country for three centuries.

Even before the United States became a nation, Virginia, Maryland, and the Carolinas were the breeding centers of America, for the Cavalier tradition with its love of fine horses was strongest in the aristocratic South, but the hub of racing remained always within a few miles of the cradle of the American turf established by Niccols and his gentlemen-adventurers in the midst of Long Island. Even today, three hundred years after they built their racecourse, when there are racetracks in some twenty-seven states from coast to coast, horsemen identified with the nation's most famous stables often say, "When you're not racing in New York, you're racing at a bull ring."

The vast importance of New York racing to the sport throughout the country and throughout the world is best evidenced by the panic conditions that prevailed during the two years that followed the enactment of the Percy-Gray Laws against race-track betting in the state in 1911. The banning of New York racing resulted directly in the English Jockey Club listing a vast majority of American race horses as cold bloods or half-breeds rather than thoroughbreds. This was true from 1913 right through 1949. Thus Man o' War, a descendant of England's "first thoroughbred," Matchem, and a horse still regarded by many authorities as the greatest champion of all time in all countries, was not a thoroughbred, according to the English. The English feared that racing in the United States would collapse because of the ban in New York and that the moneyed men who owned great stables would descend upon England and win all the stakes. They also thought other American owners might sell their stables in England at any price and so destroy the bloodstock market completely. This fear was heightened when James Ben Ali Haggin, who owned more thoroughbreds than any other one man in the world, began to sell his stock at auction in England, and Rubio, a Haggin-bred horse who had won the Grand National of Aintree in 1908 under the silks of Major F. Douglas-Pennant, went for the incredible price of seventy-five dollars. He was a gelding, of course, and thus had no stud prospects, and he was well advanced in age, but he was still a good jumper and prospective hunter and the price at which he was sacrificed seems to have scared the Savile Row breeches off members of the Jockey Club.

They hastened to pass a ridiculous protective measure known as the Jersey Act which denied thoroughbred status to all American horses who did not trace back in all lines of their pedigree to horses already listed in the English Stud Book. This meant that twentieth century American horses who had not previously invaded England or did not trace to ancestors who had raced in England bore a typographical bar sinister beside their names in the form of a Maltese cross in the English Stud Book, making them virtually valueless as bloodstock in the British Isles. This act was the worst blot on English sportsmanship in the history of a horse-loving people, but it was in effect for thirty-six years.

This seems as good a place as any to pose an obvious question: What exactly is the definition of a thoroughbred? It is surprising indeed how many veteran horsemen will blush and hem and haw and become as inarticulate and evasive as a guilt-laden witness under cross-examination when they are asked that simple question. The truth would seem to be that a thoroughbred originally was a horse who was arbitrarily listed as a thoroughbred in one of the stud books of the world, particularly the English Stud Book, first published in 1808, the year that the term "Thoroughbred" came into general usage. In the earliest Stud Books, horses were included or excluded for reasons that were often capricious or venal, since the Jockey Club members who controlled the Stud Book also owned most of the best breeding stock.

Very early it became apparent (although this does not seem to have been a stipulation originally) that all thoroughbreds must trace in the male line to one of the three oriental taproot stallions known as the Godolphin, the Byerly and the Darley. As time went on, it was established through natural selection and the preference of breeders that all thoroughbreds went back to these stallions in the male line through three foundation sires of mixed blood named Matchem, Herod, and Eclipse, the last two bred by Cumberland.

The Epsom Derby of 1804 was won by Hannibal, who descended from the Godolphin through Driver, Trentham, and Sweepstakes, rather than through Matchem. Since then every single winner of the Epsom Derby has traced to one of the three orientals through Matchem, Herod, or Eclipse in the male line.

The first four horses listed as thoroughbreds in the English Stud Book to come to America were Diomed, winner of the first English Derby in 1780, Medley, Shark, and Messenger. All trace back in the male line to the three orientals, but only one traces through Matchem, Herod, or Eclipse. This is Diomed, a son of Florizel and descendant of Herod. Medley went back to the Godolphin through Gimcrack and Cripple rather than Matchem. Shark and Messenger both descended from the Darley, but they did not descend through Eclipse. Shark was by Eclipse's sire, Marske. Messenger traced to the Darley through Blaze, founder of the hackney line, and through The Flying Childers (who was piously reported to have run a mile in one minute flat). The exportation of Shark, Medley, and Messenger to the upstart nation called the United States makes it plain that as early as the eighteenth century English breeders wanted their oriental blood filtered through Matchem, Herod, and Eclipse and regarded other racing stock as culls. Herod's Derby-winning son Diomed was shipped here at a price of a mere $250 when he was twenty-one years old and believed to be impotent at stud.

The male lines of the three imported stallions who did not go back to Matchem, Herod, or Eclipse thinned out fairly rapidly, but Shark's "tail male" can be followed right down to another horse named Shark in 1891, and Medley's male line descendants did not die out entirely until the advent of a horse named Quicksilver in 1910. Messenger exerted some influence on the thoroughbred succession, but his great feat was establishing the line of standardbreds, or trotters, through his descendant Hambletonian.

Virtually all of the earliest pedigrees must be washed down with a large draught of saline solution, for the men who devised them were sometimes more inventive than accurate. Many of the pedigrees published in the first Stud Books of both England and America are taken at face value from the advertisements of a stallion's stud services. Even the pedigree of Eclipse is drawn largely from an advertisement circulated by Dennis O'Kelly, since Cumberland's stud records had been burned by the naughty little princess. And when you get as far back as the Byerly, the Godolphin, and the Darley, you stop as abruptly as if you had run smack into a brick wall or a large policeman.

We would have had some fanciful pedigrees indeed had we depended upon Arab horse traders to supply them, for the lineage of the Arabs, Turks, and Barbs has always been pure mythology. Had you asked for a pedigree of one of the orientals, you would have been told, "He descends by twenty generations from the filly who caught the cloak of the fleeing sheik upon her upraised tail." Or you might have been informed, "He comes in a pure, unsullied line from one of King Solomon's blue-skinned mares." For reasons of ignorance or venality, or for sheer love of lying, the Arabs have always confused a horse-breeding sheik named Salaman with King Solomon, the Hebrew patriarch, a fact that the anti-Semitic Egyptian dictator Nasser might find galling.

We are far more likely to accept the authenticity of an illustrious pedigree without question when it contains such typically English names as "Smith's Son of Snake" or "Bloody Buttocks," both of whom played important parts in the making of the thoroughbred. Such names are reassuring through their very homeliness.

It is interesting to compare the price of $250 that Colonel John Hoomes of Virginia paid Sir Charles Bunbury for Diomed, winner of the first Epsom Derby in 1780, with the price of $672,000 that a Kentucky syndicate headed by A. B. Hancock, Jr., paid for Tulyar, winner of the 172nd Epsom Derby in 1952. Diomed came to America in 1798, and he must have liked the climate of the new world. Despite his advanced age and supposed impotence, he produced fifty-five sons during his eight years at stud, and founded the line of Herod and the Byerly Turk in America. Hoomes, who operated a stagecoach line and a breeding farm and was a member of the Virginia legislature, sold Diomed soon after his arrival to Thomas Goode, another Virginian, for fifteen hundred dollars. He was the last of the four thoroughbreds to come to America. He was preceded in 1784 by the small horse Medley, who stood barely fourteen hands and was named for the Mr. Medley who conducted the most famous coffeehouse and gambling rooms in England, once a favorite haunt of both Cumberland and O'Kelly. Medley was imported by Hart and McDonald, horse dealers of Louisa, Virginia, for five hundred dollars and was bought from England's famed Tattersall, still the leading dealers in thoroughbred flesh in England. Shark was bought for six hundred dollars out of another Tattersall auction and was brought to America in 1786. Messenger was the only one of the four who came to the North. He was bought by Thomas Benger of Philadelphia in 1788. The sum paid for him is in dispute, but it was most probably about two hundred dollars, almost certainly no more than that. Thus, the total price of the basic thoroughbred stock imported to America before the turn of the nineteenth century was only $1,550. You could not buy four good stable ponies for that price today.

It is significant that only Messenger remained in the North.

He made his rounds at stud under various ownerships from Pennsylvania to New Jersey to New York. It was in these Northern states and New England that trotting had its inception and Messenger is noted more as a sire of standardbreds than thoroughbreds. The trotter is a rougher breed than the thoroughbred because Messenger had less refined mares to serve in the North.

Although most of the early stallions stood at the studs of the South, particularly Virginia, their progeny would run many of their famous races at the tracks of Long Island, all of them within a short distance of the "Round Course" where the Cavalier jockeys had ridden. Over the three centuries that elapsed between the course founded by the Cavaliers and the opening of modern Aqueduct, the Colossus of the Crossroads, there were many racetracks on Long Island, all of them hallowed by the hoofbeats of great horses. The original New Market seems to have existed as a racecourse for at least a century, and another course, also known as New Market, stood on the same spot until it was replaced by the patriotically named Washington course in 1804. The famed Union course opened on Long Island in 1821. In the nineteenth century great tracks like Sheepshead Bay, Brighton, Gravesend, and lesser tracks like Jamaica and the old Aqueduct, whose clubhouse was described as "a shanty on stilts," followed. Then in 1905 came Belmont, most beloved of all American racetracks, the undisputed dowager queen of the turf, even though Morris Park, which opened in Westchester County in 1889, had previously been considered America's answer to Royal Ascot.

The prerevolutionary courses of Manhattan Island itself have a peculiar interest because of their location. There was one known as Church Farm. On this property Kings College, which would become Columbia University, was built. There was a racecourse in the section that would become a gaudy legend of American folklore—the Bowery. Today "mission stiffs" sleep off their drunks on the spot where horses raced in colonial America. In Greenwich Village unbarbered beatniks strum guitars and beat bongo drums in coffeehouses built on the site of a colonial racetrack which was located near the potter's field and hanging tree that became Washington Square. At the nothern end of the island the teeming ghetto we call Harlem was the site of a race-track both before and after the Revolution. The academic motif recurred when fashionable Jerome Park opened in 1866 on land now owned by Fordham University.

In the colonial South racetracks were called "race fields" for good reason. Most of them were merely outworn tobacco lands. It is from this source that courses like Lincoln Fields in Chicago and Golden Gate Fields in California derived their names. These "fields" were precursors of the typical American dirt courses of the nineteenth and twentieth centuries, for the early races on Long Island were run over turf, as has always been customary in England. Also, the fields foreshadowed the circular or elliptical shape of modern tracks, for they usually followed the patterned furrows of the tobacco farmer's plow.

Despite the English heritage of America, it seems odd indeed that thoroughbred racing should eventually have become far more of a national pastime than baseball has ever been. The post-Revolutionary American was independent to the point of eccentricity, a cocky, extravert individualist in all of his behavior patterns. These characteristics were even more pronounced after the War of 1812 when the hated British had burned the White House, and old Andy Jackson, who owned the famous racehorse Truxton, had whopped the daylights out of the flower of the English Army at New Orleans (with a slight assist from Jean Lafitte's pirate crew). The early nineteenth century American was stubbornly determined to be an original in all aspects of his life. When he threw off the English yoke, he threw off virtually all English customs and traditions with it. It was natural to expect that he would belittle the animal the English called "thoroughbred" and develop his own breed of race horse.

He did, in fact, establish three breeds of typical American horses. The first was the quarter horse, who did not evolve in the West as most people believe, but in colonial Virginia. In the West, Virginia blood was merged with that of the cow pony, or pinto, and it proved a perfect combination for the quick, fast horse required for short dashes. The most typically American of all horse sports is trotting, and that evolved from the standard-bred line of Messenger and his descendants, Rysdyk's Hambletonian and Hambletonian. English squires had mounted their hackneys and trotted them over country lanes in friendly contests, and this is the way Americans first raced the rough-hewn stock they lovingly called "jugheads." But soon they added a Yankee touch and hitched sulkies to the trotters and pacers. So racing came full cycle, for millennia before man mounted horses, he raced them hitched to chariots.

The third American breed was the most engaging of them all, for it came out of the nowhere into the here and its founder was as prepotent as the great Eclipse himself had been. This was the Morgan horse, derived from a stallion called Justin Morgan, which was also the name of his owner, whose peculiar combination of professions was that of schoolmaster and tavernkeeper in New England. The original Justin Morgan appeared suddenly in Massachusetts and later in Vermont in the early 1820s (even the date is inexact). No one, including his owner, knew where he came from, although tall tales were told about him in his time. He was a pony-sized bay horse of fourteen hands, round-barreled, pouter-chested, his fetlocks fancily fringed, his feet small and dainty. He raced as a trotter and proved formidable. He raced as a runner and proved invincible against the cold bloods, though he never met a thoroughbred. He was a perfect performer under saddle or harness. He was a tireless work horse. He could do almost anything a horse is asked to do. The Morgans of today are often dead ringers for their ancestor in conformation, though they stand a hand higher and weigh more in proportion. The descendants of Justin Morgan were favorite mounts of Civil War commanders. Phil Sheridan rode a black Morgan named Rienzi. Stonewall Jackson rode a chestnut-roan called Little Sorrel, nicknamed Fancy. The Morgan helped to make the line of standardbreds and it is most probable that there are Morgans in the female lines of American thoroughbreds. The pedigrees of the early nineteenth century in the United States are widely confused, however, and this is pure assumption.

All of these three American breeds raced, but in the horse country of Virginia and that portion of the state that became Kentucky in 1792, the Cavalier tradition of the Stuarts was not despised, even though the Germanic Hanovers who ruled England at the time were looked down upon as gross and vulgar pretenders. The English race horse, the thoroughbred that traced remotely to Charles Stuart's Royal Mares and the oriental stallions that came to Stuart England, was the horse of the South and he became the race horse of America and every other land.

In the very early days of racing in the United States it seemed unlikely that the little foal who arrived on All Fools' Day at Cranbourne would play much part in the development of the American thoroughbred. It seemed much more likely that the line of Cumberland's other stallion, King Herod, would prevail, for his grandson Diomed achieved a more illustrious record at stud than the other importations. And indeed it still appeared the line of Herod might reign supreme in America until well after the Civil War.

Diomed's direct male-line descendant Lexington, by Boston-Alice Carneal, often has been called the greatest thoroughbred of the nineteenth century in America, although long before the Jersey Act was passed the English were casting aspersions upon the validity of his pedigree. Despite the fine contempt the British showed for his family tree, Lexington was the leading sire of his country for sixteen years, fourteen of them in succession, a feat no other stallion in any other land has ever achieved. His career on the turf was brilliant but brief, for he went blind very early in life. He was, in fact, known as "The Blind Hero of Woodburn." Woodburn was the great Kentucky stud founded by Robert A. Alexander, who had once been Benjamin Franklin's teen-aged secretary.

During Lexington's short career on the tracks, his owners were of more interest than his record. Strangely enough (and we encounter similar ironies more than once), Lexington began racing under the name of Darley, although his male line did not trace to the Arabian Mr. Darley had brought from Aleppo but to the Turk that Colonel Byerly had ridden in battle. His real owner for his first two races in 1853 was, quite unbelievably, a Negro known only as "Mr. Burbridge's Harry," who had recently bought his freedom from slavery with his earnings as a horse trainer. Harry leased the horse from Dr. Elisha Warfield, but the rules of the turf in the 1850s did not permit a Negro to own a race horse and "Darley" ran in Warfield's jacket.

At the old Kentucky Association track in the town for which another owner named him, Lexington won two races in rapid succession for Harry, then Dr. Warfield quite unfairly withdrew the lease the Negro held. There was no legal recourse for a former slave and Dr. Warfield sold the three-year-old colt to one of the most colorful figures of the nineteenth century, Richard Ten Broeck. When you look at portraits of Ten Broeck, you encounter the same cold, appraising gambler's eyes that were the most notable features of Doc Strub, the man who founded modern racing. All of Ten Broeck's inclinations were those of an antebellum Southerner, for he was a dashing figure of a man and he made a fortune as a steamboat gambler. But he stemmed from the Dutch stock of New Amsterdam and was born in Albany, New York. His name is best known today because the last of the great four-mile runners, Ten Broeck, was named for him. One of the most famous match races of all time was that at Louisville in 1878 when Ten Broeck beat the great mare Mollie McCarthy.

Ten Broeck, the man, was a mysterious figure. His clouded legend has it that he resigned from West Point in order to fight a duel with one of his professors, and that after killing his adversary, he fled South, where men of his kidney were appreciated. Ten Broeck himself never denied this story and rather seemed to relish it, but many commentators contend he merely slugged his teacher and was expelled from the Academy.

Lexington ran only seven races during a career that extended into 1855. He was by Boston and traced to Diomed in the male line through Timoleon and Sir Archie. Lecomte, the great horse against whom he ran three of his seven races, was of exactly the same male-line breeding. Lecomte was owned and bred by Thomas D. Wells of Louisiana and his three races against Lexington were run at the fashionable Metairie Course in New Orleans, then a rival of Long Island's Union Course as the most important racetrack of America. The sons of Boston first met in 1854 in the Post Stakes, which had been heralded as the most important race ever run in America. One of the judges was Millard Fillmore, former President of the United States. Sectional rivalry was then the breath and life of racing, and the contest was designed to attract at least one representative of every state in the Union. That did not quite work out. Only four horses from three states went to the post. Lecomte and Arrow carried the hopes of Louisiana, Lexington was considered a "Northern" invader because he was from Kentucky, and Highlander, the extreme outsider in the heavy betting, was from Alabama. Lexington beat Lecomte in straight heats in their first meeting, with the others never important factors.

A rematch was demanded and it came a few days later in a two-thousand-dollar Jockey Club purse. The conditions called for at least three starters and a nondescript horse named Reube was obligingly entered by an amiable New Orleans sportsman, one Judge Hunter. This time Lecomte won in straight heats. In the second heat Lexington came to his rival, looked as if he would pass him, then suddenly changed leads, broke stride and fell back beaten. We know now that the horse was completely blind in one eye and that the other eye was failing badly. It is probable that he merely shied when he sensed the closeness of the other horse. But Lexington's impending blindness was kept a dark secret by Ten Broeck. An adherent of Lecomte, it was claimed, had run out on the track and shouted at Lexington's jockey, a boy named Meichon, "Pull up! Pull up!" The rattled Meichon obeyed, it was said. Owners and trainers often did rush out on the track during the course of a race in those days to signal their riders, and sometimes spectators also vaulted the rails in their excitement.

For a year, there were challenges and counterchallenges between Ten Broeck and Wells. For some peculiar reason, although Ten Broeck still owned Lexington, he allowed him to race against Lecomte in the jacket of A. L. Bingaman. It was the doughty Ten Broeck who issued the challenges, however. Before Lecomte and Lexington met again, Lexington ran "against the watch" with a whole relay of horses to pace him, and set an American record of 7 minutes, 19½ seconds for four miles. In 1855 Lexington ran his final race and beat Lecomte soundly despite the fact that he was virtually stone blind when the drum signaled the start.

Although Lexington's record was wildly acclaimed by his enthusiastic contemporaries, it was not really impressive, since he started only seven times in three years and won only six races. Boston, sire of Lecomte and Lexington, had won forty races in his time. It was at the stud that Lexington proved his true greatness. Lexington's winning total of fifty-six thousand dollars on the tracks was huge in the light of his times and the few races he ran. And the total of bets that Ten Broeck won must have been many times the amount of the purses, for he was one of the first of the great plungers the American turf produced. He sold Lexington to Alexander for fifteen thousand dollars, and that, too, was a tremendous price for a horse in the 1850s.

Lexington was at stud for twenty-one years and he lived always in the total darkness to which Eclipse had been born. In those years of darkness he sired at least 600 horses and 236 of them were winners. The cash value of race horses has increased twenty times in the century since the get of Lexington was racing. Even today, however, headlines are made when John Galbreath pays two million dollars for Swaps, and a syndicate of ten owners buys Gun Bow for a million dollars. Lexington sired at least three horses who would have been valued at close to a million dollars by the 20 to 1 ratio of today's prices, and he sired them all in a single season at stud. They were Norfolk, Asteroid, and Kentucky. Kentucky sold for forty thousand dollars. Fifty-thousand-dollar offers were refused for both Asteroid and Norfolk. By today's standards this means that one stallion in one season produced two horses worth more than a million dollars and another that brought a price of eight hundred thousand dollars. In the years that immediately followed Appomattox the feats of these three horses alone were enough to make the turf, which had been stagnant during the Civil War, prosper again. And Lexington also sired the greatest mare of her time in Idlewild. For fifteen years virtually every champion of the American turf was a son or daughter of the blind horse of Woodburn.

Norfolk, Kentucky, Asteroid, Idlewild and many other of Lexington's most brilliant progeny descended from mares by a fabled stallion called Glencoe. The Lexington-Glencoe "cross" in the male line of Herod was as famous as the Fair Play-Rock Sand cross that produced Man o' War for the Matchem line. Glencoe, oddly enough, also had sired Reel, the dam of Lexington's great rival Lecomte. Glencoe was a son of Sultan in the line of Herod and he had been imported from England in 1837. He finally found his way into the stud of a dashing Kentuckian named Keene Richards. Glencoe's progeny was a vital force in racing in the nineteenth century and his line of broodmares was unsurpassed, but it was a gelded son of his who never raced that most captured the public fancy.

Richards was a firebrand and an ardent Southern sympathizer. When John Hunt Morgan, the plumed knight of Kentucky, recruited his regiment of Civil War raiders in Lexington and rode out to fight the Yankees, Richards presented the general with this gelding as a war horse. He had no name and Morgan simply called him "Glencoe," after his sire, to the later confusion of pedigree experts. Many contemporaries of Morgan believed the Raider was riding the great English stallion himself, even though Glencoe had died at the age of twenty-seven, as totally blind as Lexington, the year Fort Sumter was bombarded. This gelding was captured along with Morgan and his men during the daring raid into Ohio and Indiana in 1863 and he was presented to General Winfield Scott, the aged hero of the Mexican War who was still technically commander-in-chief of the Union armies, although he spent most of his waking hours eating huge meals at the Willard Hotel in Washington instead of planning battles. Old Fuss and Feathers may have looked his gift horse in the mouth, but he could not have looked elsewhere. He fondly believed the gelding was the great stallion Glencoe who had died two years before and had been totally blind for five years before his death. He rode him proudly in parades in Washington. Edward Troye painted a heroic canvas of General Scott mounted on the captured horse which is now in the National Museum of Racing in Saratoga. Troye carefully titled the painting "General Scott on a Son of Glencoe," but even now some Civil War historians will state that Morgan's war horse and Scott's parade mount was the original Glencoe.

It is completely incredible that the great male line of Lexington and the Diomed branch of the Herod line were allowed to die out completely by 1918 through the callousness and stupidity of American breeders. Or perhaps we should say it *almost* died out—and thereby hangs one of the pretty tales that help make racing the most fascinating of the entertainments man has devised for his beguilement.

A direct male-line descendant of Lexington and Diomed named Lantados was foaled in 1918. He eventually went to stud, but he got nothing of importance and by 1930 it was said that the line, which had been dying through neglect for two decades, was dead at last. Suddenly in the late 1940s news of a lone surviving male-line descendant of Lexington came from the most unlikely of places—South Dakota. South Dakota has legalized racing. It has a racetrack called Park Jefferson, which seats only 1,500 persons. There are eleven breeding farms in the state with exactly a dozen rather nondescript thoroughbred stallions spread among them. One of these stallions, foaled in 1945, was named Rey El Tierra. He stood at D. G. Frame's Raceland Ranch near the tiny town of Reliance in Crow Indian country, and no one paid him the slightest attention until the breeding pundits suddenly realized that here was the very last surviving male-line descendant of the immortal Lexington. The line had not stopped entirely with Lantados after all. At the age of twenty-five Lantados had had a son named Rey El Rio in 1933. And Rey El Rio had been bred to a mare named Ever Graceful and had sired Rey El Tierra. In April of 1964 Rey El Tierra died, and it was once more reported that the greatest American line of thoroughbreds of the nineteenth century was finally gone beyond recall. Then Mr. Frame casually announced in October of 1964 that Rey El Tierra had left five colts behind that could possibly carry on the line. All were still at the Raceland Ranch in 1965. One was a four-year-old named Rey El Tesoro who was to make his first stud season in the spring of 1965. Four others became two-year-olds in 1965.

The windswept plains of South Dakota are far removed from the meadowlands of Woodburn where the Blind Hero held court. The probability of reviving the line of Lexington, as legendary a horse as Eclipse, is very small indeed, but as long as these five animals continue to exist on a little ranch in South Dakota, there is at least faint hope of correcting the greatest mistake the American thoroughbred breeder ever made. When a great breed dies out through natural causes, it is tragic; when it dies out through human neglect, it is criminal.

The American of the early nineteenth century was a romantic fellow, intensely loyal not only to his country but to the particular region of the country he inhabited. In his time horse races were far more than contests between animals. They were affairs of honor and they were governed by conditions as strict as those of the *code duello* which stipulated pistols for two and coffee for one. A challenge for a horse race could no more be disregarded than a challenge to meet an opponent at daybreak on the field of chivalry. A horse owner who refused to accept such a challenge was a pariah among his fellows. The most famous races of the early nineteenth century in the United States were matches between North and South, a kind of prelude to the Civil War. And the most famous match of all was that between American Eclipse and Sir Henry at Long Island's Union Course in 1823.

American Eclipse belonged to Cornelius Van Ranst, a New York State Dutchman. Sir Henry, who was usually called merely "Henry," was the darling of Colonel William Ransom Johnson, a bushy-haired Southerner who lived just over the Virginia border in North Carolina and seems to have resembled Dickens' Mr. Pickwick, since he was an inspired busybody who loved to arrange the affairs of men and horses. His contemporaries compared him to a sterner character, however. He was called "the Napoleon of the Turf." Early in the century, Colonel Johnson started sixty-three horses in two seasons of racing and won with sixty-one of them. He was regarded as a great sportsman, but his challenge to Van Ranst was hardly sporting, since he invited American Eclipse to meet a Southern horse, but reserved the right to name any horse he wished, giving him a stable of all the thoroughbreds south of the Potomac.

Lexington and Lecomte had both been sons of Boston. American Eclipse and Henry were both grandsons of Diomed, Boston's ancestor. American Eclipse was by Duroc and Henry was by Diomed's greatest son, Sir Archie. In his days as a race horse and stud, Sir Archie had been called "the Godolphin of America," and here again we encounter that anomaly of nomenclature peculiar to the early American turf. Lexington had begun racing as "Darley," though he traced to the Byerly Turk. Sir Archie also traced to the Byerly horse, but he was called "Godolphin." And American Eclipse went back in his male line, not to Eclipse, but to Eclipse's stablemate at Cranbourne, Herod. If pedigree experts sometimes make mistakes in the early records, the reason is obvious.

It is highly probable that no race of the twentieth century has ever been the medium of such enormous individual bets as the match between American Eclipse and Henry in 1823. The owners of the contestants posted twenty thousand dollars a side, but these bets increased as the big day neared. One Southerner bet his tobacco crops for the next five years. For some eccentric reason, John Randolph of Virginia, who became the great rival of Henry Clay in the U.S. Senate, not only wagered a huge sum of cash but bet his complete wardrobe, elegant garments made by the best tailors of London. Banks in New York and throughout the South were apprehensive of the outcome, since many of their heaviest depositors had bet all the cash they had in the vaults on the race and had borrowed more for the same purpose. (One hundred and four years later, in 1927, the bank of Midway, Kentucky, would close its doors when a horse named Rolled Stocking, belonging to the local citizen J. W. Parrish, finished twelfth in the Kentucky Derby.)

After the race, even though he had literally lost his shirt (and pants) on Henry, Randolph said it wasn't a horse named Eclipse that had beaten him, but "a red lobster." He based this theory on the fact that Colonel Johnson's strategy would have won for the vaunted Southern challenger, but that the Colonel was too violently ill to attend the race because he had been feted with lobsters and "high wines" by his Yankee hosts the night before.

The total population of New York City in 1823 was 150,000, but turf writers of the time, who were never given to understatement, wrote soberly that sixty thousand persons were at the Union Course and that twenty thousand of them came from the South. This would be an enormous crowd even for modern-day Aqueduct. Niblo's famed pleasure gardens on the Battery arranged to run up a white flag if the Northern hero won and a black flag of mourning if he was defeated.

The race may have drawn more truly distinguished citizens than any other turf event that has been decided in the three hundred years of American racing. Although many of the early Presidents owned horses and raced them, they were sensitive of the fact that there was a strong Puritan strain among the voters and few of them went to the track during their terms of office. (No President goes to a racetrack today.) But James Monroe sent Vice-President Daniel Tompkins as his representative. Andrew Jackson, who would be President in six years, was there. So was Aaron Burr, who had almost defeated Jefferson for the presidency.

Relay riders were posted to carry the news of the race to the city, heat by heat. When Niblo raised the black flag to signal Henry had taken the first heat, several investment houses in Manhattan closed down, fearing a panic. But American Eclipse came through for the North in the next two heats and it was reported that a thousand Southerners walked home, since their compatriots were too broke to lend them stagecoach fare. If the rather vivid reports of the time can be believed "several of the ruined Southrons took their lives in black despair; one plunged a poignard into his vitals when Henry lost."

If Colonel Johnson's strategy really could have saved the day for Henry and the South, he ate the most costly lobster dinner in the annals of the gourmet on the night before the race.

The nineteenth century racegoer's love of match races had a sound psychological basis. Playwrights learned long ago that there is more dramatic impact to two actors playing a tense scene on a small stage than there is in a panoramic view of the Battle of Waterloo, for the human mind and human eye are limited in their perceptions. If we wish to experience the sight and sound and smell and very *feel* of racing, we must view it selectively, recall a few vivid scenes in sharpest focus, contemplate men and horses frozen in time like prehistoric mammals preserved in an eternal ice field.

Oh, there are history books, of course. The shelves of libraries groan beneath their weight. We can follow every mile and every stride of a hundred thousand horses, but we cannot really see and hear and smell and feel statistics.

Man o' War ran twenty races in two years, but he was actually running on the tracks for a little over thirty minutes. The experience of racing, like all delightful things, is fleeting, a rush of colored birds before the eye, the sound of music in the night, a scent of blue grass on a passing breeze, the sweet, warm glow of physical satisfaction. Such things come of a sudden and are gone, but they are remembered.

Books will give you every detail concerning Man o' War. Charts will show you just how far back or how far ahead he was at every pole in all his races. You can trace his ancestry through Fair Play and Hastings and Spendthrift and West Australian and Melbourne and Humphrey Clinker and Conductor and finally reach old Matchem, and then go farther back to the King's horse who pulled a water cart. But if you wished to know all you need to know about Man o' War, you would have visited Faraway Farm in Kentucky when he stood at stud. A wonderfully dignified old Negro stud groom named Will Harbut would lead out the great-muscled, golden-hided horse nicknamed "Big Red" because of his bright chestnut coat, and he would make a little speech: "Ladies and gemmun," he would say, "this is Man o' War. He's the mostest hoss there ever was."

Harbut was a pious man and a deacon of his church. When he spoke of Man o' War, there was true reverence in his voice.

Man o' War ran twenty races and was beaten only once. If you did not see him run, if you never saw him leap away from the start and draw off and off and break the hearts of those who challenged him, you might know him best by listening to the words of the jockey who rode the one horse that beat him:

"I heard something right behind me and I knew it was Big Red coming at me now. . . ."

Ichabod Crane must have felt like that when he heard the hoofbeats of a ghost horse ridden by a Headless Horseman on a fearful midnight.

There may be something to superstition after all, for it was the thirteenth of August, 1919, when they ran the Sanford Stakes for two-year-olds at Saratoga, the only race in which Man o' War was ever beaten and the seventh start of his career. They said he was beaten because a substitute starter, an inexperienced man named Judge C. H. Pettingill, was at the tape, and that the champion was left at the post. This is not quite true. Man o' War broke fifth in the six-horse field. The horse that won the race, a thoroughbred of Harry Payne Whitney's presciently named Upset, had taken the lead at the stretch, and as they moved down the brown lane to the finish Johnny Loftus had Man o' War on the rail, and he was moving now, right behind the leader.

Let Willie Knapp, who rode Upset, tell the story. He is a small, graying man with a wrinkled face and a young boy's clear eyes, and in the 1960s you could find him any morning in the horsemen's room of Aqueduct when they were running in New York.

"We'd passed the quarter pole and were going to the eighth pole, I guess it was, when I heard something right behind me and I knew it was Big Red coming at me now. I looked back and there he was. Johnny Loftus was riding like a crazy man and he yelled at me, 'Move out, Willie! I'm coming through!' So I yelled back at him, 'Take off! Take off me, bum, or I'll put you through the rail!' Then I set down to riding and we won."

You remind Willie that he's often been quoted as saying that if he'd known what kind of horse Man o' War would become, he'd have taken out and let Loftus through, so the champion's record would not be marred.

Willie snorts with laughter. "If I ever said a thing like that I must have been drinking and kidding some green-pea sports reporter. Hell, I rode great horses and I always rode to win. If I had it to do over, I'd do just the same. I'd win."

Man o' War's great year was his three-year-old season in 1920. He started in eleven stakes, won them all, set American records in five of them. In three races he carried more than 130 pounds, the weight that separates the men from the boys. In one race he carried 138 pounds, a burden few horses ever shoulder today.

He beat Hoodwink by a hundred lengths, Donnaconna by twenty lengths, Damask by fifteen lengths.

There were two flaws in his golden armor. He retired too soon. And he met only one older horse, Sir Barton, whom he defeated in the last race of his career, the Kenilworth Gold Cup in Canada.

The 1920s were called the Golden Age of sports and they began with a golden horse.

There was another hero horse as the 1920s began and some horsemen still believe he was greater even than Man o' War. His name was Exterminator and Willie Knapp rode him, too. Certainly he was the greatest gelding of all time—until Kelso came along forty-two years later. He was the greatest Cup horse of all time—until Kelso came along. And I happen to believe he was the greatest race horse of all time—until Kelso came along.

Exterminator was a five-year-old and at his peak in Man o' War's great three-year-old season. The two never met. Sam Riddle, who owned Man o' War, was a conservative gentleman and although he took all weights with his horse, he seemed to want no part of Exterminator at weight-for-age.

Exterminator was owned by Commodore Willis Sharpe Kilmer, a newspaper publisher of Binghamton, New York, who had the lowest boiling point of any man in the history of the turf's eccentrics. He would boil over if you mentioned a patent nostrum called Swamp Root, which had been the basis of his fortune. He boiled over in a Chicago hotel room one day in 1931 when his Sun Beau, who was once the greatest money-winning horse in the world, was running in the $100,000 Caliente Handicap in Mexico. Sun Beau had to be rated back of the pace to run his best. When the radio announcer stated that Jockey Frankie Coltiletti had broken him on top, Kilmer destroyed the radio in his rage.

In 1920, the terrible-tempered Mr. Kilmer was at a perpetual boiling point. He pursued Riddle from track to track and club to club, shaking fifty thousand dollars in his face and demanding he put up the same stake for a race between Man o' War and Exterminator at weight-for-age. Riddle would merely smile and suggest that the two might meet in the normal course of their engagements, but they never did, a fact that has proved a boon to saloonkeepers for four decades, since the relative merits of Man o' War and Exterminator is a classic theme of barroom arguments.

Exterminator had one of the longest careers on the American turf. He raced for eight seasons, retiring when he was nine years old. He ran a hundred races and won fifty of them at twenty-six tracks in three countries over all distances and under any weight the handicapper put on his back. Kilmer's trainer, a gentleman of the old school known as Uncle Henry McDaniel, had bought Exterminator on the eve of the 1918 Kentucky Derby for the ostensible purpose of using him as a workmate for the Commodore's great horse Sun Briar. The gelding had started once in Kentucky and three times in Canada as a two-year-old and had won two unimportant races for small purses. The price that Uncle Henry paid the Kentuckian Cal Milam for Exterminator has always been in dispute. A couple of other horses seem to have been involved in the trade and it would appear that Milam received about ten thousand dollars in cash and thoroughbreds. Uncle Henry probably went that high because he knew Exterminator would have to replace Sun Briar in the Derby. Sun Briar suffered from a ringbone and was going gimpy in his trials, but Uncle Henry did not wish to bring on a Kilmer tantrum by reporting the fact.

Sun Briar broke down before the race and the big, ribby gelding carried Kilmer's green and orange silks. At almost 30 to 1, he was the longest odds on the board. Knapp took him to the lead at the mile, lost the lead at the stretch, but came on again to win handily and begin one of the most amazing careers on the American turf. Exterminator's great saga ended sadly in 1924 when he was nine years old. He finished third in an unimportant handicap at an unimportant Canadian track called Dorval that afternoon.

Exterminator was called "Old Bones" by a public that loved him as few turf champions have ever been loved. He was slabsided, knobby and ungainly, standing sixteen hands, three inches. His coat was a rather muddy chestnut. He was by McGee, a stallion in the branch line of Eclipse and the Darley that stems from Whalebone, Birdcatcher, and The Baron. Regardless of comparisons to Man o' War, who had brought new and much needed prestige to the fading line of Matchem, Exterminator was far and away the greatest descendant of Eclipse to race in America in the twentieth century—before Kelso came along.

Old Bones was credited with human qualities, not only by the crowds that cheered him but by stable hands and the nine trainers he had in the course of his career (trainers were highly expendable with the volatile Commodore Kilmer). Even in his racing days he showed an affection for Shetland ponies as mascots. When he retired, he would not eat unless the little fellow alongside him ate, too. Exterminator wore out a Hapsburgian succession of Shetlands, for he lived to be thirty on Kilmer's green pastures. The stable help always praised him for being too polite to reveal he was aware that they were bringing him a new Shetland, but they said he knew when each of his companions died and that although he tried not to show it, he was distraught and grieved for days, all the while putting up a pretense of believing the new recruit was the same pony.

He hated to take medicine and was expert at avoiding it. "Balls," as capsules for horses are called, are carefully hidden in the mash and most horses will swallow them without knowing it. When they tried to feed Exterminator a ball in this manner, they simply found it in the feed bag after he had eaten his mash.

No other horse in American turf history ever ran so well so long, and none was ever more beloved.

Willie Knapp, who rode Exterminator to his first great victory in the Derby and in many other races, says, "When he was at his best Exterminator could have beaten Man o' War or Citation or Kelso or any other horse that ever lived on any track doing anything."

That is about the highest tribute a man can give a horse.

The Dominican Rosary contains 165 beads. Were we to count over the turf champions of America one by one and hail each of them according to his due, we would find our beads more numerous and our devotions lengthy beyond the span of human life. Like the Icelandic sagas, such a task would require generations of storytellers. To dismiss a champion with a sentence or a phrase is irreverent to the point of heresy. In a modest chronicle like this we can only hope to freeze a few horses and a few men who loved them in the great ice field of time. In seeing these few at some significant moment, we may, perhaps, see the sport, the art form and the way of life that men call racing.

In the United States in recent times there has been at least one other horse of such superlative quality that when we breathe the names of Man o' War and Exterminator and Kelso his name must be spoken, too. The color of the 1920s was the chestnut shade of Man o' War and Exterminator. The 1940s and early 1950s were devil-red, the hue of cans that contained a famous brand of baking powder. The baking powder was called Calumet, and its manufacturer, Warren Wright, gave the same name to the most successful breeding farm and racing stable in Kentucky. There in the 1940s stood the stallion Bull Lea, a son of Bull Dog in the line of Eclipse, and his sons and daughters swept the tracks, winning more money and more famous stakes and setting more track records than the representatives of any single racing stable in the history of the turf. The greatest of all of them was a colt named Citation, foaled in 1945. He was a bay in color and was out of the mare Hydroplane II, who was a daughter of England's immortal Hyperion, a stallion also in the line of the foal the Royal Duke despised.

Each season for nearly thirty years some colt, often a youngster who had burst into flame at two and burnt to a cinder at three, had been hailed as "another Man o' War." Or astute horsemen who had not been blinded to Man o' War's faults by the blaze of his glory and had not been deceived by the raw-boned ugliness of Exterminator would spot some rangy horse with knobby knees who looked as if he could run all night and they would say maybe another Exterminator had appeared. Over the years there had been very great horses, of course, some of them enormous money-winners. But none of them was Man o' War and none Exterminator.

After he had been acclaimed the leading two-year-old of 1947, Citation had the most brilliant three-year-old season that any colt had enjoyed since Man o' War. He ran twenty times that year, as many starts as the golden warrior from Glen Riddle had had in two years. He won all but one of the races. His upset came in the form of an unknown colt named Saggy who would gain more fame in the 1960s as the sire of Jack Price's Cinderella colt, Carry Back, the horse who won the Kentucky Derby and later conquered Kelso. Citation could find no one willing to test him in the Pimlico Special and had a walkover, but since that counted officially as a victory, he had won fifteen straight races, tying the record of Colin, who retired undefeated in 1908 with fifteen races and fifteen victories. Citation did not race in 1949 because of a hip injury, but he returned in 1950 and won his first start, extending his consecutive victories to sixteen, an all-time record for modern racing. His ancestor Eclipse had won all of his eighteen starts, of course, but nine of them were walkovers.

When he returned to the races, Citation revealed his most glaring fault. He could not—or would not—carry high weight. Each time the crucial 130 pounds was put on his back he was beaten. The handicappers put 130 on him three times and assigned him 132 once. On each occasion he was second. The highest weight he ever won under was 128 and he won under that only once and very narrowly. The next time he carried it, he was beaten.

Even as a three-year-old, however, Citation did not dodge the older handicap horses as Man o' War had done. In fact, he began his three-year-old career on February 2, 1948, in a race against seasoned campaigners and won. At the time he was a three-year-old only by the arbitrary reckoning of the Jockey Club calendar which makes January 1 the birthday of all thoroughbreds. By the Gregorian calendar he was still a two-year-old, since he had been foaled on April 11, 1945. He whipped older horses again in the Seminole Handicap at Hialeah just nine days later.

Another argument of his adherents who rated him better than Man o' War was the fact that he could have retired as a three-year-old in the same blaze of glory as Man o' War, and with far more reason, since he had thrown a hip. But he came back a year later to start nine times and win only twice. He came out again as a six-year-old in 1951, but he did not start under weights higher than 123 and he won only three races. However, he became the first horse in history to win a million dollars on the turf. (By 1965 there were five millionaires.)

Like Caesar's ambition, Citation's inability—or unwillingness—to carry weight was a grievous fault, for it is classically weight that brings them all together on the turf.

Some horsemen believed Citation was the most perfectly made colt the world had seen. Others faulted him because he seemed "light behind," but this was largely an illusion. He was simply so tremendously muscled in front that his rear seemed small in proportion. Ted Atkinson, who rode him, used to claim that Citation had muscles in his eyebrows. He was constructed as a perfect machine for racing and he might have been far greater than he was had he used this enormous physical power to its fullest extent.

It would be inaccurate to say that Citation refused to extend himself. He simply refused to extend himself any more than was absolutely necessary. He was a cunning horse and he was selfish of his genius. He could see no point in giving more than he had to give to win. And quite often he did not give enough. The injured hip might have been an excuse for his inability to carry the weight that other great champions had carried, but his trainer, Plain Ben Jones, was one of America's immortal horsemen and he thought the hip had healed entirely when he sent him back. More likely, Citation just refused to give enough of his great powers to compensate for the added burden, or else he gave of himself too late, when he was beaten.

He was a very different horse in temperament from both Man o' War and Exterminator. Man o' War was a great, exuberant bully of a horse who roared onto the track for the very love of running, as Harry Greb had stormed into the ring for the very love of fighting. Big Red would never win a race by a length if he could win by a hundred lengths. He did not merely wish to beat his opponents; he wished to destroy them completely. Exterminator was one of those deceptively mild-mannered, affectionate horses and lacked Man o' War's bravura style. He was Lincolnesque, completely determined, utterly dependable. He would take the crushing weights they gave him with a shrug of the withers and do his very best in spite of the handicap and oftener than not his very best was good enough. As truly great as he was, Citation may not have realized his full potential for the same reason that many brilliant human beings fall barely short of the accomplishments of which they are capable. He would not give quite enough of himself and his talent.

It is, of course, pointless to compare the relative merits of men or horses of different generations—but, hell, it's fun, and comparing champions is a favorite pastime for men who love horses. We might have had a real test between two of the greatest had Old Boiling Point, as Commodore Kilmer was sometimes called, been successful in his attempts to match Exterminator against Man o' War in 1920. The match almost evolved, in fact. Exterminator had been shipped from Saratoga to Canada, where he won the Hendrie Memorial at Windsor on August 28. With the fat cat away, Sam Riddle decided to play and announced he would run Man o' War in the Saratoga Cup on August 31. When the Commodore heard this, he wired for his horse, and Exterminator came back to win the Saratoga Cup, despite the fact he had had a hard race three days before. When the frightening news of Exterminator's return reached Riddle, however, he withdrew Man o' War from the weight-for-age event.

I play the allegedly pointless game as zestfully as anybody else, and I would rate Citation the fourth best race horse America has seen, behind Kelso, Exterminator, and Man o' War. In my belief, he's the third best descendant of Eclipse to have raced in America, being outranked here by Kelso and Exterminator. The Lexington branch of old King Herod's line has virtually been allowed to die out and most of the descendants of Herod who race in America (a fading 4 per cent of the thoroughbred population) now stem from the French stallion Ksar, who was once the greatest money-winner in the world and was replaced only when the value of the trophies Gallant Fox had won was added to his cash prizes. The Matchem line almost everywhere stems through West Australian, who appeared in 1850 (the same year as Lexington). It was revived by Man o' War and is now even expanding a little through the feats of Big Red's sons at stud. Still, three of the four greatest horses we have known descend from the foal that Cumberland swore he'd feed to Sir Harry's staghounds.

The most interesting aspect of racing is not the effect that the sport has had on economics, but the effect that individual horses have had on individual human beings, and these mortals who come under the magic spell of a horse often have no tangible connection whatsoever with the animal. Later on we will meet Miss Heather Noble, a young lady of Alexandria, Virginia, whose childhood and adolescence have been mostly spent in celebrating the deeds of Kelso. Citation also has a champion. She is a charming and cultured lady in her seventies, Mrs. Irene McCanliss, of Chester, Massachusetts. Mrs. McCanliss, a lady of impeccable social position and considerable accomplishment, who edited several of America's best-known magazines in her younger days, suddenly discovered racing back in the 1940s when Calumet and Citation were painting the country devil-red. Since then she has visited most of the great tracks of America and Europe, making long trips to California or to Europe especially to see a certain horse in a certain horse race, although she has never owned a horse and has bet on a race only once. On that occasion she wagered ten dollars on the Kentucky Derby just to see what it felt like. She did not react favorably to the experience. She said it spoiled her enjoyment of racing as a sport, although she approaches racing more as an art form and enters the racetrack in anticipation of the same experience she seeks when she enters an art gallery or the ballet theater.

In recent years Mrs. McCanliss has spent a good part of her busy and useful life on a labor of love. She has written innumerable scholarly essays, many of them published in authoritative turf magazines, arguing that Citation is the greatest thoroughbred who ever raced. She has files and files of details on Citation's races, his ancestry, his stud career. She hopes to include this massive amount of data in a book, which, she says, she will gladly publish at her own expense if necessary.

One day Mrs. McCanliss made a special trip from Massachusetts just to meet a turf writer named Evan Shipman at New York's Idlewild airport. Shipman had been to Europe to see the great Italian conqueror Ribot, then called "The Horse of the

World." The plane came down in the middle of a stormy night, but Mrs. McCanliss was there. As soon as Shipman disembarked, she asked: "Is Ribot a better horse than Citation?"

"No," Shipman replied.

Mrs. McCanliss smiled happily and went back home again to Massachusetts.

The water towers that mark the boundaries of the course where the curly-haired jockeys rode are among the many topographical features of racing's landscape. The great horses themselves, perhaps, have been mileposts on the long road from Eclipse to Kelso. We can see the truculent American of the dawning United States in the horses that he raced—in prolific Sir Archie, and redoubtable, though misnamed, American Eclipse. Perhaps we can see the mid-nineteenth century turf of America best through the blind eyes of The Hero who spent his days of darkness on Woodburn's pleasant acres. And we see a later era when we remember Exterminator and Man o' War.

When Wall Street crashed and Doc Strub sat down to get a shave, an era of racing ended and a new one began. On that October day in 1929 the rather raffish Empire City course in Yonkers was the only track where races were being run in New York at the moment. James Butler, the Irish greengrocer who owned the plant, had painted the outside of the fence an emerald green that season to match the color of his Green Front grocery stores. Inside, the fence was weathered wood, for Butler could see no sense at all in spending money on paint the customers wouldn't see until they'd paid admission through the gate.

That day of the great Crash a horse named Crash was entered at Empire. He was beaten by a horse named Letalone, and the economic pundits said that it was the government's policy of let-alone, or *laissez faire,* that caused the Wall Street disaster.

There would be no more let-alone or *laissez faire* in racing. The takeover by the politicians began in the 1930s and it was complete by the 1960s.

For me, at least, one of the last great monuments of the past did not entirely disappear until an April day in 1963, when the New York Racing Association received reports of surveys made by two engineering firms. The reports stated the old grandstand of Belmont Park was no longer safe for human habitation and must be taken down.

The next morning I made a sentimental pilgrimage to the old course that so many people had loved so much for so long a time. Horsemen and horses stirred under the spring foliage of the backstretch, the smell of liniment was strong in tack rooms, the cook kitchen was redolent of coffee, and everywhere there was the soft, insistent sound of horses. With or without a grand-stand, Belmont remained the great training grounds of Long Island, of course.

I walked across to the infield and stood there for a while and looked at the huge old stand, as vacant now as the stare in a dead man's eyes.

Belmont had been the dowager queen of American racetracks. She was not so old as queens and racetracks go. She was born in 1905, in the days of a sporting monarch named Edward VII and a toothy President named Teddy Roosevelt. On this day in spring she had stood proudly and spaciously for fifty-eight years, for she had opened in a sumptuous age when true elegance was considered neither foolish nor vulgar. The New York Racing Association said the old stand of mellowed brick and time-sil-vered wood would be replaced and that its character would be reproduced as accurately as possible, but there is always something missing in a copy, whether it is Williamsburg in Virginia or Belmont Park in New York.

The character of buildings derives from the people who inhabit them. And it was the Grand Seigneurs and Great Ladies of the turf, an expansive breed of human beings that has disappeared as tragically as the line of Lexington, who gave the ranging stands of old Belmont their peculiar character and their compelling charm.

I stood gazing into the awful emptiness of the old stands and suddenly they were filled with ghosts, and I could hear a distant cheering and the muffled sounds of horses as the Handy Guy Sande jockeyed for position with the great Grey Lag in the Suburban, or Man o' War, running as if the devil were at his flanks, finished twenty lengths ahead of Donnaconna in the Belmont Stakes.

I could almost see them there in their boxes near the finish line. There was August Belmont, whose family gave its name to the greatest of America's racetracks, a man of charm and dignity and a son of the iron-willed sportsman who had been the absolute monarch of American racing. Surely that was not some trick of the pale spring sunlight on a pane of glass, but the glitter of the flawed jewels that Diamond Jim Brady wore for buttons when he took ostrich-plumed Lillian Russell to the racetrack. Or was it the sparkle of the eyeglasses worn by red-haired Herbert Bayard Swope, who was called the greatest reporter in the world?

The old betting ring where a hundred bookmakers, fabulous fellows known as the Old Mets, had posted odds was a black and yawning cavern underneath the stands. A dark, slim man with a saturnine face moved among them, "shopping the odds." His clothes were expensive but somehow not quite right, and he had the strained, uneasy air of a pretender posturing as a gentleman and sportsman. It was Arnold Rothstein, gangster, owner of the Redstone Stable. There were the great bookies themselves. Tom Shaw had always had the Number One post and he had faced down famous gamblers like Whitey Ellison, called the Blonde Plunger; Chicago O'Brien, the millionaire bricklayer; and Pittsburgh Phil, for whom the Kentucky Derby winner George Smith had been named. I could remember Ambrose Clark in that betting ring, dressed to the nines as if he were attending a Royal Day at Ascot, complaining to the bookie Johnny Ferrone that the long odds he quoted against one of his steeplechasers were an insult, and how Johnny had offered to bet old 'Brose a hundred against his gray bowler hat that the jumper would lose. There was the exuberant Dancer Hyams, too, a bookie whose signals to his runners made him look like a Javanese entertainer performing a ritual dance. Gambling was a man-against-man affair in those days, not a transaction with a big machine that spits you out a little ticket.

My restless eyes were back in the box area now, hungry for the sight of people I would see no more. There was the First Lady of the Turf, Mrs. Helen Hay Whitney, owner of Greentree Stud, her piquant, kindly face serene and lovely beneath one of the little bouquets of clustered flowers she wore for hats. I remembered the time that a very young exercise boy, his face scrubbed and his hair slicked for the occasion, had been sent by her trainer to break the tragic news that one of her champions was ill and could not race in a great stakes on Saturday. "Mr. Murphy says to tell you your horse ain't feeling good," the boy said.

It was bitter news, but Mrs. Whitney's answer was typical of the lady. "Jimmy," she said, "you should say 'he isn't feeling well.' If you don't spend more time studying, I won't let Mr. Murphy put you on any more horses in the morning."

And then I scanned the upper rows of the yawning clubhouse, where the old press box used to be, and I remembered a relatively recent day in 1940 and somehow that was the best memory of all. Colonel Edward Riley Bradley of Kentucky was eighty years old and a very sick man that year and his doctors had forbidden him to go to the races. He had won four Kentucky Derbies and in May of 1940 his colt Bimelech had suffered a heartbreaking defeat at Churchill Downs when the longshot Gallahadion beat him. Now it was June and Bimelech was in the Belmont Stakes, and Bradley had decided to see him run despite his doctors, for he must have known that this last son of Black Toney would be his last great horse. This stern-faced old man had defied fate many times. He owned the vast Idle Hour Stock Farm in Kentucky, but he chose to list his occupation as "Gambler" on his Internal Revenue forms. And so he came to Belmont that June, wrapped in blankets, seated in a wheel chair, a male attendant and a nurse accompanying him. They roped off a whole row of seats at the top of the clubhouse so the Colonel could see the race without being disturbed.

When Bimelech won, they sent a messenger with the floral wreath up to the Colonel. The crowd pressed around the Pinkertons at the rope, calling congratulations to Colonel Bradley. Bradley did not smile too often, but he was smiling now. "Let them through," he told the Pinkertons—and they came through, one by one, to shake his hand and mumble compliments to his horse, and the stern old Colonel picked a blossom from the wreath as each approached and said, "Have one of Bimelech's flowers."

At last the wreath was plucked clean and the people had gone away and the old man wrapped in blankets looked up at me and he was still smiling. "Are you going to write something nice about him?" he asked. "Bimelech's a real good horse, isn't he?"

The sight and sound of ghosts had faded now and it was an April morning in 1963 again. The old queen stood there waiting for her executioners with the serene dignity of the young Queen of France who had waited for brutal men to push her in a tumbril and send her to the guillotine.

The old queen waited calmly, for she was about to join the ghosts who loved her.

4

Yes, *Virginia*, There Is a Kentucky Derby

"What's the Derby got that's so special? I'll tell you what it's got. It's got the first Saturday in May . . ."—COL. MATT WINN

The Kentucky Derby is the oldest horse race that has been run consecutively in the United States.

It began on a spring afternoon in 1875 at Churchill Downs in Louisville and it has been renewed ever since on a Saturday in early May. According to the publicity, exactly one hundred thousand persons attend the Derby every year, never one less, never one more. Since there is no official turnstile count, a more accurate estimate of the Derby crowds may be gathered from the figures of the Internal Revenue inspectors who check the government tax on tickets. Such figures are not released to the public, but if you're persistent enough and exploit your nuisance value to the fullest extent, you may annoy some tax man into hinting that the actual count of tax-paid admissions usually runs between seventy and seventy-five thousand, and there are very few tax-free passes issued for the race. This one event supports the entire spring and autumn racing seasons at Churchill Downs.

The stands of Churchill Downs extend for half a mile and they are things of shreds and patches, additions and extensions, a jigsaw structure of wood and cement that has just growed like Topsy and the Derby without a master plan. The grandstands have been extended upward as high as possible without falling of their own weight and in the years since the first rude gingerbread stand with twin towers was constructed they have crept lengthwise until they now stretch all the way from the lower turn to the upper turn of the racetrack. Churchill Downs is a great white elephant that eats tons of fodder 364 days a year and performs its breadwinning act on only one afternoon— Derby Day.

Despite the fact that some seventy-five thousand people, many of whom have never seen a horse race before and will never see one again, travel to Churchill Downs from all parts of the United States and even from Europe to see the Derby, despite the fact that the Derby is certainly the most widely known horse race in America, despite the fact that more newspaper space is given to it than any one sporting event except the World Series, there is a strong body of opinion that holds the Kentucky Derby really doesn't exist.

Many persons who travel thousands of miles to see the Derby and view it from one of the most expensive seats in a front-row, finish-line box are not quite sure they've really seen the race at all by the time they return to the familiar surroundings of their homes and offices. This is not solely because of the two-dollar mint juleps they imbibe at Churchill Downs. These juleps, served on a kind of assembly-line system, do not, as rumored, contain plastic mint, but they have barely smelt the cork of the bourbon bottle and are hardly more intoxicating than lemonade. They are largely symbolic, a part of the involved rituals of Derby Day.

The Derby guest may have all kinds of circumstantial evidence that he has been to the race. He will have a souvenir program with the winner's name circled. He will have a receipted hotel bill for at least ninety dollars, the minimum rate charged for the minimum three-day occupancy of a Louisville hotel room that normally rents for eight dollars per day. He will have the stubs of plane or railway or bus tickets. He will even have the badge that admitted him to the racetrack. Still, he's never quite sure he's seen the Derby.

The strange effect that the Kentucky Derby has on human beings might afford a rich field for study by psychiatrists. It is pre-eminently not a horse race at all but an emotional experience.

Betting on the Derby is tremendous and begins, several months before the race, in a winter book in Mexico, since such future books are illegal in the United States. Betting at the racetrack on the Derby begins at the advance-sale Derby windows the day before the race. It continues right up to post time and sometimes the amount of money shut out because thousands of bettors simply can't get to the windows runs to more than many racetracks realize on a nine-race program.

Yet the betting is made up for the most part of relatively small wagers. The big professional gamblers consider the Derby a bad betting race because the fields are overcrowded and "anything can win it." Often "anything" has won. Brokers Tip, the fourth and last of E. R. Bradley's Derby winners, won only one race in his life—the Kentucky Derby. Alfred Vanderbilt's great horse Native Dancer lost only one race in his life—the Kentucky Derby. Morvich, a sprinter who had won eleven straight races as a two-year-old, sprinted for a mile and a quarter to win the Derby of 1922, and never won another race. Exterminator and Citation won the Derby. Man o' War and Kelso did not even start in the race.

Many owners whose horses have no chance whatsoever in the classic pay large entry fees to start because having your colors up in the Derby is a status symbol in racing, even though your horse runs last. Some of the horses with no chance whatsoever win. Donerail carried the silks of T. P. Hayes home in 1913 and paid $184.90 to a two-dollar win ticket. Gallahadion carried the silks of Milky Way Farm, a stable named for a candy bar, to victory in 1940 and paid $72.40 when Bradley's last great horse Bimelech went wide in the stretch and finished second.

The wrong horse won the first Derby in 1875 and over the years other wrong horses have won. The first wrong horse was an undersized thoroughbred traditionally referred to as "little red Aristides" because he was small and a chestnut and was named for some old Greek. In our own peculiar, upside-down fashion we'll get to him last, because properly the first Kentucky Derby was the climax rather than the genesis of all the other Kentucky Derbies that have ever been run or ever will be run.

In 1920, when I was thirteen years old, I stood on the steps of the old Seelbach Hotel at Fourth and Walnut Streets in Louisville on the night of May 7, for this was the favored vantage point for watching the Derby Eve crowds go by. A car roared past, its occupants blowing New Year's horns and sounding the klaxon. A large banner streamed from the car reading "Bet on Blazes." The car was filled with raucous Marylanders who were sampling a bit of Kentucky corn instead of Maryland rye, and its higher proof had stimulated them to this public manifestation of their devotion to a Maryland horse. Blazes was an outsider in the betting. He belonged to a great sportsman of Maryland's Eastern Shore, Major Ral Parr, whose family's silks were at that time the oldest registered with the Jockey Club. Parr had another horse in the race named Paul Jones who had won five times the year before, but nobody paid him a bit of attention, including the Major himself. Parr loved Blazes and had his heart set on winning with the colt.

I had no particular choice in the race that year, although Man o' War's conqueror, Upset, was the favorite. It seemed to me that the passing car was nothing short of a sign from heaven, and I bet two dollars on Blazes the next day. Blazes ran sixth, but I collected $34.40. It had come up mud and Paul Jones, the gelding who was coupled in the betting with Blazes, splashed home merrily in front of Upset. I felt rather like Chicago O'Brien, as I had two years before when I had won $61.40 on Exterminator and bought myself a new bike with carbide lamps and other stylish accessories.

My betting in those days was always intuitive, as most Derby betting, including mine, still is today. I liked Blazes because the passing auto was a hunch. I had liked Exterminator, who didn't figure to have a chance, solely because a horse with such a name could not possibly lose. People still bet like that on the Kentucky Derby. It's part of the ritual. It's kind of sacrilegious to handicap the race and bet on the logical horse. There is no logic of any kind involved in any aspect of the Kentucky Derby. It's not the statistics but your emotional reaction that counts.

If you think I was a juvenile delinquent or a precocious gambler because I bet at so early an age, you just didn't grow up in Kentucky in those days. Any kid who didn't save his money and bet on the Derby was considered to be some kind of sickly freak who needed a good stiff dose of sulphur and molasses. A kookie kid who didn't bet on the Derby might even grow up to like Scotch better than bourbon. I'd actually won my first bet on the Derby at the age of eight, when I sat on my dad's shoulder to see the triumph of Regret, the only filly who ever won the race.

Twenty years after Paul Jones won I got to know Ral Parr rather well, and he still wasn't happy over the result. The wrong horse won, you see. Paul Jones had won a purse of over thirty thousand dollars for him, the biggest Derby prize up to the time, but he said he'd never felt much empathy with poor Paul and that Blazes was the horse he loved more than any he had ever owned, and he'd owned a lot of them. He'd had his heart set on winning with Blazes and when Paul Jones won for him instead, tears came to his eyes, and they were tears of sorrow, not tears of joy.

There was an even costlier wrong-horse victory for Colonel Bradley the following year. He had a horse named Black Servant in the race and Black Servant had run the fastest mile that any two-year-old had ever run in Kentucky the year before. The Colonel had been encouraged to bet an enormous amount of money in the winter book on Black Servant at long odds. You get long odds in the winter book, for there are no betting couplings in such wagering and if your horse doesn't start, you lose. Bradley never talked about his bets, but he'd bet so much on Black Servant that his winter book odds eventually became far less than the 8.65 to 1 that the Bradley entry, which also included the unheralded Behave Yourself, came up at post time. Most accounts had it he'd bet $50,000 and had received from 15 to 4 to 1 for his money. Colonel Bradley, as we have seen, listed his occupation as "Gambler," and when he bet, he didn't just fool around.

At the mile Black Servant took the lead and killed off the pacemaking Leonardo II. He held off determined bids from both Prudery and Tryster, the Whitney entry, and as they came into the final quarter, he had it won. But there was another horse with green silks on his back coming from nowhere—the other Bradley horse, Behave Yourself. He hooked up with his stablemate in the final run and they came down the stretch with first one head and then the other showing in front. At the end it was Behave Yourself's head in front and the $48,500 first and second money the Colonel won didn't even make up for his winter book losses.

Bradley's Derby luck was proverbial—for everybody but the Colonel himself. Betting on Bradley horses in the Derby virtually became standard operating procedure with Kentuckians. He won four, the most anybody had won until Calumet came along and took seven Derbies. But Bradley had another personally disastrous Derby the very next year, in 1922. The Colonel always rated endurance in a thoroughbred more highly than he rated mere flashy speed over a short distance and he had a low opinion of the champion two-year-old of 1921, Ben Block's Morvich. He said Morvich would never get the classic routes—and he never did but once. That was in the Kentucky Derby. Bradley must have made that observation to Block, who was a betting man himself. Block bet the Colonel a large amount (again rumor set it at $50,000) that he couldn't send out a horse to beat him. This gave Bradley the choice of all the three-year-olds at his Idle Hour Farm, just as old "Napoleon" Johnson had had the choice of all the thoroughbreds of the South in the match with American Eclipse a century before.

Bradley sent out three horses. The only one with a chance was Busy American, and he broke down on the first turn of the race.

Block had said he'd "sprint" his horse all the way, and that was what Morvich was doing, winging along far in front. When Busy American broke down, another Bradley horse, By Gosh, was last and obviously wasn't going to improve his position. A third forlorn hope, Bet Mosie, was next to last, but he started moving when the big horse collapsed.

I have never seen any horse at any racetrack undergo the punishment that Bet Mosie took from the tough rider Jimmy Burke that day. It's the only time I ever saw a horse's flanks actually spewing blood from the whip and spurs. Bet Mosie ran second, far closer than he had any right to be in such a field, and his feat in doing that was just about the gamest ever seen on a racetrack. But the Colonel lost another bet and this time he didn't even have a winning purse to console him. Block won the big one, but his horse never won again.

Stories like this may account in part for the fact that a great many people won't believe the Derby really exists, even after they've seen it with their eyes. The Derby is such an elusive thing that even when you win it, you lose.

Colonel Bradley himself was completely unbelievable. He was a Kentucky colonel from Texas who had made a fortune in mining properties and at the gaming tables in the West. He wore sober suits of mortician black, ear-high choker collars and a flat-topped black bowler. His face was forbiddingly stern even when it was relaxed. He resembled the most sanctimonious deacon in a Fundamentalist church, but he listed himself as "Edward Riley Bradley, Gambler." He supported half the orphanages of Kentucky and his Orphan's Day burgoo picnic and one-day race meet at Idle Hour Farm was one of the gala events of the Blue Grass annually. He named Burgoo King, his 1932 Derby winner, after James T. Looney, who was the burgoo cook at these occasions.

He owned a no-limit gambling house in Palm Beach and built

149

the biggest Catholic church in town right across the street from it with part of his gambling profits. The dining room of Bradley's gaming house was famous. There was no menu. You just ordered anything you wanted and if it was in season and the house could not supply it, you won $1,000 without buying a chip. Once a Hollywood celebrity got drunk and lost $100,000 at the dice table trying to make Little Joe the hard way. He accused the house of using loaded dice. Bradley was called. "Throw the man out," he said. "And give him back his chicken feed." From that time on, no Hollywood producer or actor was ever admitted through the doors of Bradley's.

No great thoroughbred breeder in history except the Colonel would have received the Indian woman from Oklahoma who visited him at Idle Hour one day in 1921 and certainly none would have considered her suggestion that Bradley's great stallion Black Toney should be bred to an unknown Western mare named Useeit by an unknown Western stud named Bonnie Joe. The lady's name was Rosa M. Hoots and she wanted to breed her mare to the greatest stallion in Kentucky because her husband had dreamed on his deathbed that this would happen and that Useeit's foal by Black Toney would win the Derby. Mrs. Hoots told Bradley her husband had been ruled off the turf for refusing to part with Useeit when she was claimed out of a cheap race in the West. Bradley hardly resembled a starry-eyed romantic, but he was, of course, as all real gamblers are. He consented to the mating.

Three years later the colt by Black Toney-Useeit, named Black Gold after the oil of Oklahoma, won the Kentucky Derby. One of the horses he left behind him was Beau Butler, who finished third under Colonel Bradley's silks. When the Churchill Downs management ceremoniously presented Mrs. Hoots with a check for $52,775, she refused to accept it. She had made a gracious

H.R.H. William Augustus, Duke of Cumberland, who bred Eclipse and King Herod, two of the three foundation sires of the thoroughbred line.

This plate recording the birth of the most remarkable horse the world has known, direct progenitor of 90 per cent of our race horses, was erected on the site of Cranbourne Lodge in Windsor Great Park by H.R.H. Prince Christian of Schleswig-Holstein in the nineteenth century.

The only known likeness of Dennis O'Kelly, the picaresque Irishman who raced Eclipse and stood him at stud, is this cameo from a "funeral ring," made by one of Josiah Wedgwood's fine craftsmen, Lochee.

George Stubbs' famous painting, "Eclipse with Mr. Wildman and His Sons." According to contemporary commentators, Eclipse is highly romanticized in this portrait. Mr. Wildman, a meat dealer in Leadenhall Market, bought Eclipse as a yearling.

Compare this "primitive" painting, "Eclipse at Full Gallop" by J.N. Sartorius, with Stubbs' elegant portrait of Eclipse. Sartorius reveals the ugly head and the sprawling gait of the hind legs that were the subject of much contemporary comment.

The great caricaturist Thomas Rowlandson supposedly depicted Dennis O'Kelly in the villainous figure of this drawing, "Tricks of the Turf." Compare with the amiable gentleman of Lochee's funeral ring.

Dr. Charles Strub, a former dentist with a gun-fighter's eyes, lost a million dollars on the stock market and conceived the first of the great modern racetracks, Santa Anita Park, while he was reclining in a barber's chair for his daily shave.

A heroic statue of the beloved Seabiscuit stands in the garden entrance of Santa Anita Park.

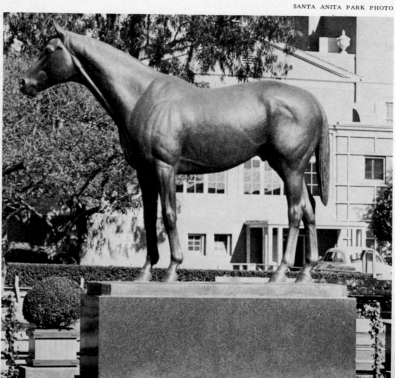

Tall palms and breathtakingly beautiful architecture feature Santa Anita, the track that Doc Strub built in a barber's chair.

Santa Anita Park, at the foot of California's Sierra Madre Mountains, has one of the most beautiful natural locations of any racetrack in the world.

This rare photograph was taken by a man named Schreiber in 1872 and is now the property of the Keeneland Library, Lexington, Kentucky. It reveals the blindness of Lexington, "The Blind Hero of Woodburn," who was proclaimed the greatest American thoroughbred of the nineteenth century and led the country's sires for fourteen years. All the other artists and photographers who depicted Lexington concealed his affliction.

The great gelding Exterminator is shown with the first of a long series of Shetland ponies who were his companions in retirement. All of the ponies bore the name of Peanuts.

In 1965 there were only five male-line descendants of Lexington in the entire world and all of them were at the Raceland Ranch of D. G. Frame in Reliance, South Dakota. El Tesoro, pictured above, was at stud. The other four were two-year-olds. In these five horses rests the last faint hope of reviving the greatest of all American bloodlines, which has almost died out completely.

Man o' War, who has become as much a legend as a race horse, is shown at stud with his personal groom Will Harbut, who described him as "the mostest hoss there ever was."

An enterprising artist of the nineteenth century celebrated Aristides' victory in the first Kentucky Derby in 1875 with this design of clover leaves made of racing plates and a horseshoe nail. At top is Aristides. At left is Price McGrath, his owner, who raced out on the track to wave his hat as a signal to Lewis, the jockey, shown at right.

Louis B. Mayer, the Little Napoleon of Hollywood, became the Little Napoleon of California racing when he discovered that thoroughbreds were a good tax deduction.

The great American jockey Willie Knapp in the days when he rode Upset to victory over Man o' War and won the Kentucky Derby with Exterminator.

Col. Edward Riley Bradley owned the great Idle Hour breeding farm in Kentucky, but he insisted upon listing his occupation officially as "Gambler."

(ABOVE) *This is the famous edition of Walter O'Hara's* Star-Tribune, *now a collector's item, that marked the beginning of the end for the proprietor of Narragansett Park. O'Hara's headline states that the Governor of Rhode Island should be lodged in an institution for alcoholics. He contrived it cleverly* (BELOW) *so that when the paper was folded on the newsstands it indicated that the Governor was actually in the institution.*

James Todhunter Sloan, the King of Jockeys, relaxes in regal fashion after a day at the races. Sloan devised the "monkey-on-a-stick" crouch that all American riders use today, largely because his legs were exceptionally short. He was a famous Beau Brummel who changed his costume from the skin out at least six times a day. But he died broke.

Jockey Johnny Pollard was known to his intimates as "The Cougar." After Pollard was crippled in a spill, he rode Seabiscuit, the crippled hero-horse of California, to the money-winning record of the world.

Troye's painting of General Winfield Scott on a gelded son of Glencoe, a horse captured from Confederate General John Hunt Morgan, is in the National Museum of Racing at Saratoga. Old Fuss and Feathers could not have examined his gift horse too closely. He fondly believed the gelding was the great stallion Glencoe himself, who had died two years before Scott obtained his son.

Avelino Gomez, a Cuban jockey, injects a bit of Latin-American gaiety into racing by jumping straight up in the air when he wins a race. Here he "dismounts" from Bupers after winning the rich Futurity at Aqueduct.

John Oliver (Jack) Keene, "The Compleat Horseman" from the Blue Grass of Kentucky. A frog croaked in Russia and he returned to the United States to look for rocks to cap his gateposts, then he built a barn, and then he built a racetrack.

The Well Gap is among many passages for horses cut through the Devil's Dyke that the ancient Iceni built as fortifications at Newmarket before Roman times. This engraving is in the British Museum.

A party of Americans watches horses work over a turf gallop called the Lime Kiln on the great heath of Newmarket.

FOX PHOTOS, LTD.

BRITISH TRAVEL ASSOCIATION

A field races past the great Queen Elizabeth II grandstand at Royal Ascot, which was dedicated in 1961. Ascot was the first of England's tracks to have a modern stand. A similar structure was built for the Royal Enclosure and was opened in 1964. Boxes in both stands are small apartments with dining rooms and kitchens.

A field races past the elegant old stands of Longchamp, outside Paris in the Bois de Boulogne. The belle époque *structure was replaced by modern stands in the middle 1960's.*

FRENCH GOVERNMENT TOURIST OFFICE

FRENCH GOVERNMENT TOURIST OFFICE

At the beautiful Chantilly course in France fields virtually race over the drawbridge of a great baroque chateau.

These are the gateposts to Jack Keene's Kentucky estate that began so many things. He searched for rocks to cap the posts and had so many left over he built a barn, and the barn grew into a racetrack.

SKEETS MEADORS PHOTO

PRIVATE
ENTRANCE

The Keeneland racetrack in Lexington, Kentucky, as it looked when it opened in 1936. Clubhouse at right was Jack Keene's elaborate stone barn.

Saddling entries under the trees is one of the pleasanter customs of the race meeting in August at Saratoga. The lady on the bench at left is Mrs. Henry Carnegie Phipps, proprietor of one of the nation's greatest stables. Seated next to her is the great trainer Sunny Jim Fitzsimmons, who finally retired from the turf at the age of 88.

These are the first white thoroughbreds ever born in America and
although the odds were trillions to
one against such a happening, both
were born on the same Kentucky
farm. The colt at right developed
chestnut freckles and was officially
registered as a roan under the name
of War Colors. The filly at left remained pure white and was registered as such under the name of
White Beauty.

THOROUGHBRED RECORD

One of the closest finishes ever seen was that between Gun Bow and Kelso
in the Woodward at Aqueduct in 1964. This is the photo-finish camera
picture. The stewards decided that Gun Bow (No. 2, inside) had an eye-
lash margin. A mirror is placed at the finish to furnish a reverse picture.

NYRA PHOTO

Mrs. Richard C. duPont brushes away a tear and Jockey Ismael (Milo) Valenzuela attempts to reassure her after a foul is claimed against Kelso in the International at Laurel in 1964, the champion's greatest race. The stewards did not allow the foul claim.

WASHINGTON POST PHOTO

Kelso, the champion whom the author calls the greatest race horse in history, is led by his groom, Larry Fitzpatrick.

NYRA PHOTO BY PAUL SCHAFER

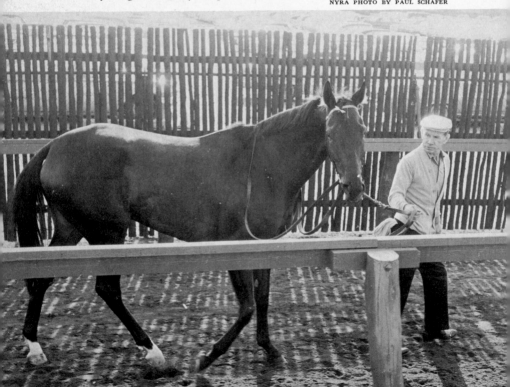

speech in accepting the trophy, but she didn't trust checks. She wanted it all in cash. She was finally persuaded it was dangerous to carry that much cash all the way to Oklahoma and she took the check, but she made them certify it.

Her trainer was an Indian known as Three-Finger Webb, and he never said anything, not even "Ugh." They arranged a press conference for him after the race, another of the Derby's rituals, and an enterprising reporter asked, "Mr. Webb, how do you feel about winning the Kentucky Derby?" Three-Finger finally said something. He said, "I gotta stummick ache."

Black Gold was as unbelievable as his owner, trainer, Colonel Bradley, and the Derby itself. He ended his saga on the proper melodramatic note in 1928 by finishing a race on three legs at the Fair Grounds in New Orleans and he is buried in the infield of the track.

No horse has ever been disqualified for a foul after placing in the Derby, but the 1933 renewal won by the Colonel's one-race winner Brokers Tip was the occasion of the foulest riding ever seen in an American turf classic. Don Meade, on Brokers Tip, and Herb Fisher, on Head Play, came into the stretch far in front of the field, locked together. They began to grab each other's saddlecloths. Then they grabbed each other's reins. Finally, midway of the stretch, in full view of the packed thousands, they began to slash each other over the backs with their whips and to slash each other's mounts over the muzzle. Meade was the more talented grabber and slasher and Brokers Tip finished a head in front of Head Play. The stewards let the result stand. There was no point in disqualifying both horses, since they hadn't interfered with other entries, and they didn't know whether Meade or Fisher had begun the rodeo riding.

Colonel Bradley's Derby-winning record of four victories ended in the devil-red era of Calumet, which won in 1941 with

Whirlaway, a horse remembered for his fly-whisk tail; in 1944 with Pensive, in 1948 with the immortal Citation, in 1949 with Ponder, in 1952 with Hill Gail, in 1957 with Iron Liege and in 1958 with Tim Tam. That record may stand for generations. The red barns of Calumet in Lexington, where these seven winners were bred, became as famous as the green acres of Idle Hour, which have now been subdivided into several stud farms.

The legends that make many persons believe the Derby is a myth and not a horse race are not the work of the man who was the Derby's press agent for twenty years. His name is Brownie Leach and he is a Kentuckian who stands as high on the hoof as a percheron in elevator shoes and a top hat. It seems almost inevitable that Leach should have served his apprenticeship as publicist for America's biggest gambling race by attending an institution of higher learning known as Transylvania, the College of the Bible. There he learned to hold his bourbon like a gentleman and never tell a lie. Leach's prose about the Derby was always terse, informative and statistical, and he avoided the superlative suffix in the way a WCTU lady avoids the Demon Rum.

Still the legends grow, for they derive from the race itself. In some inexplicable fashion, the Derby is touched with magic each time it is run. For fifty-one weeks a year practical horsemen belittle the Derby. They say it comes too early, that the three-year-olds are not mature, that the Belmont in June at the classic distance of a mile and a half is the real test of a colt.

Then the fifty-second week, Derby Week, arrives, and suddenly they would rather win the Derby than any other race on earth. They can't tell you why, any more than the fellow from Ottumwa, Iowa, who has never seen a horse race and never made a bet can tell you why he suddenly comes down with an irresistible compulsion to take all his savings out of the bank and go to Louisville to see the Derby on the first Saturday in May. In the popular fancy, seeing the Derby in May is akin to seeing the Taj Mahal by moonlight or the chestnut trees on the Champs Élysées in April.

Many students of the Derby trauma believe the mystique of the race was created by a pudgy little man named Colonel Matt Winn, but this is not true, either. When he was a stripling, Colonel Winn saw Aristides win the first Derby. According to this carefully nurtured legend, he stood up on the seat of his father's grocery wagon that was parked outside the Downs to watch the little red horse win. Later he became head of Churchill Downs. He was a hardheaded, tough-minded, practical man who liked to make money and never gave a damn about his public image. His idea of public relations was to open up a case of bourbon and let the newspapermen help themselves. He fought the elders of the Jockey Club or anybody else who got in his way when he was making money.

The picture of him as a genial, Jorrocks-like gentleman whose nose was constantly buried in a mint-sprigged julep cup was created by a sportswriter named Bill Corum, who lived to pay for his deed. Corum was a columnist of such tremendous talent that he is ranked with Frank Graham, Grantland Rice, Red Smith, and Damon Runyon. Talented sportswriters often glamorize favorite sports figures into personalities their wives and mothers wouldn't recognize, and Corum did this with Winn. For a time the whole legend of the Derby became the legend of Colonel Winn. When Winn died, it was only natural that Churchill Downs should appoint the man who created him as his successor. Playwrights seldom can play the characters they create. Corum did his best, but he always seemed faintly uncomfortable in the role he had written for Colonel Winn.

Today the head of Churchill Downs is a pleasant, intelligent and highly capable man who is constantly being plagued by people who want to fit his feet into secondhand shoes. His name is Wathen Knebelkamp. He insists upon having the Derby itself overshadow the personality of the man who operates it. But whenever he is introduced at a public function, the toastmaster describes him as the man who is filling the shoes of Colonel Winn. This must be highly annoying, since he wears his own well-shined and well-fitting shoes, but Knebelkamp always manages to smile.

A dying Indian's dream came true when Black Gold won the Derby in 1924 and a nightmare came true when Gallant Man lost the Derby in 1957. Gallant Man was owned by Ralph Lowe. He had engaged one of the country's best riders, Willie Shoemaker, as his jockey. Lowe had a dream on Derby eve that Shoemaker had mistaken the finish line when he was in front and had pulled up Gallant Man. The next day Gallant Man had the race won seventy yards out. Shoemaker mistook the seventy-yard pole for the finish line, stood straight up in the saddle, and by the time he realized what he had done, Iron Liege had passed him and won the race.

Shoemaker had won three Derbies through 1965, but his luck in the race was almost as bad as that of Colonel Bradley, whose horses won four Derbies. Willie blew one by finishing too early and he blew another in 1964 by choosing the wrong horse. He had ridden Northern Dancer in several races and trainer Horatio Luro wanted him for the Derby. But Willie thought Hill Rise was a better horse and accepted the mount on him. Bill Hartack rode Northern Dancer to victory.

There are Cinderella stories and hard-luck stories connected with the Derby, but in one case there was stark tragedy. In 1962 there semed absolutely no way of beating Christopher T. Chenery's brilliant three-year-old Sir Gaylord in the race. On Derby

Eve I was on the backstretch of Churchill Downs to watch Sir Gaylord's final blowout early in the morning. I was standing very near his trainer, Casey Hayes, a bluff and genial man and a fine horseman. Sir Gaylord suddenly faltered in his stride. It was barely perceptible, but the clockers up in their stilted stand said, "Uh-UH!" and knew something was very wrong. Casey knew, too. I looked at his face when Sir Gaylord took a wrong step, and I thought of a photograph I had seen in some magazine of a Frenchman weeping while Hitler's legions entered Paris. The Frenchman's face was unforgettable, and Casey's face was just as memorable at that stricken moment. Sir Gaylord had cracked a sesamoid, and he would never race again.

For many years I have tried to determine the exact moment when the Derby trauma sets in and some unseen Merlin goes about his magicking. I think it occurs at twilight on the Sabbath before the Derby, at an hour when thousands of starlings swoop down upon the buildings of Fourth and Walnut Streets in Louisville and burst into an insane chorus as an overture to an insane week.

It is at this moment, I believe, that all the citizens of Louisville and all the Derby guests pick up a small bottle labeled *"Drink Me,"* swallow its contents, disappear into a rabbit hole and enter a land whose scenery has the arcane quality of the monoliths of Stonehenge. Bank tellers with eyeglasses and bald spots are magically transformed into swaggering Rhett Butlers. Shopgirls suddenly wear crinoline and wait tremulously for their gray-clad swains to ride back hell-for-leather from First Manassas. State of Maine Yankees develop sorghum-thick Southern drawls. The smell of carbon monoxide gives way to the scent of magnolia blossoms. The cement sidewalks of Fourth Street become pasturelands of blue grass. Office buildings turn into pillared manors with lawns solidly planted in fragrant mint. A hitching post appears on every corner and at each a blooded descendant of Matchem, Herod, or Eclipse paws the ground impatiently, eager for the Derby post. You can't explain it and you really don't believe it when it's over any more than you believe the visions that a hallucinogen like mescaline induces, but it happens every year.

All of racing's roads lead backward. The first Derby winner Aristides descended from the foal named Eclipse who was born to darkness. Seventy-two of the winners of the first ninety Derbies descended from Eclipse. Eleven trace back in the male line to Kind Herod, another of Cumberland's stallions. And seven come down from old Matchem. Three of Herod's brood among the winners are in the line of Lexington, Kentucky's Blind Hero. The last of these was Manuel, who won in 1899, and unless the forgotten colts at the Frame ranch in South Dakota achieve a miracle and establish a line, Manuel may be the last of all the Derby winners in this hallowed family.

My tenderest memory of a Derby winner, of course, is my faint childhood recollection of Regret, not just because she was the only filly who ever won (and probably the only one who ever will) but because she was the first for me. In 1962 I heard Cornelius Vanderbilt Whitney, who is better known as "Sonny" on the turf, tell a story and it's the best Derby story of them all, so far as I'm concerned.

He was a young boy when Whiskery won the Derby under his father's Eton blue and brown silks in 1927. That night there was a big party at the manor house of the Whitney farm in Lexington and young Sonny grew very bored with the antics of the adults. He wandered out into the soft Kentucky night and he heard music in the air and saw a bonfire burning on a distant hill. As he approached he saw that a horse stood on the hill, silhouetted against the flames, and he realized the Negroes on the place were clustered about the horse and singing spirituals. He approached one of the older Negro hands and said, "What's going on? Who is that horse?"

"Why, Mister Sonny," the old man replied, "that's Regret. She was the first one ever carried home the blue in the Derby race and we been waiting twelve years now to have another celebration."

"I always think of racing in terms of that singing, that bonfire and that dark mare against the flames," said Whitney.

It's a lovely way to think of racing.

There have been many Derbies to remember, but the first one is remembered best by those who never saw it. A rawboned hardboot horseman named Price McGrath had a three-year-old named Chesapeake in 1875 and he had high hopes of beating the mighty Ten Broeck (named for the river-boat gambler who owned Lexington) in this new race called the Derby at a new track called Churchill Downs. He had another little horse, a nothing kind of horse, named Aristides. He was a shrimp with a scampering gait, but he could run fast early and make the pace and maybe tire out Ten Broeck before Chesapeake made his charge down the stretch. And so the old hardboot entered Aristides, too.

Chesapeake was left flat-footed at the post. The little red horse called Aristides scooted off in front, with the feared and mighty Ten Broeck far behind him. As they neared the turn for home, Ten Broeck, the terror of the tracks, had lengthened stride and he was gaining now, and Chesapeake was beaten. Aristides was laboring and slowing down, for he had gone as far as anyone expected him to go.

Then old McGrath ran out on the track. He waved his hat frantically to signal the hundred-pound boy named Lewis who was riding Aristides that he couldn't quit now, that Chesapeake had lost, that Ten Broeck was sweeping to him, and Aristides must break his heart to win. And you can still hear Lewis's whip sing down, still see Ten Broeck falter as the pace grows faster, still skip a heartbeat as Volcano roars up to Aristides' flanks, and still rip your throat with cheering as the little red horse with a heart that wouldn't break comes on again, inch by inch and yard by yard, until he has it won.

It may be well that there are old men who walk straight and proud and old trees that have watched the ages pass and leaf again each spring. And it's good that we still have the Kentucky Derby, an uninterrupted record of man's devotion to an animal called the thoroughbred. It's a nice word, thoroughbred. It still has meaning in a day when meanings are confused.

The same horse always wins the Derby, no matter what name he bears. Always the winner is the ghost of the little red horse Aristides, who answered when his owner waved his hat.

5

The One-Legged Cougar and
the Three-Legged Horse

"However we brave it out, we men are a little breed."
—ALFRED LORD TENNYSON

Any ambitious American boy who stops growing and stops eating at the age of twelve can earn an income of from $10,000 to
$250,000 a year before he's old enough to vote. He also has to
learn to ride a horse, but that's the easy part.

With the exception of Bill Hartack, who resigned from the
organization because of a dispute over its treatment of another
jockey, every licensed rider of any standing in the United States
belongs to the Jockeys' Guild. The Jockeys' Guild has the power

to set minimum pay scales, to approve contracts and working conditions and to call strikes, but its officials grow frothingly angry if you call the Guild a labor union. It is not affiliated with any labor union and is not officially recognized as such. Nevertheless, its members earn higher pay per capita and they earn it at a far earlier age than the members of any labor union that ever existed. There are some twelve hundred jockeys who ride fairly regularly in the forty-five thousand races in the United States each year. About twenty of them usually make as much or more than the basic salary of the President of the United States. Riding fees vary according to the quality of the racing, but they average out to about twenty-five dollars for a losing mount and fifty dollars for a winning mount. It is technically possible for a jockey to ride two horses a day for a year, lose on all of them, take a two-week vacation and wind up with earnings of $15,000, which is a fair salary in almost any profession, especially for a teen-ager.

There is no maximum limit on what an owner and trainer may pay a boy to ride a horse. Top jockeys whose services are in demand may ask and get up to a hundred dollars a mount, win, lose or dead-heat, for throwing a leg over a horse in a race that has no great purse value. In addition to the riding fee it is customary (and expected) that the owner will stake his jockey to 10 per cent of the purse he wins. In stakes of $100,000 upward, this runs to a great deal of money indeed for riding a horse for a minute or two.

The contract rider for big stables is rapidly disappearing from the American turf scene because most boys can make more money free-lancing. When a boy does "ride contract," he is usually paid a stipend that rivals that of a vice-president of a great corporation. "First calls" and "second calls" on a jockey's services over a period of time or for a single race are far more common. Big-name jockeys may increase their annual incomes considerably through such semicontractual arrangements. This means, of course, that a certain owner has first call on a jockey's services for certain big races. If his horse doesn't start, an owner who has taken a slightly less expensive second call may use the jockey.

The really important jockeys, however, dislike even giving calls to owners. They know that in a race like the Derby or the Preakness or the Belmont Stakes half a dozen stables may be clamoring for their services, and they like to keep them dangling until the last possible minute when they can judge the racing condition of the horses and take the highest bid. Oftener than not they choose the wrong horse in such instances, as Shoemaker did when he took Hill Rise in preference to Northern Dancer in the Kentucky Derby in 1964.

Only one out of every 166,666 inhabitants of the United States is a jockey. There are even less crowded professions on the race-track, however. There is, for instance, a young man at Aqueduct who climbs to the top of a nine-foot ladder nine times a day, sticks his head in a glass box on top of the totalisator board and punches a panic button if a gaggle of sea gulls flies through an invisible light beam. This watchdog is employed by the Teletimer Company which clocks the races in fractions of a second with an electronic device that is activated when the first horse breaks the beam at the various poles on the track. If the sea gulls who poach in large numbers on the swan lakes of Aqueduct went through the beam first and it was not reactivated before the horses reached it, there would be a turf crisis that might cause the speed-chart gamblers to commit mass suicide. Thus far no sea gull has broken the light beam, but runaway horses, outriders and careless grounds-keepers have. Once, at the Fair Grounds in New Orleans the beam was broken by a displaced pelican from the Louisiana bayous.

It isn't just the ability to ride horses well that limits the number of jockeys and keeps their incomes at an almost incredible maximum. Even in this mechanized day thousands of people ride horses exceedingly well. There are horsemen at almost any racetrack who are actually better riders than jockeys. It's doubtful that any man on earth sits a horse more handsomely than the dashing Argentinian Señor Horatio Luro, who trained both Decidedly and Northern Dancer to win the Kentucky Derby, or the cowboy Mesh Tenney, who trains the horses of another cowboy, Rex Ellsworth, owner of a stable that frequently wins as much as a million in a year. But Señor Luro stands over six feet and weighs proportionately and Tenney, while smaller, is still not small enough to make a jockey.

Size, or rather lack of it, not horsemanship, is the first requirement of a jockey. You can teach a man to ride a horse, but you can't shrink him unless you possess the magic formula that enabled Alice to enter the rabbit hole. The plain truth seems to be that man is outgrowing the race horse.

It is reckoned that the thoroughbred grew an inch every twenty-five years during the first century of his development. Bend Or, foaled in 1877, was considered an exceptionally large horse. He stood sixteen hands, one inch—three inches taller than Eclipse and the exact height of Kelso, who is deemed a small horse today. By 1913, Hurry On, of the Matchem line, was regarded as a giant at seventeen hands, still good size for a horse, but a height we now encounter frequently. The weight of the race horse, of course, developed proportionately. But the size of man was growing at a much faster rate than the size of the horse.

The first organized pre-thoroughbred horse racing was at

catchweights, meaning any weight the rider happened to be at the moment, since the jockeys were almost invariably the horses' owners, usually the courtiers of Charles II or the King himself. Even then, however, there was some attempt to place a maximum on the weight carried. This was usually 168 pounds, which must have been regarded as the maximum weight of a man fit to ride a horse. This maximum was maintained a century later when Cumberland's Jockey Club was formed, even though the Duke himself varied between 280 and 300 pounds and could not ride his own horses. But in the eighteenth century the use of professional jockeys became common and a scale of weights was adopted for races in which horses were not ridden by their owners. It was remarkably similar to what we have today except for "the feather," an indefinite weight assigned to young horses that varied between fifty-nine and seventy-seven pounds.

Before the Civil War "the feather" was also fairly common in races for younger horses in the United States. Most of the jockeys who could make such weight, however, were Negro slaves, and there were cases where their owners had bred them for size in much the same way they bred horses for certain qualities. These horse-owning slaveholders most probably kept these small boys on a strict diet to assure they did not become too large. Usually they were known only by their first names, sometimes only as their owners' "boys," and there is little record of them. "Abe" was a famous slave jockey. He apparently belonged to the Mr. Hawkins who gave his name to the expression "Mr. Hawkins' horse," meaning an especially favored animal. Another slave who is frequently mentioned as a jockey in early American races bore the patriotic name of "Washington."

The Negro jockey was an important factor of the American turf right up to the twentieth century, but it rapidly became evident after the Civil War that he could no longer make the absurdly low weights of the specially bred and specially fed jockeys of slave days. One of the greatest jockeys of all time in any land was the Negro boy Isaac Murphy, who lived from 1859 to 1896 and was called "the Colored Archer" because the nineteenth century English rider Fred Archer was considered the world's greatest jockey. Murphy won 628 races out of 1,412 mounts and no great jockey has come within miles of that lifetime record of 44 per cent winners. It has been said that there are 16,268 ways of losing money on the races and the surest way of all is to bet on jockeys instead of horses, a practice of many modern race-goers who have a lemming-like compulsion for economic ruin. Murphy is the only jockey in the entire history of the turf who would have shown a profit for gamblers who made a flat bet on every horse he rode.

Murphy came to the racetracks when he was fourteen, although he gave his age as sixteen. He died at thirty-seven of pneumonia. Lung ailments, particularly tuberculosis, were virtually an occupational hazard with jockeys up to a very few years ago, for rigorous dieting, strenuous exercise and sweat baths to reduce weight weakened their resistence to virus diseases. Murphy went up to 130 or 135 pounds immediately after he began eating anything like normal meals. He won three Kentucky Derbies, a record that stood until the great Earl Sande came along in the 1920s and Eddie Arcaro came along in recent years.

The Negro jockey has disappeared from the turf almost completely. In popular belief this is due to race prejudice. There may have been such resentment among the white riders, many of whom came from the lower economic and social levels where prejudice is most common. This is not the real reason, however. The real reason is that the Negro has been growing at a greater rate than the white man over the generations. Except when he was purposely stunted in order to make a jockey (one slave boy was reputed to have walked around with a load of bricks strapped to his head to keep him small), the Negro of slave days was well fed. Aside from all humanitarian considerations, it was sound economic policy for the slaveholder to keep his human possessions healthy. Although the Negro existed on the lowest economic level after he was freed, he remained well nourished for the most part. For several generations he was employed as a house servant or field hand and his keep was part of his pay. Usually he ate virtually the same food as his employer. Today's Negro is large physically. He may become heavyweight boxing champion of the world, but he is seldom anatomically fitted to become a jockey.

For some years now the Jockeys' Guild has been urging that a slightly higher scale of weights be adopted merely as a recognition of the facts of life and human development. Even the proposal that certain minimum weights of 112 be changed to 114 has been bitterly opposed, however, on the grounds that it would increase the already frightening number of breakdowns among young horses. However, an owner or trainer may take up to five pounds over the weight assigned his horse in order to get the jockey he wants, and the number of "overweights" posted on the infield board in each event is ample evidence that most horses are carrying the minimums suggested by the Jockeys' Guild. A great many horsemen oppose higher weight scales on the grounds that they would break down horses, but they really object to slowing down horses, for high speed in America has become the criterion of a thoroughbred's worth. In England only about a quarter of the races that are run are even timed.

The greatest of all American racing officials, Walter S. Vosburgh, believed that it was high speed, hard tracks and too much racing which were responsible for breakdowns, especially of young horses. That view is shared by one of the greatest of all

American trainers, Sunny Jim Fitzsimmons, who did not retire until he was eighty-eight and was still happily around at ninety in the middle 1960s. The records would seem to indicate the horses that have carried the highest weights have often been the most durable, notably Exterminator, Man o' War and Kelso. There is no really valid evidence that two-year-olds of stakes quality who carry higher weights break down more frequently than cheap two-year-olds who carry low weights. Seabiscuit was a crippled horse, but he went wrong before he was assigned high weights and he carried 130 pounds to victory despite his bad leg.

As long ago as 1938 when the former great jockey, Earl Sande, trained Stagehand, a three-year-old, to win the Santa Anita Handicap, he had to send across the country and pay a whopping fee to get Nick Wall as a rider, because Wall was just about the only experienced jockey in the country who could make the hundred pounds assigned Stagehand. Stagehand beat Seabiscuit by only a nose, and even one pound of overweight might have changed the result. (In the involved mathematical equations of handicapping, five pounds equal one length at one mile.)

During the last two decades we have been drawing more and more upon Latin American countries, where poverty and under-nourishment have been prevalent for generations, or upon the Puerto Rican population of the United States for our jockeys. Now about one fourth of the jockeys who ride in America are of Spanish-American origin. Recently Panama has been one of our principal sources of jockey talent.

We still have a few small but perfectly proportioned men, of course, but they are growing rarer and rarer. John Rotz, one of the truly great riders of our time, is relatively tall for a jockey, but he has no trouble at all in making weight. He eats as much as the horses he rides, almost never dons a rubber suit and still can make 112 without the slightest trouble. Willie Shoemaker, who seems to have succeeded to Eddie Arcaro's mantle as the Little King of the Little Men, is a doll-like figure, as exquisitely proportioned as a perfect miniature, standing under five feet. Another beautifully made and very small jockey is Ron Turcotte, who, unbelievable as it seems, began life as a lumberjack in Canada. One of the most enormously talented riders of our time, a self-made *enfant terrible* named Bill Hartack, suffers more from psychological maladjustments to his size and his profession than he does from the physical problem of making weight. Hartack seems to have a persecution complex that is directed mainly against the press and racing officials. Since he is jockey-sized and his name is William, it is natural to call him by the diminutive "Willie," but this infuriates him into a wild display of his touchy temperament. He is constantly denouncing newspapermen and racing officials and accusing them of a lack of integrity, so his public image is a not too pleasant one. This in no way detracts from the fact that he does about as many things right on a race horse as any jockey of our era.

The affluence and welfare protections that the Guild affords its members have not always existed. Many of the greatest jockeys of all time have lived in poverty after their brief moments on the turf. Earl Sande, who in my estimation ranks with George Woolf as one of the two greatest jockeys in American history, was existing on meager Social Security payments in a room above a small Long Island store in 1965. Tod Sloan, who virtually founded the modern crouch school of riding, tried his hand as a motion picture actor and later as a racing official at Agua Caliente, but when he died he was being supported by a kindly family of moderate means in Los Angeles and he had been living on their charity for years.

Winnie O'Connor, who rode for many of the great noblemen of Europe and for the Czar of Russia, lived out his old age as the nonpaying guest of a family on Long Island. I knew him well in the 1930s and his plight was heartbreaking, for he was a good man and he was trying so desperately to save his pride and earn a living. He wanted to start a jockey school at the Long Island tracks, for he believed he still had something to offer the world. The school died a-borning, largely because of lack of interest among young apprentices who wanted to start at the top. I often lent nickels for carfare to this great rider who had won many famous classics of Europe on the greatest horses of his time.

The fate of Red Pollard, who rode Seabiscuit to the money-winning record of the world in 1940, has been less heart-rending. He has a wonderful wife and two fine children, one of whom is a talented musician, but he has not been too proud to take any work that has offered within recent years. In 1964 he was a valet in the jockeys' room of the little Green Mountain track in Vermont, pulling on the boots of kids who weren't born when he won the Santa Anita Handicap. Before that he sorted mail in the secretary's office of Lincoln Downs, a small track in Rhode Island. Today's young men who walk the earth with the touchy dignity of small aristocrats and have old-age benefits stored up for them may not realize how lucky they are to have the Guild.

There is one utterly self-dependent jockey who doesn't need the Guild, apparently, although he is a member. He is Johnny Longden, the first man in history to ride 5,000 winners. At the age of fifty-eight in 1965 he was still riding, often in stakes, although he almost certainly is a millionaire. He had no trouble at all in making weight at such an advanced age, either. He began life as a coal miner in Canada.

Longden still rides at many of the country's biggest and most important tracks. When Johnny was young, the oldest jockey in

America was a man known as Uncle Bill Obert, who restricted his activities almost solely to the half-mile bull rings. Uncle Bill finally hung up his tack in the 1940s, but nobody ever knew for sure how old he really was. "I quit getting old when I was fifty," he'd tell questioners.

One of the most fabled jockeys of our era saw the handwriting on the wall in 1963 and retired after he had had trouble making weight and had been involved in several spills that almost cost his life. Eddie Arcaro was a man of wealth when he retired, although he has continued to work at various jobs. He has been connected with a sports television program and he was a kind of ambassador of good will for the American Totalisator Company. Actually he would make a perfect ambassador of good will for all jockeys and for the sport of racing. He is still as slim as an adagio dancer, beautifully dressed, exquisitely poised. He is a man of keen intelligence and wonderful wit and he possesses that rare human quality called grace. He is one of the few great jockeys to live on to enjoy life and the fruits of his labors.

In France, where racing is operated by the government, jockeys are virtually wards of the state. At the age of fourteen they enter the great jockey school in the forest of Chantilly where they live lives as Spartan and disciplined as those of the cadets of St. Cyr. Here they not only learn to ride horses but continue their formal education. They live in dormitories not greatly different from those of English public schools. And they do not begin at the top. They begin by rubbing horses and mucking out stalls before they are even allowed to exercise thoroughbreds in the morning.

Those who can stand up under such training are thoroughgoing horsemen by the time they first put a boot in an iron as apprentices. France is one of the few places where jockeys have not adopted some form of the short-stirrup, hunched-over American riding style. French jockeys still ride with long stirrups, sit straight in the saddle, come into the stretch swinging their whips in the way Bazaine's *chasseurs* swung their sabres. It is well worth a trip to France for a horse lover just to see one French jockey ride. His name is Yves Saint-Martin and if there is a better rider in the world today, I haven't seen him.

A 300-pound former All-American football player named Tom Thorp, who became a racing steward, established a jockey school at New England tracks in the 1930s. Others were tried at Santa Anita and in Florida. None lasted very long, for there is no requirement here as there is in France that jockeys must have such intensive training.

The real jockey college of America resembled Fagin's informal school for young pickpockets far more than it resembled an educational institution, but it produced some of the most brilliant jockeys America has known. It was conducted by a villainous-looking old man called Father Bill Daly, one of racing's more fabulous rogues. Like the turf's first arrant rascal, Dennis O'Kelly, Daly was of Irish descent. He had few qualifications as a mentor of the young, since before he came to the racetracks he had worked in a stone quarry, where he lost a leg, and later had served as a bartender. His artificial leg was often an asset to Daly, who loved sharp practice just for the hell of it and was in constant trouble with the stewards. He believed that crippled horses could be cured by thrusting their legs into tubs of boiling water. One day an inspector of the SPCA caught him doing this and threatened to have him arrested. Father Bill rammed his artificial leg into the boiling water to prove it wasn't really uncomfortably warm.

Daly owned and trained horses, but his main fame came from developing jockeys. He liked to catch them when they were very young and bring them up under the hard discipline of a barrel stave, which he carried with him whenever he conducted his classes. He was one of the turf's more disreputable characters and was living proof that the bad die old, since he lived to be ninety-four. He did not die until 1931, but he operated for the most part in the nineteenth century. Daly did not spare his jockeys and his pupils did not spare their horses. Father Bill had used his barrel stave on them and they took it out on their mounts with the whip.

Father Bill's most famous protégés among the dozens he schooled were all whip riders. Snapper Garrison's name still lives on in the term "Garrison Finish" which has become a part of the general language as well as turf terminology. The great Domino hated his rider Fred Taral, another Daly pupil, so much that he would fly into a wild temper and try to stomp him every time he came in sight, but Taral always mastered him with the whip. Jimmy McLaughlin, Danny Maher and Winnie O'Connor were among other *cum laude* graduates of Father Bill's college of the barrel stave. Nearly all of Daly's students were strong, well-muscled boys who had great trouble making the weight. Father Bill solved that problem readily enough, one of his students, Winnie O'Connor, told me once. "He just cut off the food," he said. "We couldn't sneak off and eat when we were overweight, because he'd take every cent of our money. Also, he'd lock us up and keep us starving behind a locked door until we reached the weight he wanted."

Daly's methods were drastic and would hardly have been approved by the Jockeys' Guild. But they worked. The rough boy graduates of his academy were the greatest jockeys of their time.

Father Bill's own horses were mostly cheap and crippled platers that got to the post and won bets for him by virtue of boiling soaks and strong dope, but no trainer of truly great thoroughbreds that raced for famous stables has ever developed so many top-class jockeys. Father Bill didn't boil or dope his jockeys. He just beat them with a barrel stave and half-starved them.

Daly never succeeded in knocking the high spirits out of his boys, no matter how hard he plied the barrel stave. O'Connor was a mild-mannered and wonderfully gentle man when I knew him in his old age, but he always claimed he had been a real hellion in his prime. He used to chuckle over his youthful exploits during the time he was wearing the most famous racing silks of Europe. He said his fellow students in the Daly Finishing Academy were the same. "Cocky, that's what we were," he'd say, "throwing our money around and drinking the bubbly and courting the pretty girls and never so much as tipping our hats to the millionaires and dukes and kings who hired us to ride for them."

None of Father Bill's pupils seemed to bear him any ill will after they flew from the nest. O'Connor used to show me a scar that he said the barrel stave had made decades before, but he was proud of it. "Father Bill was rough, but he made us all rich," he'd say. And then a wistful look would come into the eyes of the little man who seldom had as much as a dollar in his pocket. "The only thing he didn't teach us was how to save our money," he'd add.

The bantam rooster is traditionally the most truculent fowl in the barnyard, and the Breed of Little Men has never been noted for its modesty. The brashest of all, perhaps, was the Little Man who invented the modern riding seat that has even been adopted in a modified version in conservative England and prevails nearly everywhere but France. He called himself James Todhunter Sloan, he traveled from track to track with a personal valet and more trunks full of clothes than Lillian Russell or the present Duchess of Windsor ever carried, he pre-empted the best suite in the best hotel at Saratoga from his own millionaire employer, he changed his silk underwear at least six times a day and his outer garments as often, and he once shocked a usually genial and democratic gentleman by telling him, "Eddie, my boy, you look like a bloody fat walrus in that bloody tailcoat you're wearing." The gentleman in question was his employer, the Prince of Wales, who would soon become Edward VII of England.

Sloan had the amazing faculty of making all of his defects into virtues, and that, in a sense, was the way the modern high-crouch riding style was born. To begin with, his middle name wasn't Todhunter. He appears to have been obnoxious to his fellows even as a brat and his playmates called him "Toad." When he came to the tracks, he converted that into "Tod" and said it was an abbreviation of his fancy-Dan middle name of Todhunter. The Todhunters, he claimed, were a race of aristocrats from tidewater Virginia. Sloan's people were actually Indiana farmers.

The nickname "Toad" had derived in part from Sloan's physique. He was not really deformed, but in one respect he rather resembled the artist Toulouse-Lautrec. His stumpy legs were out of all proportion to the length of his barrel. One of the best tailors in London devised a short jacket with two buttons and a flyaway waistline to compensate for his physical proportions, and it was known for a while as the "Sloan swagger." It was a precursor of the "Continental" jackets that appeal to the sharpie set of adolescents today.

Because of his abnormally short legs, Sloan had to use the shortest stirrup leather of any jockey on the racetrack. The short stirrups thrust him forward and upward, and he virtually perched on his mount's neck. In England, where the Virginia aristocrat from Indiana did much of his riding, he was booed and jeered and called "The Monkey on a Stick," but he won race after race, including such great classics as the Ascot Gold Cup.

In 1898, his best year, he won nearly half the races in which he rode, scoring 166 victories with 362 mounts, a percentage that only the Negro Isaac Murphy had ever achieved. Gradually horsemen began to suspect that this forward-thrust high crouch might be partially responsible for his success, since it took weight off the horse's back and placed it forward on the neck and withers. Every jockey in America began to imitate Sloan's seat, although every jockey in America, including his own older brother Cash, hated his guts and tried to foul him up every time they rode against him.

His monkey-on-a-stick style deeply offended the British sense of dignity and tradition and horsemanship, but it is interesting to note today that although English jockeys have not quite gone all the way, they have developed a kind of compromise half-high, half-crouch Sloan seat on a horse. All American jockeys now ride the Sloan way, of course.

Sloan offended the English even more by demanding—and almost always getting—the Royal Suite at every hotel he chose to grace with his presence. It must have gladdened the heart of the descendant of the mythical Todhunters when a small country inn near Ascot, at which he stopped briefly when he won the Gold Cup, changed the name of its best accommodations. For years they were known as the Tod Sloan Suite.

It is said that a full belly and a sense of security make conservatives of radicals. During the last two decades, due to affluence and the welfare plans of the Jockeys' Guild, perhaps, many of America's leading jockeys have lost the gaudy protective coloration that the Breed of Little Men flaunted in the days of Sloan and have become sober young financiers in gray flannel suits.

We can thank Latin America not only for supplying us with urgently needed replacements for the disappearing Breed of Little Men, but for furnishing our turf with the last of the ebullient and uninhibited eccentrics whose antic conduct is in the classical pattern of horsebacking.

One of the first of the larruping Latins to arrive was an engaging Chilean named Mike Villena, who came to the States with a shipment of South American horses consigned to a gambler named Clarence Shockley in the 1930s.

Shockley had a mare named Sahri II, and he put over several betting coups with her at New England tracks with Villena as his rider. The only English that Villena spoke was a phrase that went, "No spik, señor," whenever the stewards called him in for some infraction of the rules. One day Villena had Sahri II in the gate at Suffolk Downs for a stake with important money on which his boss had an important bet.

The mare's head was sideways and Villena sensed that Starter Jim Milton was about to send them off and leave him at the post. Under that stressful circumstance, he suddenly broke into perfect English. "No chance, Mr. Milton!" he screamed. "No chance!"

A present-day Panamanian, Mannie Ycaza, who is known as "Yak-Yak" because of his hair-trigger garrulity and his compulsion to deliver a theater-of-the-absurd monologue to any available audience, is a remarkably talented rider—when he gets a chance to ride. Unfortunately, his overflowing spirits and his win-or-die riding style have caused him to receive so many suspensions that he spends almost as much time on the ground as he spends in the saddle. Ycaza, however, serves a purpose in playing the role of an old-time swashbuckler in a jockeys' quarters that often resembles a bleak accounting office with busy little bookkeepers making business on office stools all day.

Avelino Gomez, a Cuban jockey, is a young man who must have coiled springs concealed in the seat of his silken jockey pants. When he wins a race, he bolts straight up from the saddle, rising at least three feet in the air and emitting wild war whoops, before he descends to the ground and turns several ceremonial somersaults.

Many of the Latin Americans are quiet almost to the point of self-effacement, however. Braulio Baeza is a Panamanian of Chinese ancestry, which shows in his slanted eyes. He is tall for a jockey and sits straighter in the saddle than most Americans. He never says a word when a shrug of the shoulders will serve as well. He has the classic, inscrutable features you find on a pre-Columbian Chimu portrait jar.

The quietest and gentlest mannered of them all is a little Mexican boy who was born on a scrub ranch in Texas and who is already assured of immortality because he has been the regular rider of an immortal horse named Kelso. Ismael Valenzuela, better known as Milo, learned to ride thoroughbreds on the back of a shaggy little burro, a pet he shared with his twenty-one sisters and brothers on the parched acres of the ranch out West.

The root derivation of the word "jockey" is far from complimentary. It traces to the Scottish nickname "Jock," the equivalent of the English and American "Jack." As early as the seventeenth century "jock" became a slang verb to describe sharp practice, especially in horse deals, since the Scots were supposedly extremely astute and sometimes downright unethical in such business transactions. In time the phrase "jocking a man" came to mean cheating him. In early races it was accepted practice to interfere with an opponent's horse by bumping him or cutting over in front of him. In many races the conditions specifically stated that "crossing and jostling" were permitted. Such tactics were always forbidden in races in which King Charles II himself rode, however. In the vernacular of the early turf "crossing and jostling" was termed "jocking a horse." When the professional race rider evolved, he was called a "jock" and the smaller ones were called by the diminutive "jockie" or "jockey."

This etymology is particularly amusing in view of the fact that membership in any of the world's jockey clubs confers considerable prestige and social distinction upon a man. As we have seen, the term was valid for the English Jockey Club, formed by bibulous horsemen at a Pall Mall pub, since many of them actually rode their horses in races. Members of the New York Jockey Club (which in a *de facto* sense is the United States Jockey Club) are dedicated horsemen, but they do not ride in races. In France the Jockey Club (for which one of the world's more expensive perfumes is named) has little or nothing to do with racing. The real Jockey Club of France is the *Société d'Encouragement pour l'Amélioration des Races de Chevaux en France,* which is a mouth-filling name in any language. The French Jockey Club is actually a very, very exclusive social club. Once a year its members put little blue flowers in their handmade buttonholes and sponsor the running of the Prix du Jockey Club at Chantilly, a race that is better known throughout the world as the French Derby. The rest of the year members of the French Jockey Club occupy themselves by turning up their noses at the *bourgeoisie* and sighing for the dear, dead days of the Second Empire. It's odd indeed their exclusive cabal should take its name from the slang term for a crooked horse trader.

Of all the jockeys I've known over the years, the one I knew best was Johnny Pollard, and he was a very good jockey indeed to know the best, for he was one of the most completely fascinating and delightful characters the turf has produced. On the racetracks he was known as "Red." His best friends called him "Cougar."

Pollard was one of the most tremendously talented riders of

a day when many of the great stars were in their ascendancy, and he has never been given his just due in the chronicles of horsemanship. His own flippant attitude was largely responsible for this. He just couldn't take anything too seriously, including himself. Once, when a group of self-important interviewers from important publications and wire services were interviewing him about the chances of Seabiscuit in a great stakes, Pollard said reflectively, "He'll probably win if I don't fall off. I fall off a lot of horses, though, you know."

Pollard had begun in the rough-and-tumble races on the leaky-roof circuit of the West when he was fourteen years old. When he finally retired in 1955 at the age of forty-six, he called me on the phone from a long way off to announce that he was hanging up his tack. He said he had broken every bone in his body at one time or another. "The only reason I'm alive is that Satan has no stall for me," he declared.

He never gave much of a damn about what sportswriters said of him. Once, when *Time* magazine devoted its whole sports column to a story I had written about him, Pollard called me on long distance. He sang all the verses of "You Made Me What I Am Today, I Hope You're Satisfied" in a whiskey tenor, then hung up.

Those who remember Pollard today are inclined to dismiss him with the observation that great horses make great jockeys and that Seabiscuit made Pollard. The fact is that Seabiscuit was a crotchety cripple and that only two jockeys ever managed him perfectly. One was the immortal George Woolf, who may well have been the greatest of them all. The other was Pollard, who rode The Biscuit many more times than Woolf. There were a great many tricks involved in riding Seabiscuit. He had a lot of meanness in him, partly because he was hurting most of the time that he was running. He liked to come from behind because he seemed to enjoy humiliating other horses by passing them at a time when they were winging along in front. He was often criticized for "hanging" in the stretch. He would almost never surge right by a pacemaker and widen out on him. He liked to tease. He'd get to his rival's flanks, pull himself up and play with the other horse before he drew off to beat him. If he did go by and widen out, as he would occasionally, he'd slow down and wait for the other horse to come to him again before he'd go on to win.

When Kayak II, Seabiscuit's stablemate under the silks of Charles S. Howard, a San Francisco automobile dealer, came up in the stretch of the Santa Anita Handicap of 1940, exactly this happened. Seabiscuit had been waiting for him. For a tick of time he let Kayak II draw alongside, then came on to beat him. Half the reporters in the press box wrote that Kayak II could have won if his rider, Buddy Haas, hadn't had instructions to let Howard's favorite take the race. They said Haas eased up. He didn't. Haas rode Kayak II as hard as any boy could ride a horse, but Seabiscuit and Pollard were just too much for him.

Seabiscuit played his favorite game too long in the Santa Anita Handicap of 1938, and lost the $100,000 purse by a nose to Stagehand. The Biscuit was driving harder at the finish of that race than he had ever driven in his life, but he had not reckoned with the featherweight of a hundred pounds that Stagehand carried when he started drawing it fine, and when he realized he wasn't going to pull away easily this time, it was too late, for he'd given out of ground. He also had played around too long in the same race the year before and he was beaten a nose by Rosemont.

Woolf's great race on Seabiscuit came in 1939 in the match with War Admiral at Pimlico. Pollard had a broken leg and was laid up at the time. I wrote before that race that Seabiscuit would most probably make the pace, and took a good deal of kidding for doing so. War Admiral had tremendous early speed and Seabiscuit liked to come from off the pace, and I was predicting an exact reversal of their running styles in their most important race. The match had been sought for a year, since the two had never met, and it was certain to determine the year's champion. I hadn't purchased a crystal ball. I had simply been present, by special permission of both jockeys, when Woolf and the injured Pollard talked over strategy. Pollard had known all along that Seabiscuit possessed tremendous early speed if you wanted to use it. He thought the time to use it had arrived. He believed that the stable plans for War Admiral would be upset if Seabiscuit made the pace unexpectedly. He told Woolf that. "I'd come out of the gate on top and set the pace if I could," he said. "But I wouldn't let him stay too far in front too long, or he'll pull himself up and sulk. Let War Admiral get to you at six furlongs, race him into the ground, then move off in the stretch."

The race was at a mile and three sixteenths, and that's exactly what Woolf did. It is impossible to overpraise a jockey of Woolf's quality, but the writers who gave him credit for devising the brilliant and unexpected strategy of outrunning War Admiral early were misinformed. They weren't misinformed by Woolf, who always gave the credit for the strategy to Pollard.

Neither Woolf nor Pollard objected to my "guessing" in print that Seabiscuit would make the pace, as long as I didn't quote them, because they fully realized that War Admiral's connections would pay no attention at all to the pipe dream of a mere newspaper columnist. Earlier I had conducted a two-way interview for a radio network between Woolf, in a Boston studio, and Pollard in his Winthrop, Massachusetts, hospital room, and they certainly would not have revealed such plans over the air.

In fact, at one point of the interview, the script called for Woolf to ask Pollard if he had any suggestions as to how he should ride The Biscuit. The written dialogue called for Pollard to answer to the effect that if Woolf just nursed Seabiscuit along and let him run his race, his mount would give him the best he had in the stretch.

Pollard's leg was up in traction and the bulky script was resting on his chest. When Woolf's question came over the two-way hookup, Pollard turned the page and the script spilled to the floor. I scrambled to recover it, but it was no use. I had seen the evil gleam in Red's eye and I knew he was going to ad-lib. I feared they'd throw the switch and cut us off the air, because I knew Pollard all too well.

Pollard said, "Why, Georgie-boy, just ride your usual race. Get left at the post and louse it up from there on in."

They didn't cut us off the air, but Woolf was so convulsed by laughter that he could hardly finish the broadcast.

The line of Matchem, incidentally, was enjoying a peak year in 1938. War Admiral was a son of Man o' War. Seabiscuit, by Hard Tack, was Big Red's grandson.

Pollard's hard luck in suffering a crippling injury at this crucial point of Seabiscuit's career was typical of the jinx that pursued him for most of his long years on the turf, and it was also typical of the redhead's compulsive generosity, a quality many of the racetrack drifters imposed upon shamelessly whenever The Cougar was in the chips. Seabiscuit was at Suffolk Downs in Boston when the accident occurred, training for a stake. Red had just galloped him one morning and when he jumped off his back, he felt happy, because he knew the horse he always called "Pops" was feeling good and acting well, and a big one was coming up. He ran into a friend of his, Bert Blume, who owned and trained a few cheap horses, and Bert was upset because a jockey who had promised to work one of his two-year-olds had failed to show up. It was a cheap horse pointing for a cheap race, but Bert was in financial difficulties and he needed the purse, and the workout was vital to the horse's condition.

Red jumped on the horse's back, said, "I'll work the bum," and galloped off. The horse, named Modern Youth, threw him and broke his leg.

I saw Blume some twenty years later and he said he'd never forgotten that day. He said he'd hated himself so much that he'd gone out on a week's drunk after Pollard broke his leg. "I'll never forgive myself for letting a great jockey with such an important engagement take a chance by working a green horse for me," he said, "but it all happened so quick. Red was like that. Impulsive. He'd been broke often enough to know what it was like and he was trying to do me a favor. You know something? I cried like a baby for a solid hour after it happened."

Pollard grew up in Butte, Montana, and had no formal education beyond grade school, since he started riding at the half-milers when he was fourteen. He had been called "Cougar" when he entered the prize ring as a ham-and-egg preliminary fighter to supplement his meager income as a jockey. He was a great reader and his two favorite authors were about as many poles apart as literary gentlemen can get. He loved quoting Omar Khayyám, whose philosophy of taking the cash and letting the credit go appealed to him as being well adapted to the gypsy life of a racetracker. And for some odd reason he was fascinated by the essays of the Transcendentalist philosopher Ralph Waldo Emerson, whom he always referred to as "Old Waldo." The Cougar said that breaking his leg proved Old Waldo was right when he wrote his essay on "Compensation." The prettiest nurse in the Winthrop hospital was a girl named Agnes. Pollard married her, and they were still happily married twenty-seven years later.

Shortly after I got out of the Army in World War II, I encountered Pollard at Narrangansett Park in Rhode Island. I hadn't seen him in five years, since his great days of 1940 when he rode Seabiscuit to the money-winning record of the world at Santa Anita. He had announced his retirement after that race and had tried training for a while, but it wasn't long before he was riding again. (In the fifteen years between 1940 and 1955 he retired at least three times before it finally took.) At the time I encountered him, he was undergoing one of his periods of retirement, because he had found it almost impossible to make the weight. He was doing the best he could, which wasn't very good, since he was scraping a living by exercising horses in the morning and trying to win a few bets with what dollars he could earn. He had great confidence in a horse that day and had borrowed all he could to bet on him. When the horse lost, he turned to me and shrugged his shoulders and quoted Omar. "Maybe I should have heeded the rumble of that distant drum when I was riding high," he said. "But I never did. Trouble is, you never hear it if you're a racetracker. Horses make too damned much noise."

I had sought Pollard out originally in the 1930s not only because he was the regular rider of one of the great horses of the era but because he was reputed to be a rugged individualist, and I always have been an admirer of rugged individualists. One story about him appealed to me particularly. When he was very young, he had been the leading rider of a meeting at the Tia Juana track. A little Indian apprentice boy had developed a hero worship for him and followed him about like a pet dog. One day Pollard's mount came into the stretch last and the little

Indian's mount was right in front of him. The apprentice had a very high seat on a horse, and The Cougar could not resist the tempting target. He smashed the Indian across the backside with his whip.

After the race the aggrieved apprentice demanded an explanation. "I was getting even for what you guys did to Custer," Pollard told him.

During the war Pollard tried to enlist in the Army, Navy, and Marines and was enthusiastically rejected by all of the services because of the numerous injuries he had received in spills on the racetrack. He finally took a job in a defense plant. "I knew how to screw a light bulb into a socket, so they made me an electrician," he said. "The boss told me to keep walking around and look busy. This little man kept following me, so I told the boss they were on to us and had a spotter checking up. 'Don't worry about him,' the boss said. 'He's your assistant.' I figured if I needed an assistant I must be overworked, so I went back to riding."

Knowing Pollard had fringe benefits, for he attracted as camp followers many of the more delightfully zany figures of the tracks. One was his agent, known as Yummy Allen, who is still around. Yummy and The Cougar had a similar background since the jocks' agent also had begun life as a preliminary box-fighter under the name of "The Tiger," although he hardly merited so ferocious a ring name. Yummy was later agent for the great George Woolf. He is a small man with a round head who rather resembles Charlie Brown of the comic strips. He is very gregarious. He is likely to walk up to a stranger at the track, stick out his hand and say, "My name's Yummy, not Dummy. Let's you and me have a drink together and pick a winner."

Yummy and The Cougar had half a pint of brandy and twenty-seven cents between them during a race meeting at Detroit in 1936 when they encountered a trainer named Tom Smith, whose patron, Charles S. Howard, had just purchased a crippled horse named Seabiscuit for $7,500. (The price is usually given as $8,000, but Howard himself once told me it was $7,500 and he's the man who put out the cash.) Seabiscuit would prove one of the greatest bargains of all time, since he bettered Sun Beau's world money-winning record, but he hardly looked it at the time, for he was limping painfully. Smith was known as Silent Tom for good reason. He made Three-Finger Webb, Black Gold's trainer, appear garrulous. He was a small, wiry, bespectacled man who had been a Western ranch hand. Once when Seabiscuit limped out on the track at Bay Meadows, a horseman said to Smith, "Tom, that horse of yours can't walk."

"Runs, though," Tom replied.

On another occasion, Smith, who enjoyed doing menial tasks around the barn despite the fact he was a rich trainer at the time, was chopping wood. The ax fell on his foot. He took off his boot and sock, and shook out the sock. He pointed to a small object on the ground.

"My toe," he said casually.

Tom was particularly frustrating to the gentlemen of the press. When Seabiscuit was at the peak of his fame, a young reporter asked him if he would describe the champion at length, and waited, pencil and notebook poised.

Tom thought the matter over for a long while, his brow crinkled. Then he answered.

"He's a horse," he said, and walked away.

By the winter of 1939-40 Pollard was off crutches and back in California. He had spent a year in hospitals undergoing surgery. The leg had not healed properly. It had been rebroken and reset twice. But he swore he was going to ride Seabiscuit just once more in the $100,000 Santa Anita Handicap, which the old champ had twice lost by a nose. The winner's purse would make Pops the greatest money winner of the world and Pollard swore it would be his last ride, too, and was confident his leg would hold up for one more mile and a quarter. "Look how Pops' bad leg has held up all these years," he said.

I had taken a house on top of a hill in Hollywood that season, and about a week before the $100,000 race, The Cougar visited me. He did not seem his flippant self. He was nervous and worried and distraught. I took him back to the den of the house and gave him a shot of brandy, which was his favorite drink. I told Pollard my landlady was very proud of the fact that her former tenants, who were songwriters for Bing Crosby, had written "Pennies From Heaven" in the den.

"That's what I need," The Cougar said. "Pennies from heaven. And I've got just one more ride to get 'em."

He was married now and Agnes was going to have a child and he'd been out of action for more than a year. If he won the Santa Anita on The Biscuit, his fee would be at least $10,000 and it seemed a million to him at the time.

"How's Pops?" I asked him.

"Pops' leg is no worse than usual," Pollard replied, "but how's The Cougar?"

He rolled up his pants-leg. The leg he showed me looked like a charred, knobby broomstick. "One little tap," said Pollard. "Just one. But it's got to last for one more ride."

He shrugged his shoulders. "Old Pops and I have got four good legs between us," he said. "Maybe that's enough."

But the leg wasn't the real source of his concern. Howard had brought a good jockey named Buddy Haas to the West Coast. He was also starting Kayak II in the race, but Pollard feared he might ride Haas on Seabiscuit and get still another jockey for his stablemate. I promised to see Howard.

I saw him the next day and asked him if he was riding The Cougar on The Biscuit.

"I just don't know," he said. "If Red breaks that leg again, he'll be crippled for life."

I told him maybe it was better to break a boy's leg than to break his heart. I don't know if what I said had any effect on Howard's decision, but I've always liked to think it might have. Anyway, he announced the next day that Pollard would ride Seabiscuit.

Yummy Allen was living in a Turkish bath at the time. This was no barometer of his financial condition. Rich or poor, Yummy has always liked to live in Turkish baths for some peculiar reason of his own. As late as 1964 he called me to wish me a happy Christmas from a Turkish bath in Baltimore.

Now *he* began to worry. Pollard liked to drink occasionally and he suffered terrible hangovers when he drank too much. He described the results of alcoholic excess most vividly himself. "I got to wear glued shoes when I'm hung," he said, "because I shake the nails out of the other kind."

Yummy was afraid that The Cougar was under such nervous tension and that the race meant so much to him he might hit the bottle to relax, and he said he was watching him day and night and wanted me to do the same. Pollard refused to move into Yummy's suite at the Turkish bath and submit to twenty-four-hour surveillance, he said.

On the day of the race I saw Yummy in the paddock. He sidled up to me like some character out of a spy novel and said mysteriously, "I've got it." When I asked him what he had, he showed me a tiny bottle of brandy he had hidden in his coat.

"I promised The Cougar I'd give him a drink of bow-wow wine before he even got off the horse if he wins this one," he whispered. "And I'm going to."

As the field filed down the lane to the track, I encountered Howard and wished him luck. I had always regarded him as a rather cold and imperturbable man. He was trying to light a cigarette and he had already used three matches. "You're shaking like a leaf," I said.

He grinned sheepishly. "I guess I'm a little nervous," he replied. He had a right to be nervous. I'd heard he'd bet $15,000 on Seabiscuit in the winter book at odds of 10 to 1. Between the bet and the purse he stood to win about a quarter of a million in the next few minutes.

The Cougar went by us, perched high over The Biscuit's neck. The old impish, go-to-hell grin was back on his freckled face. He had always reminded me of Huckleberry Finn and he looked even more like Twain's immortal bad boy now.

I turned to Howard and Yummy and said, "He's going to win. I wasn't sure till now, but now I'm sure."

I wondered at the time where Mrs. Howard was. I hadn't seen her at the saddling ceremonies. I found out later. She couldn't bear to watch the race from her box. She went to the backstretch and climbed up on a water tower with some stable hands, but she might as well have stayed on the ground. She closed her eyes tight when they were off and kept them closed until the finish. "I'd seen Johnny's leg," she said. "I just couldn't watch it."

For three quarters of a mile it was just another horse race. At the half-mile pole, The Cougar and The Biscuit made their move, hugging the rail. A horse named Whichcee, ridden by a tough, smart boy named Basil James, suddenly came over on Seabiscuit sharply. The crowd of 80,000 seemed to hold its breath.

For an instant the horse and the boy with four good legs between them seemed certain to go down. But Pollard had learned
to ride the hard way, in the bull rings of the West, and he managed to ease off.

Then they were in the stretch and Seabiscuit was outside and
Whichcee was inside and Pollard was squeezing the frantic
James closer and closer to the rail. "I wanted to see if he could
take it," The Cougar said that night. "He made me take it."

Whichcee collapsed, but The Biscuit had to withstand another
challenge from his own stablemate, Kayak II, before he drew
out to win. And even then it wasn't over.

James climbed into the stewards' stand and claimed a foul.
It took two minutes for the stewards to disallow the claim. Then
they threw a wreath of roses over Seabiscuit's neck and he was
the greatest money-winner of the world and his last race had
been the greatest one of all.

Yummy went up and shook Red's hand as The Cougar sat on
his horse posing for pictures, and Pollard ducked down with
his head in the rose wreath and I wondered if Yummy had
passed him the little bottle. Later I learned he had, and that
The Cougar had gulped its contents down under cover of the
flowers before 80,000 people with a dozen cameras clicking.

"Best smelling drink I ever tasted," he said.

That night I sat with The Cougar and Yummy and some
other people in a fancy saloon owned by George Woolf, who
had won the match against War Admiral on Seabiscuit.

I asked Pollard how he'd felt when James went up and
claimed a foul. The freckled flesh beneath The Cougar's eyes
crinkled and he gave me a snaggle-toothed grin.

"I'll tell you how I felt," he said. "I felt just fine. I thought
if those dudes call me up in the stand and ask me questions, I'll
sass 'em. This is one time I can get away with sassing 'em. I

thought, there are eighty thousand people here and they all love me and Pops. If those dudes take our number down, they'll burn the stewards' stand—with those dudes in it." Pollard sipped his drink and looked off into space. "You know," he said, "not a single one of those eighty thousand people was making a sound while I sat there waiting."

I thought about it, and he was right. The real drama hadn't been the 121⅕ seconds it had taken Seabiscuit to run the mile and a quarter. The drama had come during the 120 seconds that a crippled boy sat on a crippled horse waiting for three men to decide if he was, temporarily, the greatest hero in sports or just another jock who'd ridden foul.

When 80,000 people are cheering, it's just a great big noise. When 80,000 people are completely silent, it's damned impressive.

6

The Grave Beneath the Gallows Tree

Since the globular earth but resembles a race,
When mankind all start to get Fortune's embrace,
In Europe no place like Newmarket for play
Haste away to NEWMARKET! *huzza! boys, huzza!*
—POEM BY A MR. WHITLEY IN LONDON SPORTING MAGAZINE, 1793

Our flight over racing's landscape and through the turf's centuries is the course of a drunken crow.

We speed from continent to continent and century to century, heedless of many vistas that would demand our attention if time and space were a continuum. Sometimes we pause and hover, wings a-flap, to view a particular scene or a particular horse or a particular man in greater detail. Again we circle backward to recall events of another time and another place that are related to the scenes and happenings we view today.

Now we fly an ocean and alight on the gnarled limb of an ancient tree from which a gallows rope has rotted a thousand years ago. We are on the great heath of England's Newmarket, and though our calendar tells us it is the 1960s, we are in the eighteenth century, for Newmarket does not change. As we perch on our limb and look down at a small mound where The Boy is buried, we half expect to hear the clatter of Cumberland's coach as it races hell for leather toward the Round Course, its portmanteau clinking with a hundred thousand golden guineas that the Royal Duke will use as betting money.

It is April, and though the chill of winter still dwells in the mists that smoke up from the undulating heath, the songbirds are back and the air is pleasant with their timid music. A man crosses the heath and pauses at the rustic fence that encloses the little mound of The Boy's Grave beneath our limb and peers down intently, as if his eyes are hungry for the sight of wonder. He is not clad in the leather weskit of the eighteenth century stud groom, but he is a horseman. The centuries do not change the bluff and ruddy look that horsemen wear. He stands at The Boy's Grave for long moments, half reverent, half eager, his eyes searching the moist earth to see if wildflowers have bloomed.

When flowers bloom on The Boy's Grave in April, a Newmarket horse will win the Derby at Epsom in June. The grizzled horsemen of the great heath will swear that this is true, that the prophecies of the grave flowers have never failed over all the years since 1780 when the first Derby race was run and won by King Herod's grandson, Diomed, who was sold out to the States when he was very old, but not too old to found a line of horses.

No one knows the name of The Boy who is buried here. He was a Saxon shepherd who lost a sheep. Human life was cheap in those cruel times and a sheep was far more valuable than a boy. The Boy's master hanged him from the very limb that serves us as a crow's-nest. On that long-ago night the other shepherds found The Boy and cut him down and buried him. And then they planted wildflowers on his grave, and each year the wildflowers bloom again. When they bloom in April a Newmarket horse will win the Derby. This is a thing the horsemen of Newmarket know for sure, for nature has her ways of imparting knowledge to men, and you learn those ways when you live your life out on the green heath that changes only with the seasons.

When the Romans came millennia ago, there were bloody battles fought at Newmarket, but since then the great heath has been an island in time, remote from history's convulsions. North, south, east and west of the turf gallops and sand gallops that stretch off into infinity, men fought for power and cannon sounded, but peace dwelt on the heath and the great events were always the accomplishments of horses.

There were horses and horsemen here long before The Boy was hanged by a vengeful master. One of the most civilized tribes of early Britain inhabited Newmarket. They were engineers of amazing skill, and brave warriors, and they had a coinage of their own that was the first in the isles. Their coins always bore the image of a horse.

They may well have been the most skilled horsemen of their times. At least Julius Caesar, who conquered them, thought so. They were called the Iceni and the legionnaires of Rome waged a long and bloody war to subdue them. In his *De Bello Gallico* Caesar writes at length of the tactics of their horse troops. He calls them "nimble horsemen" and remarks upon "the very terror of the horses and the noise of the wheels" that often broke the Roman ranks. Historians first thought that the sophisticated

Romans must have built the eight-mile ridge of fortifications that still runs through the heath like a great mole's hill and is called "the Devil's Ditch" or "Devil's Dyke," but now they seem convinced that it was the Iceni themselves who reared this redoubt. Over the years gaps have been cut through the Devil's Dyke. Many are narrow, barely wide enough to admit a string of horses walking single file. Others are large enough to accommodate the trains that carry racegoers from London and nearby Cambridge.

Even today horses pawing the ground at Newmarket will unearth the Iceni's coins engraved with the image of a horse, or a stone arrowhead that flew against the Romans, or a spear, or a part of a chariot's wheel. Sometimes the skeletons of Iceni warriors who manned the ramparts of the Devil's Dyke are surfaced. Antiquity breathes just beneath the turf of this ancient heath. There was racing here in Saxon times. The Venerable Bede, historian of the Saxon Chronicles, tells us how a party of travelers came upon the heath in the sixth century and how the younger members were so excited by the limitless expanse of turf that they "proved their horses on the greater course."

It was Charles II who established organized racing at Newmarket but it was an earlier Stuart, his grandfather James I, a peculiar fellow who not only never bathed but was disinclined to wash his face and hands, who first exploited the sporting possibilities of the place under kingly dominion. He spent much of his time here "hawking and coursing." He first took over an inn near the heath, but during his occupancy the foundation shifted so abruptly that all of the doors and windows on the leaning side fell open and he was forced to build himself a palace with covered "rides" for the Royal Horses. James was both a sportsman and a literary fellow. He wrote many poems, several of which celebrated the feats of his horses. He wrote a

Book of Sport, and forced all the clerics of England to read passages from it at every service. The passages read from the pulpit urged the King's subjects to profane the Sabbath by engaging in such sports as "racing, wrestling, and falconry" on Newmarket Heath and at other suitable places to improve their physical condition and make them into better soldiers when they were called to arms.

The Puritan movement was strong in the time of the first James and the Puritans objected to their king setting his *Book of Sport* alongside the Bible at church services. Parliament complained that James frittered away too much of his time in "hawking, hunting and racing over the Great Heath of New Market Town," but the King replied that he often devoted no more than three or four days a week to such pastimes.

James I was a Scotsman and he was surrounded by Scottish courtiers. Oddly enough this led to another of the stories connecting horses with the sea. We have noted the connection before in Greek mythology, in the stories of Ranger and Moifaa. According to legend, the Royal Horses owned by James I descended from Spanish steeds washed up on the shores of Galloway in Scotland from the wrecks of the great Armada.

In the early seventeenth century Newmarket was a favorite resort of sporting lords. It may be noted in passing that in 1617 a great fête was held there for sporting men by the sporting King James I, and that Rare Ben Jonson's masque, *The Vision of Delight,* was performed, but that this spectacle paled beside the banquet which was featured by "foure huge brawny piggs" supplied by Sir George Goring. The pigs were arrayed in the gear of race horses, bitted and saddled, with strings of sausage serving as the reins.

The banquet was a birthday celebration for a young prince named Charles who would not celebrate too many birthdays, for as King Charles I he was dragged to the scaffold by the Roundheads and was decapitated by the headsman's ax. He was an accomplished horseman as a youth and was delighted by the divertissement of Sir George's pigs. His father, James, was a devoted horseman, but a poor rider. In his *Book of Sport* he had set down the curious dictum that "a horse never stumbles except he is reined" and he was thrown into many a ditch because of his fond belief in this equestrian principle.

The town of Newmarket itself is fairly new as history goes on the great heath. It was a mere huddle of huts until 1237 when a plague drove the citizens of Exning to set up their market cross in the tiny settlement. A market cross still stands in the square, not far from the place that was once the Coffee House and is now the headquarters of the Jockey Club. Newmarket is the cradle and the historic center of the Western world of horses and it has been since the Iceni built their Devil's Dyke to thwart the Mercians and Romans. Cumberland and his cronies took over the Coffee House when the premises of the Star and Garter in London proved too small and too inconvenient for them. At first the Jockey Club at Newmarket was mainly a place where lords and gentlemen gambled on the races.

Just up the road that runs beside The Boy's Grave, half a mile away, is Cheveley Park. In the time of the first James it was owned by Sir John Carleton, who was gamekeeper for the king. Cheveley is one of the great studs of Newmarket. It had many owners before Sir John and dates back at least five hundred years. Ancient records are treasured at Newmarket, and some indicate that Cheveley Park is even older and that the horses known as *Equus Britannicus,* blocky, short-coupled animals that were remote forebears of the cobs and hackneys and other light-horse breeds, may have been raised here even in the time The Boy lost his sheep.

When I visited Cheveley Park in the spring of 1964 it was

owned by Richard Stafford Smith. The proprietor had business at Bath that morning and he had left instructions for his stud groom to show me about. There was a nameplate on the door of one of the brick lodges that read "W. Cowell" and I asked my companion, Geoffrey Webster, a racing journalist and an official of the British Race Course Association, what the initial stood for. He warned me that English stud grooms are touchy fellows, very sensitive of their dignity, and that I should not address our host by his first name. Before I could assure him that I intended no such familiarity, but merely wished the name for the record, Cowell appeared.

I liked him on sight. He had that look of utter dependability that is common to all horsemen who know their business. He seemed to belong to Newmarket in the way The Boy's Grave and the market cross and the ancient horse yards belong there. He was as sturdily built and as sublimely independent as John Bull himself. He had been stud groom in the yards of Lord Derby, on the same great heath, not far from Cheveley, and for other famous turfmen. He told me at once that his last previous situation had not been a happy one. He said his employer had been "one of those Eastern potentates who tried to instruct me, so I told him to instruct himself and came back here to New-market where I'm happy." His eyes looked off over the great green washboard of turf and gorse that ripples away to infinity, the best-known training ground of the world for thoroughbreds, a place described in the fifteenth century as "queachy Washes where steeds are set to coursing."

"A man gets used to Newmarket," he said. "If he's a horse-man it's the only place for him, and he should stay here."

Cowell pointed a thick finger to the ground beneath his feet. "Race horses were bred here in the tenth century," he declared. "Old King Canute bred horses right here."

He waved his hand toward a stand of trees. "Those cedars are new," he remarked. "Barely nine hundred years old, I'd guess. But that stand of limes beyond them is very old. A few thousand years, I'd think. The Romans saw those limes when they were here and they were old trees even then."

Cowell conducted us to a brick lodge built onto a small brick cottage. A plaque on the lodge stated it was erected to house the immortal Isinglass, who in the years from 1892 to 1895 won many of the greatest stakes of England and the enormous sum of £57,465, a record for the time. Isinglass held court here. His personal stud groom occupied the adjoining cottage, where he could hear his charge moving about and whinnying in his sleep. He was at the beck and call of the great stallion twenty-four hours a day and was seldom more than a few feet away from him, waking or sleeping.

The great Psidium, Mme. Arpad Plesch's son of Pardal-Dinarella, was residing in lonely grandeur in Isinglass's lodge. Flowers grew on The Boy's Grave in April of 1961, and Psidium had won the Epsom Derby that June.

Cowell summoned one of the stablemen, whom the English always call "lads," regardless of their age, and he led the stallion out. Cowell affected indifference, but he watched our faces covertly as an anxious mother might watch the reactions of adults to her talented child.

Psidium was a magnificent physical specimen. His knotted muscles and almost incredible heft of quarters and his coat of molten gold made me think of Man o' War. He is an actor of parts, too. He prances, snorts and stamps the ground while on display. According to the classic concept, great horses have the look of eagles in their eyes, but this is seldom true. Instead they have the roguish look of mischievous children who clamor for attention. Psidium was like that. He kept glacing sidewise at his stud groom as he pawed and snorted, seeking approval of his performance.

We left Cheveley and drove over the great heath. Here Matchem met Trajan, King Herod met Bay Malton, and Eclipse met Corsican. There are miles and miles of sand gallops and turf gallops. A horse could work every day for weeks and still not use them all. There are strict rules about which courses may be used on specific days, and violators are heavily fined. This keeps all of the training grounds in superb condition at all times. England is a small country in area, yet it can afford this vast expanse of real estate for the benefit of horses. In all the continental reaches of the United States, we have nothing like it.

The great heath belongs to time, but its proprietor of record is the Jockey Club. Horsemen pay twenty-five pounds a year, less then seventy-five dollars at present exchange, to train here.

We left the heath and came into the village and drove by the market cross and the Gothic clock tower and the Jockey Club and then went on to another part of the gorse lands to attend the races at the July Course. We passed the statue of Lord Derby's Hyperion, the greatest British stallion of modern times, who descended through a dozen sires from Eclipse.

This was a day in June, but to the English who call a coin worth seven cents a sixpence and who reckon their accounts in guineas which have not been minted for decades, there is nothing inconsistent in racing at the July Course in June. There are two racecourses on the heath. The other is the Rowley (pronounced "rolly") Mile, and this was probably the original location of Charles II's Round Course, where the first organized racing was conducted a century before the thoroughbred evolved. The July Course is used in summer because of its pleasant shade, but on this day the old trees were more useful as umbrellas, for a spring shower was coming down.

There are four stands on the July Course, varying from the Silver Ring, the cheaper accommodations far down the course near the hill, to the exclusive Members Enclosure. Between the

Members and the Silver Ring is Tattersall's, where most of the general public sees the races. In the Members Enclosure there is a stand built at a slant that looks straight down the course and is by far the best vantage point for watching straightaway races. It is very small and is limited to owners and trainers who have horses in a race and to jockeys waiting their turns to ride in a later event.

All the stands are of brick, with sides and roofs of silvered wood and concrete slabs for seats. Only in the Members do the seats have thin pads placed on them. English racegoers are a rugged lot.

The wooden portions of the stands must have been painted green in some remote era, for flecks of paint still remain, but they have not been refurbished in recent times. The English seem to think the color of old wood blends well into the surroundings of the ancient heath, and they are right.

We lunched in the Members Restaurant, an exclusive resort where the Welfare State has not yet encroached and class distinction is very evident. Those who dine here are mostly persons of wealth and distinction and often they are titled. The room itself is a haphazard area under the stand, square and bare, with whitewashed walls, and the food is very poor. If we offered backstretch cook-kitchens like this to stable help in the United States, there would be loud complaints.

The door of the dining room stood open and our table was near it. As I ate cold veal pie and curried eggs, I glanced out into the paddock area. A striking Churchillian figure of a man was sitting beneath a tree, clad in a tan weatherproof and a felt hat with the brim turned down against the rain. His hands rested on the crook of a sturdy ash stick and his fine leonine head was held proudly high.

Somehow he seemed a symbol of Newmarket, for he had the

face of a horseman, and the faces of horsemen change no more through the ages than the great green heath has changed.

The man beneath the tree was the grand old gentleman of British racing, Captain Cecil Boyd-Rochfort, Trainer for the Queen.

> ALL GUILTY BEFORE GOD
>
> THE WICKED SHALL BE TURNED TO HELL
>
> BE SURE YOUR SINS WILL FIND YOU OUT
>
> THE END IS AT HAND AND HELL YAWNS WIDE

The heath at Ascot is always packed solid on the four Royal Days in June and among the human beings who pack it are many eccentrics of the type who make speeches at Marble Arch and attempt to Ban the Bomb by sitting down before the government offices of Whitehall. They wear beards and shoulder-length hair and sometimes don the flowing robes of early Christians, and the placards that they bear furnish a sharp rebuke to the elegantly attired gentlemen in gray toppers and the ladies in their mad, mad hats who assemble in the Royal Enclosure and the reserved areas across the racecourse. But even these eccentrics wave their signs in respectful salute rather than indignant protest as the Queen's landau, drawn by the matched team of four Hanoverian Creams, leads the Royal Procession down the course from the Golden Gates to the Royal Box on one of the four great days of English racing. Across the course, in the privileged areas of the aristocracy, gentlemen place their toppers reverently against their hearts and ladies wave enormous chiffon handkerchiefs as the Queen goes by. These handkerchiefs are often family heirlooms, stored in lavender for most of the year and used only for Queen-waving on the Royal Days.

The "sharks, greeks and blacklegs" of London hounded poor

Cumberland to his grave largely because of the sums he had borrowed from them in order to preserve Ascot racing in the eighteenth century. It was at Ascot in 1769, four years after the Duke had died, that Eclipse ran his second race, distancing the one rival who had the temerity to test him, a bay horse named Cream de Barble (also known as Creme de Barbade), belonging to a gentleman delightfully named Mr. Fettyplace, in the Noblemen and Gentlemen's Plate. It was on this historic occasion that the wily O'Kelly managed to buy a half-interest in Eclipse from little Mr. Wildman.

Racing at Ascot predates both Cumberland and the thoroughbred. It was begun in 1711 under the auspices of Queen Anne, and her Master of the Horse, Charles, Duke of Somerset, carefully set down such accounts in his records as "one pound, six shillings and sixpence paid to one Benjamin Culchett, for painting the posts for the Round Heat at Ascott Common in July."

In 1708 Jonathan Swift had come from Dublin to London to urge the claims of the Irish clergy to the "Queen's Bounty" upon Anne's minister Lord Godolphin, who would bring the famed Godolphin Arabian to England in 1724. At the time of the first Ascot meet Swift was editing his Tory pamphlet, *The Examiner,* in London and the Queen urged him to write a little piece about her meet on Ascot heath. Swift, always irresponsible about keeping appointments, missed his coach to Ascot and "since I would not sore-up my behind by galloping thither mounted on a horse," we lack his account of the racing that day.

Anne took residence at nearby Windsor Castle for the Ascot meet of 1711 and every reigning monarch of England since her time has done the same for the week that the Royal Meet is in progress. Ascot was in a bad way in the 1750s and 1760s, however. George II, Cumberland's father, and George III, his nephew, were willing enough to ride down the stretch in the

Royal Procession and receive the plaudits of the crowds, but they would give no money from the Royal Purse to support the course. Cumberland, as Ranger of Windsor Forest, which included supervision of Ascot Heath, deemed it his duty to keep racing alive and although he was already financially ruined by his gambling, he borrowed huge sums from the usurers in order to operate the Royal Meets.

There are many ironies in racing. The formal costume of Ascot is much the same as it has been for a century or more. There is one change. Gentlemen no longer wear Ascot ties to Royal Ascot. They wear pearl-gray or dark-striped four-in-hands instead. This is a small touch of modernity indeed. The great change at Royal Ascot occurred in 1961 when the Queen Elizabeth II grandstand was built. It was the first modern grandstand at a racecourse in England, and one of the most lavish structures of its kind in the world. A similar but even more luxurious stand was built for the Royal Enclosure in 1964. Quite by chance I was present for the dedication of both of these great grandstands.

The architects had studied both the racing plants of Doc Strub's Santa Anita and the pop-art architecture of Aqueduct before they went to work and brought a British racetrack out of the eighteenth century. The stands at Ascot differ sharply from those at American courses, however. The boxes are not really boxes at all. They are small apartments. There is a porch for watching the races, a dining room and kitchen. Boxholders bring their cooks and butlers to the course and have private luncheons in their private quarters. These boxes, rented only for the four-day season, cost about $800. The great families lease them in perpetuity and they are often inherited, along with the title, by the eldest son.

The climax of Royal Racing arrives before the Royal Racing

even begins at Ascot. The ceremonial called the Royal Procession is the high mark, and it is held fifteen minutes before the first race. The Queen and her house party drive over from Windsor Castle in Rolls Royces. They leave their cars on a road inside the racecourse at the end of the stretch. Most Americans are startled by the fact that public highways cross the courses at tracks like Ascot and Epsom. When races are in progress, gates, like those at railway grade crossings in the United States, are lowered and traffic is halted. When races are run, swatches of turf are spread over the roads like rugs.

The Royal limousines stop on a road up the course where the landaus, vehicles very similar to those in use in the time of James I, are waiting. The special breed of chunky gray and roan horses now known as the Windsor Grays, formerly called the Hanoverian Creams, are hitched to the leading coach in which the Queen and her consort ride. The Creams came to England with the first Hanovers. A circus proprietor named Sanger conducted George IV's team of Creams safely across the Irish Channel in a tempest and the King rewarded him with one of them, who became an ancestor of the famed "Liberty Horses" of the Greatest Shows on Earth. The breed is continued outside the circus solely to draw the Royal coaches.

The carriages enter through the Golden Gates, and if you ever have a close-up view of this entrance to the course, you will be sorely disillusioned. The Golden Gates are by no means as stylish as the pearly portals at which St. Peter supposedly presides. They are merely wooden gates in a farm fence, painted a rather ugly shade of mustard yellow.

The coachmen in top hats and velvet livery sit on a high seat at the back of the landaus. Postilions in green velvet jackets and billed caps ride the horses, two to each team.

The Duke of Edinburgh and other gentlemen of the retinue

wear the traditional Ascot costumes, gray toppers and dark tail-coats. The ladies wear tulle hats and lovely gowns and neither they nor the ladies in the stands ever don a wrap, no matter how bitter the English weather may be. (There is a rumor they wear woolies beneath their dresses.) The Queen traditionally wears a gown of a different color on each of the four afternoons and, also traditionally, she wears these gowns but once. They are made especially for her Royal Days at Ascot. There is a legend that the gentlemen of the Royal House Party and the titled stewards of the Royal Races are the only men in England who own their own Ascot toppers and tails. The others are rented from a Covent Garden firm, Moss Bros., Ltd., affectionately known as "Moss Bross." These London clothiers reputedly live all year on the profits of renting formal wear to gentlemen for the four days of Royal Ascot.

The Royal Procession proceeds down the course for about six furlongs to the decorously enthusiastic cheers of the multitude and a flutter of chiffon kerchiefs. Then it turns into the Royal Enclosure. One year a lady just behind me said to her escort when the Procession had ended, "Ah, me, it's all over so quickly, isn't it? Should we go home, pet, or stick around to hazard a pound or two?"

The Royal Box, on the finish line in the Royal Enclosure, is a great glass fishbowl about fifty feet wide and twice as deep. I doubt it has sleeping chambers, but it has dining tables, bars, kitchens, pantries and all the other amenities of a luxury apartment. Lackeys in knee breeches serve champagne and tea all afternoon. (I noted through my binoculars that the Queen herself usually takes tea.) Owners, trainers and jockeys of winners of the Royal Plates, Cups and Trophies are escorted to the Royal Box and presented to the Queen, and this seems to mean far more to them than the purses they win.

The Duke of Edinburgh, who is not English, of course, is said to loathe racing and he especially dislikes the ceremonials of Ascot. The Queen herself is intensely devoted to the sport. She starts her horses in many of the Royal Ascot events. The Queen Mother's horses also run as frequently as possible. Sir Winston Churchill's racers (none of whom was much good) always pointed for Royal Ascot.

I visited Ascot for the Royal Hunt Cup in 1964, the second of the Royal Days, and, as it turned out, the last afternoon of Royal Racing that year. I had seen the Royal Procession come down the stretch before, and, like the topography of Newmarket, it doesn't change. At the suggestion of David Hedges, an ingratiating gentleman who is the singlehanded public relations counsel for all of England's sixty-eight racecourses, I posted myself on a balcony at the rear of the press rooms of the new Royal Enclosure.

The Royal Procession turns off the course, proceeds through the paddock and ends directly beneath this balcony. I was some ten feet above the Queen and Prince Philip when they disembarked from the leading landau. The oldest of the Old Pensioners who serve as attendants in the Royal precincts opens the door of the Queen's carriage. He wears a long, befrogged green velvet coat and a black silk topper with a gold ribbon and gold trim around the brim. He also wears all his military decorations and they are numerous enough to suggest that he began collecting awards for gallantry about the time the Boers became obstreperous.

In the other four carriages of the Procession I recognized the Queen Mother (fondly called the "Queen Mum" by the British), the beautiful Princess Marina, and the young and devastatingly handsome Aga Khan. For dizzying moments I was even closer to a queen than Dick Whittington's cat.

The press room of the brand-new Enclosure is startling to an American who has worked on newspapers in the States. There is only one typewriter, and that is owned by Mr. Hedges, a shockingly modern young man despite the Edwardian garb he dons for Ascot. The reporters, all arrayed in Moss Bross uniforms, write out their copy longhand. There is an old gentleman in the press box whose pockets sag with the enormous English pennies. His sole function seems to be to supply the journalists with coins for the phones they use when they call in their scribbled stories. The press room is commodious, even elegant by most American standards, and there is, inevitably, a refreshment table where tea is served at the proper hour.

The best horses in Europe race at Royal Ascot, but the pomp, pageantry and just plain people are far more fascinating than the races. Moss Bross apparel is required of gentlemen in the Royal Enclosure. In the Queen Elizabeth reserved stand most males wear toppers and tails through choice. Royal Ascot is a brief annual revival of the age that died with a bluff *bon vivant* named Edward VII, the last stand of the British Establishment which flaunts its gray toppers and tulle bonnets in the austere face of the Welfare State. The great clubs of London— White's and Carlton and Cavalry—all erect huge, Chautauqua-like tents down the course for luncheon parties, and to be invited to one of these (where I suspect the food is pretty horrible) assures you a permanent place in British society.

On the informal acres of the heath across the course, the thousands who benefit from the Welfare State enjoy a glorious afternoon betting a bob or so on the runners and watching the gentlemen parade about in their rented formal wear and the ladies looking lovely in their Paris gowns.

There is always some delightful, human touch to Royal Ascot to relieve the stiffish formality. While the horses were at the post for the Royal Hunt Cup, the public announcer took time out at a very crucial moment to make an urgent appeal: "Will Mrs. Morris please collect her granddaughter Deborah from the police office on the heath?" For a brief moment little Deborah was of greater importance than the millions of pounds' worth of thoroughbred horseflesh jockeying at the barrier.

Most of the foreign dignitaries who attend the Royal meeting acknowledge custom and pay tribute to Moss Bross. In 1964 there was just one militant individualist in the Royal Enclosure, a very black African potentate who wore a flowing yellow silk robe and a bright red fez.

One of my most pleasant memories of Royal Ascot concerns a barmaid in my favorite London pub, the Swan, a Victorian tavern on Sloane Street in Knightsbridge. Some years ago she became wildly excited when she learned I was going to Ascot the following day and made me promise to come straight from the train to relate to her all the details about the toffs I saw. She confided that the great ambition of her life had been to wear a tulle bonnet out to Royal Ascot, but she was now past middle age and her hopes of realizing the dream were growing dim.

I took a cab from Waterloo Station to the pub and she looked at me with great disappointment when I arrived.

"You didn't go!" she said.

I told her I had just returned, but she shook her head.

"You 'aven't got a topper on your 'ead," she said. "A gent 'asn't been to Royal Ascot unless 'e 'as a topper on 'is 'ead."

I have always suspected that the English are the last truly civilized race on earth, and that suspicion was confirmed on Gold Cup Day at Royal Ascot, June 18, 1964. The occasion is now known to history as The Day It Rained at Royal Ascot, a date as memorable as that of the Battle of Waterloo, which also came on June 18, in 1815. For the first time since 1807 the entire card of six races and the Ascot Gold Cup were canceled because of weather conditions. I was there.

In the long past of Ascot, programs had been canceled or transferred to other courses because of war. In 1930 a bookmaker on the rail was killed by a lightning bolt, and since bookmakers are respected citizens in England, the last two races were declared off out of respect to this pillar of the turf. In 1935 the Royal Procession was canceled because of rain, but races were run. In 1955 another lightning storm erupted during the races and people on the heath were mowed down like tenpins. One person was killed and the remaining races were canceled. On the opening day of the Royal Meeting in 1960 a big wind hit the course and there was considerable lightning. The public announcer merely warned the crowd to keep away from metal railings, and the races were held. But in 1964, after a crowd of well over 50,000 persons had already jammed the stands and heath for the biggest turf event of the Royal Season and the most important social occasion of the year, there were no races at all.

Nothing can look quite so disheveled as a chiffon gown and tulle hat or a tailcoat and gray topper when they are soaking wet, and even the gentry who frequent the Royal Enclosure and arrive by Rolls Royce get soaking wet between the parking lot and the stands when it rains at Royal Ascot. The classic British brollie proved little protection against the storm that blew up on Gold Cup Day. It is anybody's guess as to how many thousands of pounds' worth of couturiers' creations and milliners' masterpieces were completely ruined. Tons of sodden tailcoats and wilted toppers were returned to Moss Bross.

My wife accompanied me to the Gold-Cup-That-Wasn't, and for this reason I was in the reserved section of the Queen Elizabeth stand instead of the press box. Elegantly attired ladies and gentlemen sat dripping steadily, like trees in a rain forest, all around us. No one complained at all. They were, in fact, cheery to the point of being chipper. At two o'clock, it was announced that the Royal Procession was canceled. There were sighs and sympathetic tuttings. One lady said, "All I really care about is the Procession, but I'm glad they've canceled it. The Queen is subject to colds."

A few moments later it was announced that the two thirty, or first race, would be postponed fifteen minutes while the stewards inspected the course. A Land Rover carrying the distinguished and formally attired gentlemen who serve as stewards drove out on the course. Stewards emerged from it in the lashing rain, and this afforded a sight indeed. There in front of us on the puddled greensward were the Duke of Norfolk, K.G., G.C.V.O., the Earl of Derby, M.C., the Earl of Halifax, K.G., P.C.O.M., G.C.I.E., and Brigadier, The Lord Tryon, K.C.B., K.C.V.O., D.S.O., all tailcoated, boutonniered and top-hatted, and all stamping their feet like irritated roosters to test the turf.

Shortly after two thirty there was a terse announcement to the effect that the two thirty was now postponed "indefinitely." Meanwhile, wind was blowing the lashing rain into the stands, but the ladies and gentlemen continued to sit dripping, bantering and completely composed. The massed crowd of simpler folk on the heath had no cover at all, but they also stood there dripping patiently.

Around three o'clock the Duke of Norfolk betook himself and all his attached initials to the glass-enclosed fishbowl that is the Royal Box. He is Her Majesty's Representative.

Seventeen minutes later there was a curious announcement over the loudspeaker. "The stewards are satisfied . . ." it began, and there was an audible sigh of relief among the dripping customers. But then the announcer continued: "The stewards are satisfied after inspecting the course that racing is not possible today." He then advised the soaked throng to wait even longer for further announcements about refunds of bets, admission tickets and the rescheduling of races. By this time £70,000 had been bet through the tote and many times that amount in the books on the course and in the city.

A lady near me, her gown as wet as wash on a line, had focused her binoculars on the Royal Box. "What a beastly shame," she said. "The Queen does look so lovely today, too."

A gentleman who had been shaking water from the brim of his topper for the last hour remarked, "I say, I'm rather glad, you know! Let's all go to the bar. It's a splendid day for getting squiffed, isn't it?"

Another gentleman of such mature years that one wondered how he had managed to totter over the woodland path to the course said, "Only thing to do, I suppose. Must think of the horses first, mustn't we?"

Finally it was announced that the wet patrons might queue up for refunds of their bets in tote and books and that "emergency tickets," or rain checks, would be issued and would be good for Friday's races (which weren't held because of the condition of the course, as it turned out). Tickets to the stand cost 50 shillings, about $7.00, incidentally. Reserved seats cost 30 shillings above the entrance fee. There were no refunds for reserved seats or the $200 Royal Enclosure boxes.

The biggest problem of all was getting out of Royal Ascot. The rain was pouring harder than ever now and there was no shelter. There are only two exits from the grandstand area, each as wide as an ordinary door to a room. They are reached by narrow, cul-de-sac alleyways that twist and turn. The thousands had to exit single-file, since each was handed his emergency ticket by the gateman. This, of course, took hours. It took me something over a half-hour to advance about ten yards up the alleyway.

You then walk over an uncovered woodland path to the tiny Ascot train station. Here there were thousands waiting for the infrequent locals, which were the only available trains since the race specials were not due for an hour or so. But I must say that the British Railways, which are by no means the best loved of England's institutions, rose to the occasion magnificently. They managed extra trains, and I even found the first-class-only limited that had taken me down. It was early for tea by British standards, but they served it in the buffet with jam and crumpets and that historic restorative was enough to revive the spirits of even the weaker souls like myself.

A Scottish couple shared our table. They had come all the way from Inverness especially for the Cup and they had to go all the way back again and had no really solid guarantee at the moment that they would be refunded any of the money they had spent for tickets. They were quite wet and quite happy, though they complained that crumpets couldn't compare to scones.

"Wonderful day, really," the Scotsman said. "Went to Royal Ascot on Cup Day and didn't lose a bob, did I?"

The monument to British patience and muddling-through that was afforded by the great press of humanity waiting to exit from the narrow gates was incredible to me. Water from ladies' umbrellas poured steadily down the necks of gentlemen. One lady apologized to a stranger after she had virtually removed his eyeball with the rib of her umbrella. "Not at all, Madam. No bother at all," the gentleman said, rubbing his inflamed eye.

There was no shoving, no pushing, no anger, a great deal of joking. At Waterloo Station in London the soaked chiffons and wilting toppers queued up in an endless line again for taxis and no one tried to get ahead or to flag down a cab before his turn.

There must be something after all to this business of living in unheated dwellings all winter, eating food that is boiled to the consistency of pablum, using tea and hot water bottles as sovereign remedies for all diseases and winning battles on the playing fields of Eton.

Had the same thing happened at any racetrack in America, the stands would have been demolished completely by the rioting crowd, and the entire Board of Stewards would have been hanged by their necks from the eighth pole. The British simply managed to enjoy the fiasco.

"Demmed glad I was there," one gentleman said. "Expect they'll be talking about this at the club as long as there's a Royal Ascot."

And there'll always be a Royal Ascot, of course.

When I was in France in 1964, the hospitable Jean Romanet, managing director of the *Société d'Encouragement* which operates French racing for the government, furnished me with a car and chauffeur to transport me to the racecourses and training grounds. They would have been difficult to reach otherwise, for public transportation is spotty and Paris taxi drivers often refuse flatly to take passengers even to such nearby courses as Auteuil and Longchamp in the Bois de Boulogne. If you can argue them into making the trip, they charge three francs above the meter. I can't believe French taxi drivers have any moral objections to racing—or anything else—and must conclude they are fearful that wolves are still lurking in the Bois.

My private driver was a delightful and interesting fellow named Jacques Cartout who had once been a professional skater and had operated a rink in Australia. He did not pretend to know much about horses, but he liked to go to the racecourses occasionally and patronize the two-franc windows, usually hazarding his money on longshots. He described French racing more accurately than any of the experts I encountered.

"I never liked to gamble in Australia," he said. "In Australia they bet on anything. They throw up something in the air and they bet you how it lands. What fun is this? At French tracks I may lose my money, but I have enjoyment. I see something that is—how you say in English?—something pretty. Yes, I find French racing pretty."

In the eyes of the beholder French racing is indeed just that—a spectacle that is expected to have the beauty of a ballet presented as a gala at the Paris Opera. The highly sophisticated people in the reserved seats of the *tribunes* (which are literally on the right side of the track) demand style and *élan* of horses and riders and they discuss the fine points of racing in the same articulate manner that visitors to the *Jeu de Paume,* an art museum named for a tennis court, discuss the qualities of the Impressionist painters whose works hang on the walls.

On the heath, or the wrong side of the track, where the general public drives its cars and spends the afternoon, there is an informal, picnic atmosphere. The best races in France are always run on Sunday, and for the middle classes racing is a family outing. The people on the heath invariably bring large baskets full of cheeses and crusty bread and red wine in long-necked bottles. They eat. They play ball games. Sometimes they unfold collapsible tables and play cards. Once I even saw a happy group engaging in a game of tenpins. But they, too, are demanding so far as horses and jockeys are concerned. The superb artist Yves Saint-Martin is their idol, just as he is the idol of the richer and more elegantly dressed people across the course. And they have their favorite horses and favorite stables. The Baron Rothschild seems to be one of their most admired *propriétaires* and when his stable is in a streak of bad luck, the people on the heath moan loudly each time his blue and yellow silks go down to defeat.

When my friend and driver Jacques Cartout saw the great French three-year-old Le Fabuleux at Chantilly that year, he nodded his head with satisfaction. "Ah, now here is a horse that's worth my francs," he said. "He has the look of a hero."

Chantilly, some thirty miles from Paris, is the great French training grounds. It is called the Newmarket of France, but there is no other place quite like it on the face of the earth.

When you enter the green tunnel of the Forest of Chantilly early on a misty morning, the fantastic play of light and shadow is as striking as the glow of stained glass upon the reliquary of the True Cross, the Blade and the Sponge which Saint Louis brought to France in the thirteenth century and enshrined in the chapel of Sainte Chapelle. The forest paths are shaded by a leafy roof of trees that must have been growing in the time of Charlemagne. It is late spring and it is warm with a hint of rain, but a few chestnuts have forgotten the season and are still in bridal-veil bloom and now and then there is a small snowstorm of white blossoms in the verdant twilight. This is a place where you might well encounter a knight in armor doing battle with a dragon. But instead of medieval knights in armor there are small exercise boys in sweaters and instead of dragons there are thoroughbreds.

The Aga Khan's string is coming out upon one of the broad, straight sand gallops. There are nineteen horses, walking slowly, single file, bays and browns and blacks and chestnuts and a lone gray, a descendant of King Herod, perhaps, whose fading line is more abundantly represented in France than elsewhere. The boys who straddle the horses' backs either have the pinched, attenuated look of figures in a Modigliani painting or they seem dumpling-plump, like children who have not quite lost their baby fat.

There are horses everywhere, even at the Lamorlaye training center a kilometer or so up the highway, but the vast forest and the open fields of greensward seem deserted because the training ground of Chantilly, which comprises more than six thousand acres, is so immensely vast. The sand gallops and turf training courses alone run for some fifty-seven miles when you add them all together and there is seldom any reason for two strings to be working over the same path, or to use any one of the courses on consecutive days. The strips are kept in superb condition, partly through the use of spraying attachments hitched to the bordering fences, each of which has a range of a hundred yards. There is a total of about five thousand race horses in all of France. On this misty morning, two thousand of them are at Chantilly. If you combined the training grounds of Belmont and Saratoga and half a dozen other U.S. tracks and then, perhaps, multiplied by fifty, you might have some idea of the extent of this amazing place. And in America we have some forty thousand horses.

Except in the great clearings where the emerald turf courses extend for miles, horses may always walk under an umbrella at Chantilly. The many sand gallops vary in length from six furlongs to two and a quarter miles, all straightaways, mind you. And they cleave their way through great avenues of trees whose highest branches clutch each other like friendly hands. Here on the hottest days, horses are protected from the sun and when the sudden showers of France descend, only drippings from the thick foliage spatter the dappled coats beneath them. And the horses at Chantilly are, indeed, dappled. I have never seen so many horses look so abundantly healthy.

"The shade is restful for a horse," says Harry Harper, my

guide. "If a horse can't do well here, he can't do well anywhere." Mr. Harper, nattily attired in riding habit and boots, once handled horses for such great turfmen as Marcel Boussac. Now he is with the *Société d'Encouragement*. He is one of the English Frenchmen who seem to comprise half the population of Chantilly. His father, a horse trainer, brought a string to France years ago and stayed in these pleasant precincts, where his son Harry was born. Harry Harper speaks impeccable and very rapid French and when he converses in English, he drops his aitches like a proper Londoner.

Chantilly became a "Ville du Cheval" in 1833 when the Duc d'Orléans and other aristocratic horsemen set part of it aside as a preserve for training, stabling and racing their horses. All of the horses did so well that the colony grew and grew, and by 1840 organized race meetings at a regular course were immensely popular with the French public.

The present course overlooks the great Château of Chantilly. In fact, one of its turns virtually runs into the front court of the château. The château is a beautiful baroque structure that seems very ancient. Actually it was rebuilt entirely on the site of the older demesne, which had been destroyed during the Terror, and was not completed until 1876. The château began as a thirteenth century fortress and then was the stronghold of the ill-fated Montmorencys. A Montmorency opposed the wily Richelieu in the seventeenth century and lost his head and his estates. Families of Orléans and Bourbon and Condé owned the property later. The chatelet, built for court favorites, antedates the present château by centuries. The stables, too, are far more ancient than the château. They are made of stone and are extremely elegant. All of the families who made their homes here loved horses. There are stalls for 240 mounts. The old stone stables are a fitting backdrop for racing at modern Chantilly.

"This is a place of horses and history," said Harry Harper, who has lived his life at Chantilly and loves every tree in the great forest.

I saw the horse my driver Jacques admired so much, the golden swashbuckler called Le Fabuleux, win the Prix du Jockey Club (French Derby) in 1964 at the Chantilly course, which borders the training grounds in the way the Rowley Mile and July Courses border Newmarket. Le Fabuleux is a son of Wild Risk and descends from Eclipse in the line of St. Simon and Rabelais. He impressed me as just about the chestiest and most muscular-looking three-year-old I had ever seen, not excluding Man o' War and Citation. He was almost beaten in the race, however, not by a horse, but by a jockey. Yves Saint-Martin just missed catching him with a horse named Tranel, who was rated pounds below France's three-year-old champion. I think Saint-Martin's ride that day was one of the most superb exhibitions of horsemanship I have ever seen. Had he been on the great Le Fabuleux instead of Tranel, the champion would have won by ten yards instead of half a length.

The Prix du Jockey Club is the occasion when members of the exclusive social cabal dress up in their best and pay a token respect to the sport from which their club derives its name. I noted that the gentlemen mostly wore dark suits and gray bowlers instead of the tails and toppers of Ascot. I remarked upon this difference to a French friend, and he said, "There is another difference. French gentlemen *own* their clothes."

Le Fabuleux was well back early and to me the strangest occurrence of the afternoon was the call of the public announcer when the shining chestnut began to sweep up and challenge the leaders on the backstretch. *"Au château Le Fabuleux est deuxième . . ."* he cried. It was odd indeed to hear the historic baroque château where the great families of France had lived described in terms of a furlong marker.

Nineteen sixty-four was the last year you could have seen the old Longchamp, symbol of France's *belle époque,* in the forest just outside Paris. Because of the computations of a distinguished French mathematician named André Carrus, all of Paris is having its face washed and Longchamp is being completely rebuilt. M. Carrus, an Academician and a distinguished intellectual, devised an off-track betting system called the *tierce,* in which bettors are required to pick the first three horses in the exact order of finish in a specified race each Sunday. They buy their tickets for three francs (60 cents) in the city betting offices called *Pari-Mutuel Urbain,* and they buy eight million dollars' worth of them every single Sunday. Twenty-seven per cent of this money goes to the government. Pay-offs to winners are, of course, astronomical at times, since they must pick three horses instead of one in order to cash. The largest pay-off through 1964 had been 20,288 to 1.

This unexpected windfall to the government of more than two million dollars a week is being used to clean everything in sight and to improve the racetracks which are the source of the money. The Opera, which wore a black coat for generations, is unrecognizable in its party dress of shimmering white and gold. The bridges across the Seine have been scrubbed as scrupulously as a moppet on Saturday night. The Louvre was being cleaned for the first time since Napoleon made an honest woman of Josephine, and it was startling to discover that beneath its smoke-gray patina the ancient palace is far from the forbidding monument that has glowered at the river for centuries. Its basic color is a sort of pale buttercup hue. Even horses have been cleaned. The rocking horses behind the puppet theater in the Tuileries Gardens are advertised as *"Chevaux Hygiéniques."*

It was announced that Longchamp would be completely rebuilt. This is the second time that this has happened in the twentieth century. In 1904 French racegoers expressed their disagreement with a decision of the judges rather vehemently. They burned the place down. The new stands were virtually identical with the old that had been constructed during the reign of Louis Napoleon, who often enjoyed the races from the Royal Box. There was no Emperor in France when the new stands were built, but a Royal Box was included for Presidential use. Charles de Gaulle has never sat in the box, however. They say he disapproves of racing, but likes the money it brings the government.

The stands I saw for the last time in 1964 were made of some glistening stone that resembled marble, but wasn't. They had a look of frivolous austerity, like a wrinkled dowager dressed in a chic frock and pert hat. The new stands were planned as a three-tiered, glowing white structure made of a material invented in France and called "iron cement." The stands will have giant escalators like modern Aqueduct, which the architects studied before submitting blueprints. A new totalisator with an electronic board like those in America was a part of the plans for the new course. The tote in use when I was there was a forty-five-year-old model. There was no odds board. The reconstruction is a sad blow to the old Heroes of the Republic. Many of these elderly gentlemen, wearing campaign ribbons, sold the odds, marked on flimsy sheets of yellow tissue in blue pencil. The fainter carbons were almost unreadable and the odds were never close to being the latest computations. Guessing the price a winner would pay at a French track used to be as much fun as guessing the winner.

My favorite French racecourse has always been one of the smallest and least important of them all. This is Maisons-Laffitte, outside a little country town thirty miles or so from Paris. The village, like Chantilly, is owned by horses and horsemen and has been for many generations. Maisons-Laffitte is also a training grounds like Chantilly, though on a much smaller scale. The best tailor of the village specializes in making jockeys' silks. Although the scale of weights in France is slightly higher than ours, the French are facing a shortage of jockeys, too, and are drawing upon Spain now for many of their riders. The Spanish colony at Maisons-Laffitte is much larger than that of Chantilly. Restaurants in the town print their menus in both French and Spanish.

The course at Maisons-Laffitte resembles Hansel and Gretel's gingerbread house in the forest and has a compelling charm that is all its own, one that is not duplicated elsewhere in Europe. The wooden stands are painted weirdly in grass green and rusty red with little pictorial panels of flowers and sheaves of wheat and other symbols of the countryside. They are crosshatched by wooden staves, like the old houses of Normandy. The pebbled walks in front of the stands are decorated by small gardens of green grass and brilliantly colored flowers and there are rather too elegant stone urns and statuary that seem as out of place as Italian marbles in the garden patch of an English cottage. The largest sculpture is that of a recumbent lion who wears the ludicrously downcast look of a disappointed horse player whose choice has just lost by a nose.

I particularly like the haystacks in the infield and the six old men in blue smocks who plod around the course after each race tamping down the turf with long-handled wooden mallets.

I have seen great horses and brilliant jockeys and beautiful women and distinguished gentlemen at French racecourses, but the memory I treasure most is that of the six old men in their long blue smocks.

7

The Frog That Croaked in Russia

The frog's own croak betrays him.—GEORGE HERBERT, JACULA PRUDENTUM

As constant readers of *Pravda* and *Izvestia* are fully aware, the Russians invented virtually every scientific device from the abacus to the zymometer. Strangely enough, the Soviets have not claimed credit for another scientific advance which Russia perfected more than twenty-five years before it was introduced into capitalist countries, possibly because it was achieved in the time of the Czars. They devised the saliva test, one of the principal means of detecting dope in race horses, as long ago as 1903.

I came across this fascinating nugget of information while doing research in one of the world's finest collections of racing lore, the Keeneland Library, which is an adjunct of the sporting little Keeneland racetrack in Lexington, Kentucky. This is the only library in the world where the librarian, a charming and hospitable Kentucky lady named Mrs. Amelia Buckley, serves sherry to the readers at cocktail time.

The revelation is made in an article by John Oliver (Jack) Keene in the November 28, 1903, issue of a long-defunct magazine called *Illustrated Sporting Life*. Had Izaak Walton written about racing instead of fishing, Keene could have served as his *Compleat Horseman*. He was a breeder, owner and trainer of thoroughbreds and a do-it-yourself veterinarian. He was not above acting in the capacity of a groom when he considered his stable help incompetent. He was too heavy to ride in races, but he served as agent for several American jockeys in Europe. He was one of the most dedicated gamblers of his time. He grew up with horses on the great Keeneland estate, now the site of Keeneland racetrack, which bore a marker reading, "Here on May 14, 1825, General Lafayette was entertained by Major John Keene, who had served as his aide-de-camp during the Revolutionary War." Lafayette's aide was Jack's ancestor.

In his latter years Keene was a Kentucky institution, a raconteur who was rivaled only by his hardboot contemporary Colonel Phil Chinn. When the two happened to meet in the Phoenix Hotel and began swapping tall tales, word spread throughout the town and they attracted such a large audience that business in Lexington was virtually suspended for the duration of the conversation. Keene always carried a fat little loose-leaf notebook around with him. He delighted in shaking it in the face of Colonel Chinn and others and declaring, "This little black book is worth more than anything I own. When I get real broke and can't borrow any more money, I'm going to sell it for a million dollars. It's got all my formulas in it." By that he meant his prescriptions for doping horses. In view of this, the outrage he expressed in his 1903 article over becoming the world's first victim of the saliva test seems a bit curious, for in the magazine he pictures himself as an innocent victim of a jealous, power-mad Russian villain.

In any event, a frog as well as a jealous Russian was Keene's undoing. In a rather complicated way the frog must be recognized as the genesis not only of the Keeneland racetrack but of the vast enterprise known as the New York Racing Association, which operates upon the same nonprofit basis as the course in Lexington.

No other racing man in history ever possessed Keene's missionary zeal. He wished to spread the word about the Kentucky thoroughbred throughout the backward countries of the world, especially if he could win a few purses and a few bets in the process. At the turn of the century many of the Kentuckians whose vast ancestral farms had not been bought up by the Eastern millionaires were land-poor and in desperate financial straits. Around 1908, when Keene was in his late thirties, he heard that there was horse racing in Japan. He had just eight dollars in cash assets at the time and it cost considerably more than that to reach the Orient, so he started betting. In no time at all he had parlayed his small stake into six thousand dollars, and he set out for Japan with three thoroughbreds.

The three thoroughbreds set Japanese racing back by decades. The Japanese were racing scraggly Chinese horses at the time, and Keene's blooded steeds won seventeen starts without being defeated. The Japanese are a notoriously chauvinistic people. They kept backing their own horses against the invaders and suffered terrific losses. Finally they rioted when all three of Keene's thoroughbreds won on the same afternoon. Many people were hurt in the melee and betting on horse races was banned by the Japanese government for several years.

Five years before, Keene had made an even more successful invasion of Russia, but that, too, ended in disaster when the frog got into the act. In the Russia of 1903 racing was a sport of the aristocracy and the immensely rich capitalists, as it had been in eighteenth century England. Keene was engaged as trainer for Michael de Lazareff, whose wife was a cousin of the Czar.

Most of the Russian owners, including De Lazareff, were men of Keene's own kidney, for they were all tremendous bettors. Keene acquired some Kentucky-bred and English-bred and Irish-bred horses for De Lazareff and by the autumn of 1903 he had won 116 races and rubles equivalent to $146,370 for him. One of De Lazareff's main rivals on the turf as well as in business and high society was Henri de Bloch, a banker who was reputed to be the richest man in Russia, perhaps the richest in all of Europe.

According to Keene, De Bloch framed him because he was winning so many races for De Lazareff. One day the Moscow Jockey Club passed a rule that all the entries in the races must be in the paddock four hours before post time. Then a chemist entered the paddock with various test tubes and other paraphernalia and a basket containing four frogs. He scraped the tongue of one of Keene's horses and injected the saliva specimens into the frogs. Keene said that three of the frogs showed no reaction at all to the injections. The fourth seemed "uncomfortable" and began to croak piteously and act strangely, although Keene's article does not specify just what a frog does when he's acting strangely. In any event, they dissected him, which probably made him even more uncomfortable, and this scientific experiment resulted in the announcement that the foreign substance introduced into the frog, namely, the saliva of Keene's horse, contained morphine. Keene was ruled off the turf in Russia.

According to his story in the magazine, Keene was completely innocent. He said he had later been fully exonerated through the efforts of De Lazareff and the Czar himself. He had been offered a job by the Imperial Russian Government and the Moscow Jockey Club, he declared, which was ample proof of his innocence. Naturally, he didn't take the job after the way he'd been insulted. Also, he added, they offered him only one thousand eight hundred dollars a year. He had been making ten thousand dollars a year with De Lazareff, plus 10 per cent of the purses he won.

The saliva test did not evolve in backward capitalist America until the 1930s. Up to then doping was a generally accepted practice among horsemen throughout the world. Actually, there's no real proof that doping ever hurt a horse. It was always against the rules of racing, of course, but men who were barred for the practice were usually barred solely because some racing official thought their horses "had a funny look in the eyes," or were lathered up too much or were acting generally as if they were overstimulated. Many old-time trainers, none of whom will allow himself to be quoted, will state categorically that virtually all of the outstanding turf champions up to the 1930s ran "with help," which means dope.

When horses went to the farm and there was no longer any reason to dope them, they did not show any distress or "withdrawal symptoms." They usually lived longer than they do today and they certainly broke down less frequently—but they did not, of course, race so much or go over such hard tracks as they do now. Horses were doped for two principal reasons. The first and most frequent reason was to keep sore horses from hurting. The second was to stimulate them to the point where they would give that little extra surge that meant winning instead of losing. Contrary to popular belief, very few horses were ever doped in order to make them lose. This is not necessarily a tribute to the innate honesty of turfmen. Horses that had been given depressants showed the physical effects of such medication by nodding heads and glazed eyes and the racing officials of the time could note these reactions far more easily than they could detect the effects of stimulants or mere pain-killers.

Even today a large number of veteran horsemen will argue that there was nothing wrong with doping. "If a fellow who's working for you has got a headache, you give him an aspirin tablet so he'll feel better and earn his money," they say. "Or maybe if you want to brace yourself for some special occasion you swallow a big belt of whiskey. What's wrong with that?"

What was mainly wrong, according to racing officials and the public, was that horses could be run "hot and cold," and that horsemen could cheat by administering dope or withholding it.

Today we have both the saliva test and the urinanalysis to detect narcotics, and dope cases are very rare. In fact, the pendulum has swung so far the other way since the day the Russian frog began to feel uncomfortable that horsemen are afraid to give almost anything to their horses. It is said the tests are so refined that even certain vitamins show up in them, and if they show up, they're illegal. Nearly all standard veterinary kidney medicines show positive in the tests. Butazolidin, a specific for arthritis, has been banned not because it is a narcotic, but because it shows up in the narcotic tests. Some veterinarians have told me they are absolutely convinced that even certain foods are likely to result in a positive test, which means a trainer may

227

be suspended from racing for a long period of time, maybe just for feeding a horse a bunch of carrots.

In his posthumous book, *A Moveable Feast,* Ernest Hemingway claims he kept himself alive in parlous times in Paris by going to French racetracks, looking over the horses and betting on the ones he deemed to be doped. This is sheer moonshine. In the first place, a large number of horses in a race, perhaps all of them, might be doped. I knew Hemingway through his close friend Evan Shipman, whom I employed as a turf writer when I was editing the *Morning Telegraph* years ago. I talked horse with Hemingway a time or two. He may have known a lot about bulls, but he knew almost nothing about horses and certainly could not have told at a glance whether one was doped or not.

The funniest story about the narcotic tests, one that has never been officially verified for obvious reasons, but is absolutely true, occurred at Hollywood Park in 1941 when Jerry Giesler, the brilliant counsel for the defense who never lost a client to the gas chamber, was chairman of the California Racing Board. Horse after horse showed up in urine tests as positive for caffeine that season. The horses belonged to many of the biggest men in the Hollywood movie colony, including Louis B. Mayer and Harry Warner. There was an attempt to hush the scandal up, but Giesler, though he knew little of racing, was an honest man and a zealous crusader and he insisted upon a series of open hearings, which rocked the power elite of Hollywood to its foundations. In the end, all of the trainers and their horses were suspended. Then a short while later, men and horses were suddenly reinstated.

There were wide reports of a "fix." This was nonsense. Nobody ever fixed Jerry Giesler. He may not have known as much about touts as he knew about torts, but he was absolutely dedicated and no one in Hollywood, including Mayer, who gave a lavish studio party for the press entirely for the purpose of vilifying Giesler, could intimidate the commissioner.

What actually happened was this:

Inspectors of the California Racing Board were paid only ten dollars a day at that time and weren't too scrupulous about their duties. One of their duties was to collect the urine specimens of horses. Horses can be ornery. They won't produce a urine sample when you snap your fingers. The inspectors got tired of being late for dinner and they came to a tacit understanding with stable hands. The inspector would turn his back and gaze off distractedly into space and the groom would suddenly produce a urine sample.

The samples were all positive for caffeine. Virtually all stable hands drink dozens of cups of coffee in the course of a day.

Because of the Case of the Uncomfortable Frog and the riots his horses caused at Japanese racetracks, Jack Keene decided he wasn't appreciated on foreign strands and his missionary zeal was dampened. He returned to his old Kentucky home. He was always a man of peculiar compulsions and he wasn't back at Keeneland long before he was totally engrossed in a strange task. He decided the gateposts of his farm needed capstones. Not just any old capstones, mind you, but capstones of the best limestone. So he started blasting on his property and for months and months the usually peaceful meadowlands of central Kentucky were hideous with the sound of high explosives.

It's no trick to find limestone in the Blue Grass region of Kentucky. There's virtually nothing but limestone and horses and bourbon whiskey in the whole section and there wouldn't be any horses or bourbon if it weren't for the limestone, because the limestone deposits in the streams make bone in thoroughbreds and give a pleasing taste to Kentucky whiskey. But Keene was looking for the Koh-i-noor of all limestones. He uncovered a whole ledge of the rock before he found two capstones to suit him. Then he discovered he had a lot of rock left over, and, being a tidy man, he thought he should do something with it.

With Jack Keene one little thing always led to another and the next little thing was always a lot bigger than the last little thing.

One day Keene stood there looking at his enormous pile of rock that might have served as a testimonial to the industry of all the convicts in all the penal institutions of the country, and he got to thinking about a thing he'd seen in Russia. The thing he'd seen had been a stone horse barn on the estate of a Russian nobleman. Keene decided he had to have a horse barn like that for himself. He didn't want just an ordinary barn, though. He wanted a Taj Mahal among stables. As he envisioned it, the stone barn would be a place where horses and the men who loved them would live together. Stalls for forty-eight horses would open off a circular eighteen-foot-wide indoor training track. In the center there would be a great dining hall with a huge fireplace. On the second and third levels there would be living quarters, where Keene himself planned to reside the year around, and innumerable bedrooms for overnight guests. As the years went by and rock began to pile on rock, Keene's conception grew and the barn assumed the proportions of a feudal castle.

But if he was to have a private barn like that and a covered training track, he might as well run private race meets for his friends, so he decided to build an outdoor track, too. First of all, though, he thought he needed a stone fence around the whole vast property to match the capstones of his gateposts. He started building the stone fence in 1914. By 1916 he was building both his track and his barn. The track wasn't designed as a measly little quarter-mile or half-mile training track, either. It was a mile and a sixteenth in circumference, larger than many of the public racetracks of the time.

The work progressed slowly and as it progressed Keene's plans became more and more grandiose. He began to fancy himself as a one-man Jockey Club. He was going to establish the great training grounds of America on his property and make Keeneland into an American Newmarket. The ambitious project proceeded in fits and starts, like the pace of a shadow-jumping horse. Keene was always finding himself completely out of cash. When he had no more money and no more credit, he'd take time out to hustle up fresh capital. He'd sell some yearlings or another piece of his property or race some horses or parlay a small stake into large gambling winnings. Then he'd go back to Keeneland and build some more until he ran out of money again.

The barn and the racetrack were in the process of construction for twenty years. By 1931 the racetrack was complete and the barn was almost finished. By that time the greatest depression America had ever known had ravaged the land. The oldest racetrack in America, the Kentucky Association course where Lexington had run his first two races, closed and the Blue Grass country, the heartland of American racing, had no racing at all for the first time in its history. Every time Keene got a couple of bucks together he put a few more finishing touches on his barn, put one or two more stones on top of one or two other stones, or built floors in the horse stalls and living quarters.

By 1936 he had spent a total of $440,000 on his stone barn and stone fence and private racetrack.

Racing was prospering, or at least undergoing a mushroom growth, all over the United States. Kentucky breeders, the very foundation of the sport, were appalled by the form it was taking, however. Doc Strub was operating great sport at Santa Anita. Joseph E. Widener was conducting fine meetings at Hialeah. But many of the newer tracks were so outright and blatantly commercial and were run upon such slot-machine principles that men who really loved horses were shocked and horrified. Walter O'Hara was operating at his highest, widest and ugliest in Rhode Island and other promoters throughout the nation were emulating him. In Illinois the sports-loving Capone family of Chicago was granted a license to open a racetrack in Cicero. The looming evil of political control had already reared its nasty head, but it was not yet too evident and the threat of the unprincipled promoters who were taking over American racing at the time seemed more urgent.

Kentucky horsemen decided to open a nonprofit, sport-for-sport's-sake racetrack and set an example for the country.

They paid Keene $140,000 for 148½ acres of his great ancestral estate, his racetrack, his stone barn and his stone fence in 1936. And they opened the Keeneland racetrack, which is still just about the pleasantest horse park in America. Keene's baronial barn became the clubhouse. Its horse stalls and guest rooms are now offices of the racetrack.

The first Keen of Keeneland had spelt his name without the terminal "e." His first name was Francis and he received a grant of one thousand eight hundred acres in what was then part of Fauquier County, Virginia, before Kentucky became a state in 1792. The grant was signed by Patrick Henry. Jack, last of the Keenes, died the way he would have wished to die at the age of seventy-three in 1943. He dropped dead of a heart attack at the Fair Grounds racetrack in Detroit and legend has it they found a fifty-dollar ticket on a winner in his pocket.

Although Keene did not arrive on earth until 1870, he was in many respects the last of the eighteenth century horsemen in his expansiveness, his utter devotion to race horses and his contempt for money as anything more than markers in a gambling game

232

or a means of obtaining better horses and better physical surroundings for horses and the men who love them. He would have felt completely at home with Cumberland and the lords and gentlemen who founded the Jockey Club in a tavern called the Star and Garter. Like Cumberland, he bankrupt himself time and again simply because he loved horses and was pursued by moneylenders for most of his life.

Keeneland is now the center of the Blue Grass horse country, and the Blue Grass of Kentucky has always been the breeding and training grounds of America, an area that resembles England's Newmarket and France's Chantilly. The Blue Grass does not, of course, include all of Kentucky. It is a relatively small section around Lexington where the great horse farms were established early in the nineteenth century, where the limestone deposits are richest and closest to the surface and the peculiar grass that feeds upon their minerals is the lushest in the world. Until very recently horses were almost the sole preoccupation of the citizens of Lexington. It has always been a horse town like Newmarket, a *ville du cheval* like Chantilly. Now modern industry is moving in and the old town is encroaching upon the blue pastures around it, its suburban area of bastardized architecture called "ranch house" and "modern colonial" creeping across the pleasant countryside. The great horse farms are going, one by one. Some have been subdivided, others have simply ceased to exist, several have been split in two by the roadmakers. National highways and state highways have sliced into the belly flesh of Kentucky's rolling land and appear as great appendectomy incisions, taped over with concrete bandages.

The older citizens of Lexington and the landholders of the great horse farms have resisted the march of wanton expediency that thoughtless men call progress. One of the most militant opponents of the spoilers has been Mrs. Gene Markey, proprietor of Calumet. Her great stallion Citation now stands in a pad-dock beside a four-lane highway and gazes curiously across the road to an obscenity called a motel which seems to be con-structed of bright orange and blue and green panels and gaudy neon lights that advertise frozen malts and cheeseburgers.

The Men of Vision who have condemned acres of the ancient land where generations of American thoroughbreds have lived say there is no reason the farms should not be smaller, that horses live better than people anyway. One of the people who did not live as well as horses showed his resentment in a curious way. This tourist stopped his car beside a post-and-rail fence where an inquisitive little yearling was frisking in the paddock. He whis-tled and enticed the youngster, who was worth at least $25,000, to gallop over to him. He pretended he was going to feed him a sugar lump, but he was only fooling. The fellow was a jokester. He thrust a paper bag over the friendly yearling's head and the young thoroughbred went mad with fear, flailed about the pad-dock, plunged into trees and fences and broke his neck. The humorist started up his motor again and exited, doubtless laughing.

There have been other incidents of the sort, though none of such raw brutality, yet the great farms, all privately owned, of course, are open to the public and during specified hours anyone may drive his car up their private roads and be guided through the stallion barns and broodmare paddocks by courteous Negro stud grooms. There is no charge, but the grooms do not refuse tips, which they richly earn. It is amazing that the Kentucky farms have been able to retain such a high quality of help, for competent stable employees are in short supply everywhere. But the stud grooms are mostly an older generation and they are im-possible to replace.

An elderly Negro took me through the great paddocks of

Arthur Hancock's Claiborne not long ago, and he spoke of the employment problem. "This young teen-age boy, he come here the other day and he say he want to be a horseman. I took him over to the barn and just let him stand there a minute, then I say, 'Boy, take a deep breath.' He took a deep breath and he turned up his nose and made a face. I say, 'Boy, you ain't never going to make no horseman. You got to *like* that smell to be a horseman.' "

The older stud grooms are mostly fine and dignified gentlemen, and lady tourists sometimes embarrass them greatly by the questions they ask. In the breeding sheds of some Kentucky farms you will find shallow ditches about six feet long and half as wide dug into the ground. The stud grooms dread lady visitors asking them the reason for these little ditches more than any other questions. But the ladies almost always ask, of course. The stud groom looks uncomfortable, averts his eyes and mumbles something about "some ole hoss pawing it out, I guess." Obviously the ditches are not accidental. They are dug for a very definite purpose, in fact. When a short stallion serves a tall mare, the mare stands in the ditch.

Breeders and stud grooms have problems other than tourists and road builders, of course. Great horses are as different in temperament and as downright cantankerous at times as brilliant human beings. Tom Fool was a champion of the tracks and one of the most devastatingly handsome bays who ever appeared on the racecourse. He was, in fact, a matinee idol of a horse that might set any filly's heart a-flutter. When he returned from the wars to make his first season as a stallion at John Hay Whitney's great Greentree Stud, there was wild excitement among the help, for it was predicted he might prove another Lexington, another Man o' War at stud.

Very soon the stud grooms had to face a horrible fact. Tom

Fool just showed no interest at all in the girls. He was polite enough to them, but that was all. He seemed a deeply introverted horse and had no time for tender relationships.

One day a stud groom said, "They ain't nothing the matter with that po' hoss except he's downright dumb. He just don't know what it's all about, that's all. I know a way of showing him."

So he led over a big, rough farm mare, a veritable Moll Flanders among horses, an earthy creature who enjoyed the physical satisfactions of life and made no pretense whatsoever of being a lady. They put her in Tom Fool's paddock. She took one look at the handsome stallion and neighed with delight.

She was a patient mare with her reluctant suitor. She tried for hours to instruct him in the facts of life. When Tom Fool finally got the idea and let her maneuver him into the proper position and he just stood there and did nothing at all but gaze about him foolishly, the mare at last became disgusted. She gave a great heave and tossed the royally bred stallion smack into a nearby water trough.

Finally after weeks of trying, they introduced Tom Fool to a slender, delicately made young thoroughbred mare of aristocratic lineage and he found romance at last. There was nothing wrong with him at all. He was just a gentleman of discriminating taste, it seemed. Ever since, he has been a successful sire.

The older sections of Lexington, America's great horse town, are not much changed. The ancient Phoenix Hotel still stands at Main near Limestone, though visitors on wheels now frequent the innumerable motels that cluster about the old town like plastic julep cups around an antique punch bowl. In the 1950s a group of militant ladies of Lexington came to the rescue in the nick of time when a wrecking crew had already arrived to tear down General John Hunt Morgan's old home, one of the most beautiful houses in the Blue Grass. They were going to demolish it to make room for a parking lot. The ladies saved it and have made the place into a museum.

Morgan's statue still stands in front of the courthouse on Main Street and still causes horse-wise folks to snicker. It is an equestrian statue, of course, since Morgan was a cavalry commander. The sculptor was a realist and he left no doubt that Morgan's mount is a stallion. In battle Morgan rode a gelded son of Glencoe. He rode a mare named Black Bess through the streets of Lexington before the war. Certain anatomical details of Morgan's sculptured horse have always made Lexington's citizenry chuckle.

As late as the 1920s there was one horseman still left in Lexington who was contemptuous of automobiles, and he rode his horse proudly through the streets almost every day. There was a hitching post in front of the Phoenix for his special benefit. His name was Colonel Dick Redd, and he was an octogenarian who had fought for the Confederacy. Once, when he was well over eighty, he rode his horse all the way to a convention of Confederate veterans in Knoxville, Tennessee. Quite frequently, when he was feeling exuberant because of an extra toddy or two, he'd ride his horse right into the lobby of the Phoenix and sit in the saddle exchanging pleasantries with friends who lounged in chairs. Once he even rode his horse up a flight of steps and into the Administration Building on the University of Kentucky campus. When the startled Dean of the college emerged from his office, Colonel Dick tipped his wide-brimmed Confederate hat politely and said he'd just dropped around to say "Howdy." Then he rode out the door and down the flight of steps.

Keeneland was a small but beautiful racetrack when it opened in 1936, made largely of the same stone that old Jack Keene had unearthed to top his gateposts. It had the first totalisator in Ken-

tucky and other modern improvements, but it disdained a loudspeaker system on the grounds that Kentuckians were sophisticated enough to follow the silks carried by horses and did not
need a public announcer's tinny voice to tell them how the runners were placed in a race. Children were not only admitted to
the track, but welcomed, and they came in large numbers, as
they had been doing for generations at the tracks of England and
France.

One of the more delightful aspects of Keeneland in its early
days was the yearling paddocks across the racetrack. The young
horses would all come dashing to the fence to watch their elders
race. Then they would stage impromptu races of their own,
galloping around and around the paddocks. Jack Keene's old
barn and his great dining room with its baronial stone fireplace
was a members' club. The library adjacent to it began to acquire
some of the finest and most beautifully bound volumes of racing
books in the world, a matchless collection of racing photographs,
and fine paintings of horses. It is one of the pleasantest retreats
in the world of racing and is used for cocktail parties as well as
scholarly research during the meetings.

There is a kind of theater-in-the-round building on the Keeneland property which serves as a sales ring and the auctions held
here now match those of Tattersall's in England and the famed
yearling sales of Saratoga. Here in 1964 the world-record price
of $187,000 was paid for a yearling colt by Bold Ruler. The colt
was promptly named One Bold Bid.

Up until very recently bookmaking, while technically illegal,
was conducted fairly openly in Lexington because the great
breeders could not always leave their farms and go to the distant
tracks where their horses were engaged if they wished to bet.
Many of the bookmakers of Lexington were sporting men themselves, not gangsters as they are elsewhere. When Keeneland

opened its gates, all the bookies in town closed their shops during the meetings voluntarily, since they did not wish to deprive the courses of customers. Keeneland is very much a community project.

Keeneland accomplished its purpose. It was a shining example to the rest of the country. Profit, quite legitimately, is the basis of nearly all American enterprise and not many tracks emulated the Lexington course in abandoning the profit motive. But the worst fly-by-night promoters who were operating the sport did go out of business all over the land, and their successors, while they may have had no antecedents in the sport, were mainly businessmen of unquestioned integrity. One track, Delaware Park, in Stanton, Delaware, financed largely by the horse-loving DuPont family, followed Keeneland's example and opened on a nonprofit basis in 1937.

And the Keeneland plan showed the way to the Jockey Club in New York when it formed the nonprofit New York Racing Association which now conducts the finest racing on earth at Aqueduct and Saratoga and hopes to have the new Belmont Park ready by 1967.

The most significant events in racing's history have all had wildly unlikely origins. Cumberland bred an ugly, swaybacked, common-looking stallion to a lovely mare of royal lineage and their foal is the ancestor of 90 per cent of the race horses in the world today. Doc Strub got a shave and Santa Anita was born. We may also follow a zany line of reasoning and conclude that an uncomfortable frog croaked in Russia in 1903 and that the remote result in 1959 was Aqueduct, the Big A, the world's largest racetrack, on the flatlands of Long Island.

If the frog hadn't croaked, Jack Keene might have remained in Russia instead of returning to Kentucky. If he had not returned, he would never have blasted his acres in search of rocks for his gateposts, and if he hadn't built the track and the barn, Keeneland might never have opened, and it was the example of Keeneland which encouraged members of the Jockey Club to form the New York Racing Association. Things happen like that in the world of racing where the laws of logic are the same as those of the Land of Oz. It is the dissertations of the Mad Hatter rather than the critiques of Immanuel Kant that govern the course of racing.

By 1965, unfortunately, racing was being governed almost everywhere in the United States by the vagaries of politicians, and if this was madness from the standpoint of the racing man, it was motivated madness from the standpoint of the politician. His motive was greed for more and more taxes. The founders of Keeneland had foreseen the results of irresponsible racetrack management. They had not foreseen the result of political control of the sport. Removing private profit from racing has not been a sufficient curb on the state legislators who rule the sport today. Politicians exact more tribute from the nonprofit New York Racing Association than they do from any profit-making racetrack elsewhere.

If the accidental occurrences that seem to have shaped the course of racing for two centuries have been mildly insane, the contrived happenings under political dictatorship have been utterly mad. At the end of 1964, for instance, the New York Racing Association presented the state with more than seventy-two million dollars in taxes. In return for this favor, the legislators of Albany in 1965 threatened to pass an off-track betting bill and an added 5 per cent tax on racing, either of which would almost certainly kill the sport in the state. By comparison, the fact that Aqueduct is an echo of a frog's croak in Russia in 1903 seems coldly logical.

Ironically enough, the New York Racing Association was originally formed in 1954 as a means of preventing state ownership of the tracks. At that time it was nothing more than a loose association of twenty members of the Jockey Club, all of whom had served as stewards of the organization, and all of whom were citizens of considerable wealth and substance. What they accomplished was nothing short of a miracle. With no corporate standing whatsoever at the time, no franchise, and for the ostensible purpose of founding a business from which they intended to derive no profit, they received solid commitments from several banks, principally the Guaranty Trust, to lend them fifty million dollars to build a racetrack and renovate two other courses. Like many other events of racing's history, this was entirely impossible, yet it happened.

In the postwar years racing had enjoyed an unprecedented boom everywhere except in New York. Crowds and betting were up 28 per cent throughout the country. In New York the increase was barely 3 per cent. This, of course, was a ridiculous situation. New York was not only the cradle of racing in America, but it was the richest and most densely populated area of the United States. Furthermore, the best horses of the country still appeared at New York tracks for tradition's sake if nothing else. The reason for the small betting and small crowds was that two of the Long Island tracks were rickety and ancient and simply could not handle large crowds. Glorious old Belmont was immense, but largely impractical because its betting areas had been designed for bookmakers instead of tote machines. The tracks were separately owned and none of them could rebuild or even improve their premises since the pari-mutuel law of 1940 had awarded them only 4 per cent of the wagering, the smallest given to racetrack proprietors in the country and barely enough to pay operating expenses.

The nonprofit association was originally the idea of a remarkable old gentleman named Ashley Trimble Cole, who served as Chairman of the New York State Racing Commission until his death in 1965. He was a political appointee, but he never hesitated to fight the politicians who appointed him when they attempted to enact legislation that would hurt the sport he loved. He was far and away the greatest racing commissioner who ever served in the United States. Oftener than not such posts are held by political hacks who are errand boys for the legislators. I saw Cole a week or so before his death and he bawled me out for libeling him. I had written a magazine article in which I gave his age as eighty-seven. He wanted me to know he was a mature man of eighty-eight and one-half, he said.

It took a long while for the New York Racing Association to obtain permission from the Legislature to hand the State of New York over seventy million dollars a year, but the franchise was finally issued, and the Big A opened in September of 1959, replacing the old Aqueduct and Jamaica courses. When Belmont was found unsafe for human habitation in 1963, the only racetrack on Long Island was the Big A, which ran for two hundred days a year, with the track superintendent keeping his fingers perpetually crossed for fear the bottom of the racing strip might fall out from the pounding of hoofbeats. The only other track the NYRA operated after the close of Belmont was the month-long August season at Saratoga.

If you find beauty in the tinted geometry of Piet Mondrian, the new Aqueduct plant may please you aesthetically. Its visual appeal is limited mainly to those who are enraptured by the design of electronic computers and the architecture of large airports, or to the most *avant* of the *avant garde* who visit the galleries that exhibit the overblown comic strips called pop art. Certainly the mountain-shaded elegance of Santa Anita, the

bougainvillaea-draped charm of Hialeah and the rustic antiquity of Saratoga are lacking. Aqueduct, however, can accommodate up to eighty thousand people in its enormous stands and
on its cement lawns; it can be reached directly by subway and
there seems no limit to the untold millions in bets its totalisator
can handle in the course of an afternoon. Through the operation of Aqueduct and Saratoga alone, the New York Racing Association pays the State of New York more than half the amount
that ninety-eight other racetracks pay to twenty-six other racing
states.

The largest crowd at Aqueduct was 73,375 and the largest betting $6,120,631 on Memorial Day of 1965. The crowd figures
fall short of the Santa Anita record of 83,000 persons, achieved
in 1947, but the betting is many times larger. Inevitably, the
Big A has suffered the fate of Santa Anita in having its enormous betting figures publicized more than the quality of its racing. There is no question whatsoever, though, that New York
racing is the very best on earth. It can be safely said that no
truly great horse ever appears in America without racing at
Aqueduct. Many of the greatest champions of recent times, Kelso in particular, have run the majority of their races at the New
York course.

The vast premises of the Big A are devoted almost entirely to
people and the stable area can accommodate only 350 horses.
Belmont has long been called, with considerable poetic license,
the Newmarket of America. Its acreage for horses, which includes a training track, is ten times that of Aqueduct. Most of
the horses that race at the Big A are vanned the few miles down
the parkway. Between March and December Belmont usually
has a fairly constant colony of some two thousand thoroughbreds
on its backstretch, about the same number that are quartered

at Chantilly in France, although they have about 1/100th the elbow room. (Horses, incidentally, do have elbows. They come at the point where the rear of the foreleg joins the barrel.)

Saratoga's largest crowd through 1965 had been under thirty thousand persons, but in spirit and atmosphere the oldest race-track in America is the closest thing to Newmarket and Chantilly in America, except for the Blue Grass region of Kentucky. Saratoga is famed mainly as a racing town, yet it assumes this character for only one month a year, in August. The century-old racecourse is built primarily for horses. Mere people occupy whatever space is left. The grandstand can accommodate about one fifth the number of people that the stand at Aqueduct can seat. The backstretch has room for almost ten times the number of horses that can be stabled at the Big A. The stable areas are two small towns in themselves known as "Horse Haven" and "Oklahoma." Oklahoma got its strange name from a horseman who was stabled at the far edge of the course one year. Someone asked him the location of his barn and he waved his arm off toward the far horizon. "They put me 'way out there in Oklahoma," he replied.

August in Saratoga is sometimes unbearably hot and humid and sometimes uncomfortably wet and chilly, but the place is heaven on earth for the real horsemen of the country. Here for thirty days and thirty nights they race, work, buy, sell, talk and live horses during all their waking hours and dream about horses when they sleep. About eighteen hundred thoroughbreds can be stabled at Saratoga and most of them belong to the wealthiest aristocrats of racing. The prices of accommodations in the town reflect this fact. Few "cottages," little private homes abandoned for the racing season by their owners, rent for less than $1,000 for the season. A furnished double room in a modest private home costs around a hundred dollars per week in August. A new motel, belonging to a chain that usually charges eight to ten dollars per day for accommodations elsewhere, demands—and gets—forty dollars per day for rooms during the racing season. The price of an unexceptional meal at one of the fancier roadhouses during the racing season runs about the same as that of gourmet fare at the Tour d'Argent in Paris. The pleasantest meals you can eat at Saratoga are breakfasts at the racetrack. Tables are set on the lawn of the clubhouse early in the morning during workout hours and you can eat the "Hand melons," a luscious fruit grown nowhere else in the world, and ham and eggs while you watch the greatest horses of the country having their morning trials.

Saratoga, like Lexington, has suffered from the cheapening process called modernization. It has not become the site of as many industrial plants as the Blue Grass and its suburban areas have not been extended so far. Frank Sullivan, the noted humorist and a patriotic Saratogian, prevented the spoilers from cutting down the elms that have shaded the streets for centuries. But the two beloved old eyesores, the United States and Grand Union Hotels, are gone. They were wooden Victorian monstrosities that had been built shortly after the Civil War and there was nothing in America quite like them. Their smallest rooms were about thirty feet square and during the racing season rented for about one dollar per square foot per day. Each room had a coiled rope for a fire escape. Their wide stairways, great chandeliers, paneling, and broad verandas, where the great financial titans, society leaders and sportsmen rocked back and forth during the August evenings for nearly a century, were the last remnants of the expansive way of life that had once been Saratoga in August. Ulysses S. Grant spent nearly every August at the Grand Union after his term as President. The vast acreage occupied by the old hotels and their spacious grounds is now a modern shopping center, full of drugstores and supermarkets. Only one of the old hotels is left. This is the Rip Van Dam. It was a poor relation of the great hostelries. Nowadays during August the wicker rockers on its porches are filled with old men who remember the great days of the spa. They sit rocking and remembering until midnight when the racing papers arrive at a news store across the street. Then they go up to their rooms and handicap the horses.

The way of life at Saratoga in August is much as it has always been, however. The Whitneys and the Sanfords and a few other of the great racing families retain their old houses and they are ablaze with light and filled with guests during August evenings. A few of the country's truly great sportsmen, notably John Hay Whitney, who owns Greentree in partnership with his sister Mrs. Charles Shipman Payson, reserve their best two-year-olds for Saratoga racing. The yearling sales in the evening are still the biggest gamble in all of racing and a great many of the older racing families continue to dress formally when they go to the sales ring.

Only 10 per cent of all the yearlings sold for fifty thousand dollars or more have ever won themselves out on the racetracks, but this does not deter the bidders. Most of the veterans of the sales ring have their own peculiar manner of bidding huge amounts for year-old, untried horses and only the spotters in the ring can even detect their gestures.

Mrs. Jack Price, who raced the great horse Carry Back, says she now holds hands with her husband when they attend the sales. "Once Jack scratched his nose and paid twenty-five thousand dollars for a colt we didn't want," she says.

There is a legend that Cornelius Vanderbilt Whitney always bids by the slightest movement of his eyebrows. I watched him closely all one evening at the sales. I never saw his eyebrows move, nor did I notice him make any other significant gesture, but he bought three horses for fancy prices. Sometimes I think the bidding at Saratoga must be a form of mental telepathy.

Saratoga is lugubriously known as "the graveyard of champions," and it is true many of the turf's Bonapartes have met their Waterloos here. Upset defeated Man o' War in the Sanford of 1919. In 1930 the two great three-year-olds, Gallant Fox and Whichone, were to battle in the Travers and the race would decide the championship of America. The mud was fetlock-deep that day and a rawboned horse named Jim Dandy came out of nowhere to beat them both. The first headline I ever wrote for the old *Morning Telegraph* concerned that race. It read: WHO IS THIS SMITER OF CHAMPIONS? JIM DANDY—AND HIS NAME IS MUD. When another Travers is coming up and rain is in the air, the old men who rock on the porch of the Rip Van Dam nod their heads wisely and say it's "Jim Dandy weather."

A month at Saratoga is a costly indulgence, but it is worth the money to anyone who loves horses and horse racing. Only at Saratoga and during the brief meetings in the spring and fall at little Keeneland can you still know racing as it used to be—and always ought to be. In the great paddock areas of the track each entrant is saddled beneath a certain tree and his admirers can get close enough to him to tighten the girth themselves. There is never much fear among horsemen that anyone at Saratoga would want to harm a horse, and thoroughbreds at the ancient spa are not guarded and sequestered as they are elsewhere. It requires a pocketful of credentials to get into most racetracks during workout hours. At Saratoga anyone who wishes to watch the trials just wanders through the open gate, and so many come that the track's caterers serve a special breakfast.

When the wind blows down from the hills the August nights are often cool and fine for sleeping, but little sleeping is done at

Saratoga in the month of August. Winners stay up late toasting their success and losers stay up late drowning their sorrows. And they are up with the sun again to see the morning trials. Breakfasts are important meals and social occasions. On the backstretch, many of the cottages have the latchstring out every morning and friends just drop in for ham and eggs and pancakes. For nearly half a century this has been true at the backstretch cottage of the great American trainer Maxie Hirsch, where an incomparable cook named Virgie presided at the griddle until her death in 1965.

The famed gambling houses like the Brook and Arrowhead, where the greatest stars of the stage once performed as an added attraction to the roulette wheels and dice tables, are gone. An old farmhouse on the Lake Road known as Smith's is gone, too. There was no singing, dancing and dining at Smith's. This place was strictly for business, and for generations the highest-rolling gambling men of the country patronized it.

It was here that E. Phocion Howard, a reincarnation of Dickens' Micawber, spent his last night on earth. Old Phoce seldom had much money in his pocket, but he belonged to Saratoga in the way the Whitneys and the Sanfords belong. He published a racing paper called the New York *Press,* and each payday it was a question whether Phoce could stake the help to the salaries that they earned. Usually he won, begged or borrowed the payroll at the very last minute. He owned a hundred suits of clothes, most of which were decades out of style, he drove a twenty-five-year-old Rolls Royce, and his retainer, chauffeur, valet, cook and spiritual counselor was a Negro known as Chicken-Fry Ben. It was Phoce who left the turf an immortal phrase—"All horse players die broke."

Phoce always shared a large house on Union Avenue during the Saratoga season with Damon Runyon. He loved Saratoga more than any place on earth, but he was seldom lucky there. During one of his worst losing streaks, the beloved sportswriter of another time, John I. Day, a gambling man and Beau Brummel himself, watched Phoce going up to Dancer Hyams' book to bet the last cent he had on a longshot. "There goes Custer to Little Big Horn," Day remarked.

On the last day of his life Phoce won a lot of money on the horses—several thousand dollars. Every drifter at the track heard the news and he gave hundreds away before he even reached his Rolls Royce after the last race. That night he went out to Smith's to play a little faro. The next morning Chicken-Fry Ben found him dead in bed. When he went through his clothes, he found $2.37 in his pockets. "Mr. Phoce didn't quite die broke after all," he told Runyon. "He had enough for a two-buck bet."

All the great gambling men of their time came to Saratoga. Bet-A-Million Gates, who had won two million dollars in bets in England once when the British bookmakers were rash enough to quote 100 to 1 against a horse of his named Royal Flush in the Stewards' Cup, was a Saratoga regular. So was his sidekick, Old John Drake. Once Drake and Gates were making a long train journey. They had no cards or dice and they grew bored, so they bet a thousand dollars a crack on the speed of raindrops rolling down a window pane. By the time they reached their destination, Drake had won $46,000 from his partner. He said rainy days were always lucky for him.

Chicago O'Brien died of a heart attack at Saratoga. Once he had bet one hundred thousand dollars against a thousand with bookmaker Tom Shaw on Man o' War in the Stuyvesant Handicap, where Big Red faced only one opponent, a horse named Yellow Hand. "It's a crazy bet," Shaw protested. "I don't mind giving you a grand, but any horse can fall down. Any man is crazy who takes one to one hundred odds."

"The grand will pay for my cottage at Saratoga," O'Brien answered calmly.

The oldest gambling house of all still stands in Congress Park in the center of Saratoga Springs. This is the famed Richard Canfield's Casino. Today it is used for businessmen's luncheons and for civic functions. The great casino is dominated by an enormous oil painting of Emperor Napoleon III mounted on a rearing charger. Somebody once told Canfield he resembled Louis Napoleon. The next day he commissioned the portrait.

In 1951 the townsfolk of Saratoga allotted space in Canfield's Casino to a group of Jockey Club members headed by Walter Jeffords who wished to found a National Museum of Racing that would preserve invaluable relics of the turf's history as well as commemorate the past of Saratoga. Today the Museum is housed in a fine building on Union Avenue directly across from the parklands of the racecourse. Its collection of sporting art and racing memorabilia is unmatched this side of the English Jockey Club's headquarters at Newmarket. The museum has another distinction. It has the prettiest curator on earth in the person of Mrs. Elaine Mann, who, fittingly enough, is the daughter of Buddy Ensor, one of the great jockeys of the 1920s.

Racing first opened at Saratoga on August 3, 1863, a few weeks after Lee's scarecrow legions had begun the long retreat from Gettysburg. In view of the fact that the richest and most fashionable turf families have always patronized Saratoga, its beginnings were odd, like so many other things in racing. The track was built by John Morrissey, a big bully boy with a billy-goat beard, who had defeated Yankee Sullivan for the heavyweight championship of America and who was known as both a fearsome barroom brawler and a political ward heeler. Morrissey also operated one of the spa's first big gambling houses. When he was in his cups, he liked to stand out in the middle of the street, wearing tails and a topper, and direct traffic on the main stem of the little town.

There was a counter-attraction to the grand opening of the Saratoga course in 1863. Mohawk Indians played a game of lacrosse just outside the track's gates that afternoon on a rutted road now known as Nelson Avenue.

It is strange indeed that Keeneland and the New York Racing Association should have descended remotely from a croaking frog and more directly from a rock on top of a gatepost, but even curiouser things have been happening in the Blue Grass of Kentucky recently.

In 1963, for the first time in the history of the American turf, a white thoroughbred was born on a Blue Grass stud farm.

J. A. Estes, one of the world's recognized authorities on thoroughbred racing and breeding, has reckoned that the odds against a thoroughbred showing a white coat were between two and three million to one before 1963. The odds against two horses with white coats appearing on the same farm the same year, he says, were four trillion to one. Kentucky hardboots have always been contemptuous of the odds. It was a hardboot trainer from Kentucky named Jim McKee who took the 100-to-1-shot Jim Dandy to Saratoga and beat Gallant Fox and Whichone in the Travers of 1930. In the spring of 1963 a white colt and a white filly were foaled on Mrs. Joe A. Goodwin's Patchen Wilkes Farm between Lexington and Winchester. Previously there had been just one white foal in the two-hundred-year history of the thoroughbred. A white filly appeared in Germany in 1925 and went to the races under the name of Woher?, thus attaining another distinction, since she is the only thoroughbred whose name includes a question mark. *Woher?* is the German word for "Whence?"

In that spring of 1963 there was yet another happening and even the statistical Mr. Estes was unable to quote the astronomical odds against such a triple miracle. A white colt was foaled in France. He would be named Mont Blanc and would bring 27,000 francs from the English owner Charles Clore at the Deauville yearling sales in 1964.

Both the white colt and the white filly in Kentucky were sired by Ky. Colonel, a chestnut horse by the black Balladier who was sired in turn by Colonel E. R. Bradley's great stallion, the dark brown Black Toney. The white foals of Kentucky are therefore in the line of Eclipse. The French colt descends from Gainsborough and is also in the line of Eclipse.

The Jockey Club spoiled the fun a bit by registering the colt (named War Colors) as a roan because he developed a spattering of reddish chestnut freckles on his otherwise albino hide. Actually, this was niggling, because roan is not a true coat color. All of the horses registered as roans before War Colors came along were actually grays, but for purposes of identification they were called roans to indicate a gray coat in which darker colors mingle in abstract-expressionist designs. In the Old West horses of this mingled color were often called "paints." Until the advent of Woher? in the 1920s, the only recognized coats for thoroughbreds were bay, brown, chestnut, gray and black, in the order of frequency. Roan is a registered coat, but only as a matter of convenience.

The filly, however, was registered as white, and she was indeed just that, her snowy coat completely unmarked. Almost inevitably she was named White Beauty. Both horses were the property of Herman K. Goodpaster, manager of Patchen Wilkes Farm. White Beauty made her first start during the early spring meeting at Keeneland in 1965 and finished ninth. She won her second start at Keeneland.

Estes says that because of the events in 1963 odds against thoroughbreds showing a white coat have now been reduced to a mere 25,000 to 1. All sorts of theories have been offered for the sudden appearance of three white thoroughbreds during the same foaling season. Radiation from atomic explosions, insecticides on pasture grass, new veterinary drugs have all been suggested as reasons for the sudden mutations. None of the theories is tenable as yet.

For some peculiar and completely indefensible reason, the purists among horsemen have always maintained that there has never been such a thing as a white horse of any breed. They base this upon the contention that one dark hair in mane, tail or coat (in Arabs or Lippizanners, for instance) makes the horse technically a gray. Nobody can even find one dark hair in White Beauty, although some close observers claim there is a very faint suspicion of chestnut at the root of the forelock. Her eyes are dark blue. Her skin seems to be minus pigment, a very pale pink.

When the unbelievable foals first made their appearance, there were stories that a philandering palomino had jumped a fence and had forced his attentions on a thoroughbred mare named Why Wander, dam of the colt, on a moonlit April night in 1962 and had found the experience so pleasant that he jumped the fence again and wooed a thoroughbred mare named Filly o' Mine, dam of White Beauty, in May. This hypothesis was refuted by careful blood tests of all the horses involved. Ky. Colonel, whose thoroughbred bloodlines are impeccable, whose racing record was a good one and whose progeny had won over two million dollars on the tracks before the white horses were foaled, is unquestionably the sire of War Colors and White Beauty.

Joseph Alvie Estes, who computed the probable odds against

the miracles of genetics that occurred in Kentucky and France in 1963, is the most distinguished of America's turf writers and turf editors and a thoroughbred theorist whose opinions are respected throughout the world. There is a general tendency to believe that Estes is at least six different persons, not only because of his considerable accomplishments, but because of the variety of names by which he is known. In his youth he wrote a newspaper column in collaboration with another budding journalist that was signed "The Simps," and he was known as "Simp." His fraternity brothers at the University of Kentucky discovered his middle name and gleefully called him "Alvie." When he came to New York to take his Master's at Columbia, he supported himself as an editor of a racing paper, where another editor thought he looked like a guy named Bill, so he became "Bill" for many years. When he returned to Lexington he was usually called "Joe" or just plain "Estes." His wife, a professor of psychology at the University of Kentucky, became so confused that she has simply addressed him as "E" for more than thirty years.

The multimonikered gentleman is now senior advisory editor of the *Thoroughbred Record,* a publication that made its first appearance in 1875, the year the first Kentucky Derby was run. The magazine is now partly owned by the Jockey Club. On behalf of the Jockey Club, Estes undertook a project a few years ago that is as fantastic in its way as the appearance of the three white horses.

Among the industries that have poached upon the peaceful preserves once sacred to the thoroughbred is the International Business Machines plant, a few miles outside the Lexington city limits. It is a startling sight to come upon these ranging industrial buildings among the rolling meadows, ancient trees and post and rail fences. A few miles away it is even more startling to encounter the stark modern architecture of the Spindletop Research laboratories on property that was once the stud farm of the famous sportsman and thoroughbred breeder W. R. Coe. The research project was originally established some years ago by the University of Kentucky. From its windows you can look out upon the barn once occupied by the great race horse and stallion Ladysman. The new building is a brood-mare barn of computers whose foals are punch cards.

Since the electronic horses were already grazing in the Blue Grass pasturelands, the elders of the Jockey Club decided they might as well put them to good use. At Spindletop they have established a thoroughbred statistical bureau under Estes' direction and are using a computer known affectionately to its manufacturers as IBM 1401 to gather a great reservoir of information concerning horses that may, they believe, eventually furnish the basis of important and even revolutionary conclusions about thoroughbred bloodlines, thus enabling the Jockey Club to fulfill its purpose of improving the breed of horses. In 1964 Estes and his assistants and Dr. Robert A. Porter, Vice-President of Spindletop, were primarily concerned with the collection of data and it was reckoned that it might be three years before any important results were obtained from the study. Five young women under the direction of Mrs. Mary Cole Palmer, widow of the great turf writer Joe H. Palmer, work for a solid year converting race result data into punch-card form.

The Jockey Club project is aimed mainly at arriving at an abstract which will afford information about the breed as a whole. They hope breeders will be able to use this information for particular conclusions about particular lines and individual horses—and pay for it, of course. It is believed the computers may also provide a general pattern that can be digested by veterinarians in relation to individual problems of horses.

255

When I was in Lexington in the late autumn of 1964, I asked Estes to put his electronic horses through a short trial so I could observe their action. I have tried to depict the look and style of many horses, but I find it difficult to describe the computer.

Its various units are rectangular in shape, stolid in mien, yet somewhat on the gaudy side, since their manufacturers, with surprising whimsy, have inserted colored panels in their bellies. They whirr and hum and tremble slightly like a jukebox on the verge of rendering music by the Beatles. Lights blink on and off and presently little cards with cabalistic perforations are spewed forth. When I saw old 1401 in its morning trial, the cards were blue and pink for a peculiar and, under the circumstances, a delightfully human reason. The young man who feeds 1401 its daily ration of punch cards is Collin Hyde. He has close-cropped hair and a short nose and wears owlish horn-rimmed spectacles. He resembles a mischievous Cub Scout far more than a systems engineer. He was an expectant father at the moment and he was celebrating the occasion by blue for boys and pink for girls. His offspring was male and the punch cards are now all blue.

It seemed to my unscientific mind that 1401 had already provided some interesting information, although Estes and the other stud grooms of this Trojan horse were inclined to belittle its accomplishments to date. It had indicated, for instance, that the average horse wins the average race by a margin of exactly 1.9 lengths. This is no help at all in winning a daily double, but in view of the fact that some forty-five thousand races are run in the United States each year, it's a fact hard to come by unless you have a little computer in your home. The whirrings, hummings and spewings have brought forth the information that there is probably a gap of at least one hundred lengths between the best horse and the worst horse. The trial runs have also indicated that the English have been eminently right in their suspicion that time itself means very little. Time will not even be a factor in the computations, it has been decided, because of the difference in track surfaces and the variance of the same track from day to day because of weather conditions. The little holes have further revealed that the shorter races bring closer finishes.

In simplest terms, the over-all aim of the project is to determine just how good a horse really was in order to establish a valid expectation as to the quality of his offspring. To achieve this, the stud grooms of old 1401 hoped to attain what they call a bell-shaped curve in which the median, the mode and the average are virtually the same. They achieved this late in 1965 and horses can be rated according to their position above or below the midpoint. It is hoped that the ultimate breakdown of these statistics may afford important information in the field of genetics.

Of course, if you find all this a bit complicated, you may always toss a coin before choosing a stallion to serve your mare.

In any event, down in old Kentucky where the meadow grass is blue, the Duke of Cumberland has undergone a startling metamorphosis.

Our friend William Augustus has become a robot who feeds on punch cards instead of rare roast beef.

8

Chocolate Sundaes and Old Shoes

The present contains nothing more than the past, and what is found in the effect was already in the cause.—HENRI BERGSON, *Creative Evolution*

DEAR KELSO GOD PUT US HERE AT THE SAME TIME, YOU TO BE A GREAT RACE HORSE, AND ME TO BE A GOOD BOY FOR MY MOTHER AND FATHER GOOD LUCK IN "1965"

JOHN PRICE EASTBURN ACRES WILM. 8, DEL

A small boy printed the above letter carefully on a piece of yellow paper. He forgot to put periods after his sentences, but he put in all the commas and spelled every word correctly. He mailed the letter to "Kelso," Woodstock Farm, Chesapeake City, Maryland, and it did not go astray, for Kelso has a private mailbox at the farm. Since 1960, the first of the consecutive seasons in which he was acclaimed Horse of the Year, Kelso has received hundreds of letters. Hardly a day passes that the mailman does not leave at least one envelope in his private box, and after he has won a great stakes event he receives dozens. Most of the letters are from children and teen-agers. This fact is very pleasing indeed to his owner and breeder, Mrs. Richard C. duPont, formerly Allaire Crozer of the Philadelphia Crozers.

Largely because of the unprecedented feats of Kelso, Allaire duPont is known as The First Lady of the American Turf. The title is not formally bestowed by an after-dinner orator at a dreary banquet. It derives entirely from the spontaneous acclaim of people who love horses. In the long history of racing in America only two other great ladies have been awarded the title. They were Helen Hay Whitney of Greentree Stud and Isabel Dodge Sloane of Brookmeade Stable. Allaire duPont of Bohemia Stable wears her accolade gracefully and modestly, as she wears her clothes. When she is interviewed by the press or on the many occasions when she has had to say a few words after accepting another Horse of the Year trophy on behalf of Kelso (trying experiences for her), she never uses the personal pronoun. It is always "we," and the "we" is by no means the mock-modest "editorial we." It means Kelso himself. It means Kelso's trainer Carl Hanford, Kelso's jockey Ismael Valenzuela, Kelso's personal groom Larry Fitzpatrick, Kelso's personal exercise boy Dick Jenkins.

"I think it even means the people who love Kelso," she said once. "I feel they have as much of an interest in him as I have."

Mrs. duPont shared her husband's enthusiasm for gliders. Richard duPont, a great sportsman, was killed in a glider acci-

dent during the war. Today Mrs. duPont is a competent airplane pilot. So is her lovely daughter Linda, who sometimes
transports her mother by plane to the tracks where Kelso is
racing. Linda duPont was a member of the 1964 equestrian
Olympic team.

"My children love flying," Mrs. duPont says. "Thank good-
ness they also love horses. I honestly don't believe that any child
who loves a horse can possibly become a delinquent."

That's why she is so pleased that such a large amount of old
Kelso's personal mail comes from children. Kelso even has a
fan club composed of a thousand children and teen-agers. It was
formed by an intense young girl who was about eleven years old
at the time that Kelso was in the full flush of his fame. Her name
is Heather Noble, and she lives in Alexandria, Virginia. She
might be perfectly typecast for the role of Enid Bagnold's hero-
ine, National Velvet. On the greatest day that Kelso ever knew,
November 11, 1964, the afternoon he finally won the Washington, D. C., International at Laurel, beating his great rival Gun
Bow and many of the best horses from Ireland, France, Italy,
Russia, Japan, and South America, Heather, then fourteen, was
Mrs. duPont's guest of honor at the course. The delightful girl
had dressed herself in Kelso's colors of gray and gold. She waved
a homemade felt pennant reading *"King Kelso, We Love You,
Win Or Lose."* She was festooned with homemade badges in-
scribed with endearments of Kelso. The Canadian Royal Mount-
ies, clad in scarlet tunics, wheeled their horses in drill forma-
tions on the track, flags of foreign nations flew from the tall
poles in the infield, dignitaries from foreign embassies sat formally attired in clubhouse boxes, the post parade was a colorful
affair called "the Parade of Champions," but Heather attracted
more attention than anybody except Kelso himself.

This young lady spends a good part of her time throughout

the year writing odes to Kelso, illustrating them with watercolor sketches and sending them off to newspapers and magazines and friends of Kelso. Kelso seems to be the very center of her life. She accords him the same uninhibited adulation that most teen-agers render to the four shaggy young men from Liverpool known as the Beatles.

Throughout the years of the thoroughbred it has been the effect of horses on humans that has been the most remarkable aspect of racing. Eclipse made a gentleman out of an arrant rogue named O'Kelly. Old, old men will challenge you to a fist fight if you take the name of Man o' War in vain. A hard-bitten, cynical gambler who watched Equipoise, one of the gamest horses in history, drive home in the 1930 Pimlico Futurity after he had gone to his knees at the start, said, "When you see a horse like that, you believe in God for a minute." A scholarly and sensitive lady named Irene McCanliss discovered horses late in life be-cause Citation represented pure beauty to her, and she has de-voted much of her time to the study of thoroughbreds ever since. And a young girl in Virginia is inspired to write poems and paint watercolors by a race horse named Kelso. No other animal has ever affected the emotional nature of man so much as the thoroughbred race horse. The relation of men and horses almost invariably has been ennobling for the human beings involved, it would seem.

We began with Eclipse and when we come to Kelso, we have gone full cycle. Not only did Kelso, the greatest horse of modern times (in my opinion the greatest race horse of any time), de-scend directly from Cumberland's foal in the male line, but his hopeless beginnings, his brilliant career, his effect on human beings, even his physical appearance are so strikingly similar to those of Eclipse that we feel we are reading an old, old story when we ponder the saga of this great modern champion.

Can you trace your paternal ancestry back for two and a half centuries and twenty generations? Kelso can. It goes like this: DARLEY ARABIAN (1698)–BARTLETT'S CHILDERS (1716)–SQUIRT (1732)–MARSKE (1750)–**ECLIPSE** (1764)– POT-8-0s (1773)–WAXY (1790)–WHALEBONE (1807)– CAMEL (1822)–TOUCHSTONE (1831)–NEWMINSTER (1848)–LORD CLIFDEN (1860)–HAMPTON (1872)–BAY RONALD (1893)–BAYARDO (1906)–GAINSBOROUGH (1915)–HYPERION (1930)–ALIBHAI (1938)–YOUR HOST (1947)–**KELSO** (1957)

These are far more than twenty names on a piece of paper. They are the snips and snails and puppy-dog tails that Kelso is made of. To racing men these twenty horses are mileposts on time's long road that stretches from the age of England's haughty Stuarts to the era of a rough-hewn fellow from Texas who wants a Great Society for his fellow Amurrrricuns.

To students of racing, each name brings a memory. The foaling date of the Darley, the fire-breathing Arabian charger known as "the Headstrong One," is largely speculative. Mr. Darley seems to have brought him out of Aleppo during 1703, the first year of Queen Anne's reign. His birthday varies with the authorities who inform us. It is also given as 1699 and 1700. All of the authorities agree that the oriental stallion, regardless of his age, made a great impression upon the horsemen of England when he arrived. Squirt, of course, was the pathetic little foal who almost became a meal for staghounds. Marske was the swayback swain of the beautiful mare named Spiletta. Eclipse is certainly the most famous horse that ever lived. Pot-8-0s was named with crude eighteenth century humor, but he was the greatest of Eclipse's sons, both on the track and in the stud. Camel was a fair race horse and established a great line, but he was sad to contemplate, for he had an outsized neck, a ridiculously small head and a humpbacked look that resulted in his name. Touchstone was the horse who showed the same sprawling gait of the hind legs that had distinguished Eclipse sixty years before. When we come to Hampton, Bay Ronald, Gainsborough, and Hyperion we arrive at the greatest modern dynasty of English thoroughbreds.

All of Kelso's male-line ancestors up to Alibhai raced in England. Alibhai was one of the horses for whom Louis B. Mayer spent his millions, and that fact alone assures Hollywood's strutting little Napoleon a lasting place in American turf history. Mayer bred his imported stallion to Boudoir II, a daughter of the great Mahmoud, and got a colt named Your Host who was sold as a two-year-old in the great dispersal of his holdings in 1949. Your Host was Kelso's sire and his own saga is so exactly similar to that of Squirt, grandsire of Eclipse, that it seemed a drama of the eighteenth century was being revived in the twentieth.

Before we consider this fascinating fact, we should remark that the blood of old Matchem and of Cumberland's King Herod as well as that of Eclipse is in Kelso's veins, as indeed it must be in every thoroughbred's on earth today. Through Kelso's dam Maid of Flight and her paternal granddam Quickly and Quickly's dam Stephanie we come to Stefan the Great and he leads us to Herod's great line through The Tetrarch. Maid of Flight's maternal grandsire was Man o' War, the greatest modern descendant of the first of the English-Arab mutations known as Matchem. It is like spinning inside the great hoop of history to follow the complicated spiderwebs that make up the bloodlines of a thoroughbred like Kelso. Always, at some point in our dizzy somersaultings, we come upon not only Matchem, Herod, and

Eclipse, but the three orientals, the Godolphin Barb, the Byerly Turk, and the Darley Arabian. Beyond them lies uncharted outer space.

The emotional pleas of a groom saved the life of Squirt in the eighteenth century and thus preserved Eclipse and most of the line called thoroughbred. An unemotional insurance agency saved the life of Squirt's remote descendant Your Host, sire of Kelso. Your Host had been a good race horse. He had won the hundred-thousand-dollar Santa Anita Derby as a three-year-old. Shortly after he began his career in the handicap division as a four-year-old, he broke his shoulder. Up to then virtually every horse who suffered such an accident had been destroyed. Lloyd's of London paid off the tremendous sum called for in the insurance policy only on condition that the company would take possession of the crippled horse.

He was saved for the stud by a new form of veterinary surgery (inevitably called "miracle surgery") but had to wear an elaborate brace in order to hobble about. He was obviously in no pain, however, and was capable of serving mares. He was purchased from the insurance company by a syndicate of American breeders, one of whom was Mrs. duPont, who had operated a modest stock farm in Maryland up to that time.

Your Host stood at Arthur Hancock's vast Claiborne farm in Kentucky, and Mrs. duPont's beautifully bred mare Maid of Flight (who won the Broodmare of the Year award in 1965) was sent there to be bred to him. The striking similarities between the dramatic stories of Eclipse and Kelso did not end with the hairbreadth escape of their respective ancestors. Kelso was not born during an eclipse of the sun and there was no obese Royal Duke present to roar with bitter laughter, but when he arrived on earth in the spring of 1957 he was as undersized and puny as Cumberland's colt. Of the entire crop of foals that year, it is probable he would have been voted the Least Likely to Succeed on the basis of appearance alone.

One of the great curiosities of the turf is the fact that the race horses painted by eighteenth century artists, with the exception of the "primitive" Sartorius, bore little resemblance to their subjects. The eighteenth century sporting painters idealized and romanticized the champions they depicted to a ridiculous degree. The eighteenth century mutation of the Arabian and English horse was short, compact, a bit on the shaggy side and ugly by the standards of the perfectionists in conformation. He was painted for the most part as taller, longer of limb, better balanced structurally, smoother of coat and far more elegant of head and neck. Paintings of him resemble the most strikingly handsome thoroughbreds of today far more than they resemble their contemporary subjects. Here, then, is a classic case of nature imitating art. Eventually the thoroughbred actually grew to the size and attained the sleekness and rhythmical beauty of physique that had been anticipated by artists two hundred years before he evolved in such a shape.

Exterminator, though much taller and heavier than the horses of Cumberland's time, had been an exception to the developing rule. He was, in a sense, a throwback. He was rough-hewn like the earliest thoroughbreds of the eighteenth century, and he was certainly one of the greatest horses of the twentieth.

Kelso, as he matured and gained stature after he was gelded as a yearling, seemed a throwback, too. He was in many ways even closer to the horses of Eclipse's day, especially in size. His ultimate height was a fraction under sixteen hands, one inch. It is an odd coincidence that a distinguished veterinary surgeon of the eighteenth century, Vial de Saint Bel, gives us this measurement as the height of Eclipse, but unfortunately for our comparison, he was unquestionably inaccurate. Saint Bel did not measure the living Eclipse. He measured his skeleton, and he made his reckoning of height conform exactly to a pet theory of his that each part of a horse's anatomy was in exact proportion to other parts. It was as simple to measure animals then as it is now by stretching a taut string from the point of the withers to the ground and measuring the string. This was done many times in the case of Eclipse when he was alive and all the measurements showed him just over fifteen hands. Even that was good size for the time. At sixteen hands, he would have been a giant for his day. A really tall thoroughbred today stands at least seventeen hands, some three inches higher than Kelso. Kelso is also extremely slight for a race horse. In training he weighs about 970 pounds and seldom gains more than sixty pounds even after he has been away from the races for months. He loses this excess poundage almost immediately when he goes back into training.

Standing or walking, Kelso is not a beautiful horse by any means, although he is far from the grotesque beast with "a stove-pipe neck" that he was once called in a widely circulated illustrated magazine. His coat is an indeterminate shade officially registered as "bay or brown." It never glints dazzlingly in the sun, no matter how much loving care his grooms give it with rag and brush. His handlers are inordinately proud of him and they accord him the same care that studio beauticians render a movie star about to pose for publicity stills. He appears as a lovable and rather shabby old fellow, completely ordinary, distracted in the paddock as if he has his mind on more important things (such as completely destroying his opponents), unworried about his public image. He submits patiently to having a little yellow ribbon tied to his forelock, but in his appearances in the spectacular "Parade of Champions" that precedes the International at Laurel he has refused flatly to wear the stylish blanket emblazoned with the national colors and provided by the management. The others in the field flaunt the handsome holiday dress, but Kelso plods along in his own bare hide, with Larry Fitzpatrick carrying the presentation blanket over his arm. To Kelso it is just another horse race.

When Kelso starts running it is a different story entirely. When he poses in the paddock or in the winner's circle for a battery of photographers, he's just another horse. When he races, he is the most beautiful thing alive, and his stride is the measured strophes of a poem. You hear music when you see Kelso run.

Kelso is an eccentric millionaire in the tradition of old Jay Gould and Hetty Green. He is the richest horse in the history of the world. Through the season of 1964 (when he was supposed to have retired, but didn't) he had earned $1,893,362 in fifty-six starts, thirty-six victories and a dozen seconds, nearly all in great stakes events. He is the leading capitalist of the equine world, yet he not only walks around in his shabby coat of uncertain hue, but often has as many as fourteen holes in each of his shoes. Despite his great wealth, his brilliant record of accomplishment, his irreproachable family background, his heavy fan mail, his rave notices in the press and the loving attention accorded him by his owner, trainer, groom, jockey, exercise boy and stable attendants, Kelso seemed a very insecure horse right through his sixth year of racing and his seventh year of life. His sense of security could be re-established in only one way: by feeding him a chocolate sundae. If Kelso were managing his own financial affairs, he'd have spent every nickel of his $1,893,362 on chocolate sundaes. His craving for sweets is insatiable. His owner always carries lumps of sugar around with her at times when it is inconvenient to obtain a chocolate sundae. Like everything else about Kelso, even the sugar lumps are very special. They are wrapped in yellow paper imprinted with Kelso's name and likeness. Kelso also drinks a special bottled spring water.

After he had finally passed Round Table's long-standing money-winning record and had virtually obliterated his most persistent rival Gun Bow in the International of 1964, Kelso suddenly seemed to gain a self-confidence he had never possessed in four other seasons as the greatest thoroughbred of America (and most probably the world). This did not decrease his appetite for chocolate sundaes, however. Instead of begging for them in the wheedling manner of Oliver Twist proffering his empty bowl, he demanded them as officiously as a prima donna demands star billing.

Mrs. duPont had planned to retire him forever at the very peak of his fame and accomplishment when he won the International in November. She said she simply couldn't stand the old boy's new personality, however. He was throwing his weight around at the farm and lording it over the lesser horses on the place. In the spring of 1965, his owner announced that she would probably run him in a few carefully selected events during the summer and fall, even though he was eight years old, a very ancient age nowadays for any race horse and practically senescence in the case of most stakes campaigners. "He's so darned cocky we just can't stand him any longer," Mrs. duPont said.

Kelso and Exterminator, both geldings, have been the most abundantly healthy champions in the history of the turf. Such a prognosis was highly unlikely for the undersized and awkward foal that teetered on spindly legs at Woodstock Farm during the summer of 1957. Mrs. duPont fell in love with the little fellow at first sight, but his appeal was mainly that which is always attached to the runt of the litter because of his seeming helplessness.

Kelso was a spry little horse, with lively curiosity and an affectionate nature, but as a weanling his qualities were more those of a friendly puppy dog than an all-conquering thoroughbred. When he scampered in the paddocks of the farm he showed a slight fault of stride that might have arisen from a strangulated condition. The small Bohemia Stable was then trained by Dr. John Lee, a veterinarian. He and other vets believed Kelso's size might be increased and his stride corrected by gelding. This was done in Kelso's yearling season, and it may become the most controversial piece of surgery since Sir Humphry Davy discovered the anesthetic properties of nitrous oxide in 1799. It is tragic, of course, that Kelso can never have progeny. On the other hand he might never have been a champion, might never have raced even, if the operation had not been performed.

Gelding Kelso did correct the fault of stride, but it did not seem to increase his size too much. He was still a scrawny and unimpressive-looking horse when he first came to the races in his two-year-old season. At that time Dr. Lee was training him. We had been waiting forty years for Kelso. Nothing like him had been seen on the American turf since the days of Exterminator and Man o' War. Those who saw him win the first start of his life in September 1959 had no reason to suspect that this was the case, however; that the career of this youngster who won an unimportant race that day would mark the glorious culmination of events that had their remote inception during the dark of the sun in a paddock of Cranbourne Lodge in 1764. In 1959 Kelso ran two more races at Atlantic City, finished second in both and earned a total of only $3,380, hardly a promising start for a horse that aspired to the estate of a millionaire.

When Kelso turned three, Carl Hanford, who had been a top jockey in the 1930s and had trained a small stable after serving a long hitch in the Army, took over. Kelso's racing record was brief and undistinguished, but he had an appealing nature that attracted Hanford to him. Carl made a close study of the horse. After consulting with a veteran blacksmith named Tom McNaboe, he decided that one of the main difficulties Kelso faced was the thin walls of his hoofs. Hanford and McNaboe solved this problem eventually by changing Kelso's shoes as infrequently as possible and by having the blacksmith punch holes between the eight holes in the standard racing plate. That's why Kelso sometimes has fourteen holes in each of his shoes. He is one of the few horses in history who ever won two stakes in the some pair of shoes. In 1963 he won both the Nassau County and Suburban Handicaps in the same racing plates.

Kelso's three-year-old debut did not come until late in June at Monmouth Park, New Jersey, long after such classics as the Kentucky Derby, the Preakness and the Belmont Stakes had been run. He was a different horse entirely. He won the Monmouth race by ten lengths, moved on to New York to run a mile in the sensational time of 1:34⅕ and win by a dozen lengths. Then came a dismal performance at Chicago. He finished far back in the rich Arlington Classic. This was the only race he lost in 1960. He wound up the year with eight victories in nine starts, earning a total of $293,310. He was not only the three-year-old champion; the polls of racing officials and newspapermen acclaimed him Horse of the Year for the first time.

He was Horse of the Year again in 1961 when he won seven out of nine races, including the Handicap Triple Crown of the Metropolitan, Surburban, and Brooklyn. That year he earned $425,565. By 1962 the weights he carried were growing heavier and he slowed down a bit, winning six of twelve races, finishing second four times and earning $289,685, and another Horse of the Year award. On December 1, 1962, in the Governor's Plate at Garden State Park in New Jersey, his earnings soared past the million mark. The season of 1963, his fourth term as Horse of the Year, was the greatest he had known from the statistical standpoint. He won nine out of twelve races, finished second twice, amassed the colossal total of $569,762. He passed Nashua to take second place on the list of all-time money-winners when he won the Suburban at Aqueduct on July 4.

At the end of the season he looked better than ever before. He seemed to have filled out a little and his coat was dappled for the first time. "Maybe the old boy's finally getting handsome," Hanford said one day.

Actually Hanford had never encountered many physical difficulties with Kelso, and it is the delicate physical construction of most modern thoroughbreds that makes neurotics of their trainers. Sometimes the modern race horse seems as expendable as the windows of a U.S. Embassy in an Iron Curtain country. Kelso had thin walls on his hoofs. His only other shortcoming had been a stiffness of the stifle. This is not a serious defect in horses. It is exactly like a stiffness of the joints in a human being who has not had his usual amount of exercise. The human being works out of it after he moves about for a while. Kelso works out of it after he races a few times. It has been costly to him, of course, for except in his earliest years he has seldom won first time out and sometimes he has lost several races before he regained his perfect stride.

This is one of the reasons he is known as a "fall horse," or one who runs best in the autumn. Stifle trouble must be treated with patience rather than medicine, and Kelso has been exceedingly fortunate in having a very patient owner and a very patient trainer. He has been brought up to his big races by easy stages during his entire career. He is one of the few champions of recent years who has not been overraced, or "sweated for the

271

brass," as the race-track phrase goes. During his first six years of racing he went to the post only fifty-six times, an average of fewer than ten starts a season. Few owners and trainers in recent turf history who had a money machine like Kelso would have used it so sparingly—and so intelligently. This, of course, is one of the primary reasons Kelso has remained a sound horse for so many years.

There are many oddities in the story of Kelso. For one thing, he is a perfect gentleman but he is named for a lady.

Mrs. duPont was actually hoping for a filly when she bred Maid of Flight to Your Host. She has a friend in Wilmington, Delaware, Mrs. Kelso Everett, whom she considers the most perfect hostess she has ever known. She thought it would be fitting to name a horse sired by Your Host for the lady. When a colt arrived, she had her heart set on naming the foal Kelso and she called him by her friend's first name anyway. During his weanling and yearling days, when Kelso failed to attain much size and showed an impediment of stride, Mrs. duPont thought she might have paid Mrs. Everett a dubious compliment.

Another oddity about Kelso is the reception he received from the public right up to his sixth year of racing. Children hailed him as the one, undoubted champion, sang his praises, formed a fan club and wrote him love letters. But children always have been far more perceptive than adults.

Right up to 1964, despite five seasons of racing, four of them as brilliant as any horse had ever known, Kelso seemed to lack a valid legend with the racegoing public. He was, of course, recognized as the greatest horse of our era; his extraordinary record of thirty-one victories and nine seconds in forty-five starts through 1963, against the best horses, and often under crushing weights, demanded that. Every time he went to the post the public accorded him the compliment of backing him down to almost unbettable odds. They applauded him politely when he justified their confidence with one of his clockwork, seemingly effortless performances in disposing of his rivals. Yet it seemed to be respect rather than adulation that Kelso commanded. It was Kelso's record of accomplishment rather than Kelso-the-horse that seemed to appeal most to the public. He had not yet stirred the deep emotional reaction in racing fans that created a gaudy *mystique* for Man o' War, the knight in golden armor who had retired to stud forty-three years before, nor had he become a Paul Bunyanish hero of folk tales like the rangy and knobby Exterminator.

The season of 1964, when Kelso was seven years old and appeared to be in the most glowing health of his entire career, was the worst in all the years of his glory from a statistical viewpoint. He started eleven times. He won only five races. Only three of these races were stakes. His first two races at Hollywood Park in California were the most disappointing he had ever run. He faced inferior competition in each and he finished eighth in one and sixth in the other. From the twenty-fourth of May until the seventh of September, when he won his first stakes victory in the Aqueduct, it seemed that Father Time had finally replaced the little Mexican boy named Ismael Valenzuela in Kelso's saddle.

And, strangely enough, this was the season when Kelso came into his own, when the public finally took him to its heart, when rafter-shaking cheers instead of polite applause greeted him, when Kelso at long last was not merely respected but dearly beloved.

To account for this queer quirk of mass psychology, we must, I think, go back to the reign of the Sun King, Louis XIV of France. The King, if you remember, became smitten with a young lady of the court who had a mole on her cheek. Other jealous ladies who had known the kingly favor laughed derisively behind their fans at the taste of a monarch who loved a lady with a mole. One of the boldest of his castoff mistresses asked the King how he could possibly admire a lady whose complexion had so obvious a mar.

"You should know, my dear," the King replied, "that there can be no beauty without a blemish and that perfection must always have a defect for the sake of contrast."

The next day there was a new fad in the court of the Sun King. All the ladies appeared with artificial moles glued to their cheeks. They called them "beauty patches."

What Kelso had lacked all along, apparently, was a defect. He had been beaten before, but only once, very early in his career in the Arlington Classic, had he been beaten so badly as he was in his two California races. Now, at last, in 1964 he even had a blemish and he was suddenly the most popular hero the sport of racing had ever known. Not even ribby old Exterminator, who had acquired many blemishes in his long turf years, or magnificent Man o' War, who had attained his vital defect when Upset beat him, had known such unadulterated adulation as Kelso knew in 1964.

By the standards of any other horse, Kelso's 1964 record would have seemed exceptionally brilliant. He won less than half his races, but he set two American records and equaled another one. He achieved an all-time American record for winning Cup races when he took his fifth Jockey Club Gold Cup at Aqueduct on October 31 over the testing distance of two miles. He bettered the money-winning record of the world that Round Table had held since 1958. He won under 136 pounds, weight that few horses in history have carried to victory. He was beaten by very narrow margins under 131 and 130 pounds. His most heartbreaking defeat came in the Woodward when the stewards awarded Gun Bow the decision in a photo-finish that was so close virtually everyone else deemed it a dead heat.

Yet Kelso raced for six months in 1964 and he won the championship and his fifth consecutive Horse of the Year honors in two minutes, 23⅘ seconds when he took the International at Laurel in his last race of the season and proved his absolute superiority over Gun Bow, his archrival, who was the greatest horse that had challenged him in six years on the tracks. This was far and away the greatest race that Kelso ever ran and it may well be the greatest race that any American thoroughbred has ever run. Kelso, carrying equal weight with his younger rival, simply walked away from him in the final quarter of the mile and a half contest and won by four and a half lengths. He ran on the turf and bettered the American records for both turf and hard-dirt courses. The previous turf record had been set on a downhill course at Santa Anita. Laurel is a flat course.

The International had been Kelso's great jinx ever since his four-year-old days. The event is an invitational affair that is designed to bring together the greatest turf champions from all the nations of the world. This noble intention does not always quite work out, of course, because the thoroughbred is a fragile animal and he suffers breakdowns in other nations of the world as well as in America. Since 1961 Kelso had been invited to represent the United States in every International. In 1961, 1962, and 1963 he ran second. He was beaten successively by the American horse T. V. Lark, the great French horse Match II, and another American horse Mongo. This led to the general conclusion that Kelso does not like to run on grass, and it is an entirely logical conclusion, which is not too convincingly disputed by his victory in 1964. Laurel, along with the rest of the nation, had undergone a prolonged drought by the time the 1964 International was run. The grass was so sparse and withered that the management sprayed the course with green dye in a frantic effort just to make it *look* like grass. Actually the turf course was as hard as the regular dirt track that encircled it.

Mrs. duPont does not think that Kelso dislikes grass courses, however. She insisted right up to 1964 that the International was a jinx for Kelso, and that was that. Even on the day of the race she was absolutely certain that Kelso, in the most superb condition of his life, could not possibly win because of the jinx.

Trainer Hanford also denies that a grass course is a disadvantage to Kelso. "He ran a magnificent race every time he finished second," Hanford insists. "It was bad racing luck and not the grass that beat him."

I have seen most of Kelso's races over the years (I am glad I was in Europe and missed his humiliating defeats in California in the spring of 1964) and I have always held that a grass course is the equivalent of ten pounds of extra weight for the champion. Tommy Trotter, the brilliant young secretary and handicapper of the New York Racing Association, once told me he concurs in this belief. If my contention is true, of course, Kelso's races over the turf on the three occasions when he finished second are even more commendable than Hanford himself deems them.

Hanford's absolute confidence that Kelso is capable of doing almost anything better than any other horse, such as running over unfamiliar turf courses, is indicative of the strange effect that Kelso has on the human beings who are closest to him. Not one of them will ever believe that Kelso can be defeated through any fault of his own. Mostly, they are inclined to blame themselves. Such an attitude is almost unprecedented with people who race thoroughbreds. Except for the Arlington Classic of 1960 and his inexplicably poor races in California in 1964, Kelso has tried so desperately hard to win, sometimes against the most impossible odds, that his connections are inconsolable when he loses. Their way of forgiving him is to blame themselves.

Eddie Arcaro, one of the turf's immortal jockeys who retired in 1962, rode Kelso in all of his great races of 1960 and 1961. Arcaro is an outspoken iconoclast, certainly no sentimentalist about horses. When he and Kelso finished a yard or so behind the superb grass horse T.V. Lark in the International of 1961, he was an infuriated young man. As soon as he jumped off his mount, he said, "If they'd run this race tomorrow, we'd win. I'd know what to do, and we'd win." He blamed himself, not his horse.

In 1962 Ismael "Milo" Valenzuela succeeded Arcaro as Kelso's regular jockey. Milo is Mexican but he exhibits no emotional Latin temperament when he is riding. Sportswriters usually describe him as "chilly." He was very emotional indeed when he vaulted off Kelso after losing the International of 1962 to the magnificent French distance runner, Match II, who had been ridden by one of the greatest of history's jockeys, Yves Saint-Martin. Little Milo raced to the jockeys' room, buried his face in his arms and sobbed for a solid hour before he even peeled off his racing silks, blaming himself, although he had ridden a brilliant race.

Valenzuela finished second on Kelso in the International again in November of 1963 when he was beaten narrowly by the talented American grass horse Mongo. This time Milo did not seek the catharsis of tears. Without consulting either Mrs. duPont or trainer Hanford, he rushed into the stewards' stand and claimed a foul against Wayne Chambers, Mongo's jockey. Mongo had drifted out on the turn for home and Kelso, outside him, had been forced to steer wide to avoid a collision course. Valenzuela insisted that the ground he lost doing this beat him.

The stewards, who were not under the magic spell of Kelso, disallowed the claim and fined Milo a hundred dollars for a frivolous protest.

Mrs. duPont's attitude toward Kelso is somewhat ambivalent. There can be no doubt that in one respect she is overawed by her horse's feats in the way parents are overawed by the accomplishments of child prodigies. On another level, Kelso seems to inspire in her emotions of fierce protectiveness and affectionate amusement. Sometimes when the champion is being saddled for one of his great races, his owner will stand near his stall in the paddock, her gaze transfixed and adoring, and she will say, almost inaudibly to no one in particular, "Isn't he wonderful? Isn't he simply wonderful?"

Then, when Kelso comes back from another stirring victory and nuzzles her and whinnies softly, demanding affection and sugar lumps as a reward, she'll say, "Oh, stop, now! You're acting like a silly kitten. Of course I know you won. What do you think I expected you to do?"

On the occasions when Kelso loses, Mrs. duPont is utterly desolated, not because of losing a great turf classic and a large purse, but because Kelso himself knows he was beaten and is hangdog ashamed, like a small boy who has been naughty or a star pupil who has failed a final exam.

"It's simply heartbreaking to see him," his owner says. "No matter how much affection you lavish on him, it's impossible to console him."

Hardheaded horsemen like Hanford often have a low opinion of a thoroughbred's intelligence, deeming the average race horse to be a wilfully stupid animal. Hanford thinks Kelso is about the smartest horse that ever lived and that he has the most competitive spirit, despite his docile demeanor. He never works Kelso with another horse, because the champion will want to run too fast when he has something to beat and "leave his race on the track." Both Hanford and Fitz, Kelso's groom and boon companion, are certain Kelso always knows the days he is going to race. The accelerated training program and altered feeding schedule may tip him off. Over the years, when Fitz has opened the door of Kelso's stall on race days, his charge will not rush up to him as if he hadn't seen him for years, as he does on every other morning. He stands tensely, nods briefly in greeting, as if he does not wish to be disturbed. He seems abstracted, like a person who has important matters on his mind.

This businesslike, no-nonsense attitude has always been evident in the paddock. There Kelso is no longer a playful house pet. In a sense, he's like an indulgent father who dismisses his family because he must attend to an urgent matter that does not concern them.

When Hanford and Kelso returned to New York in late June of 1964 after their brief and disastrous campaign in California, the champion's trainer was an obviously puzzled man. Hanford, one of the most talented practical horsemen the sport has produced, a highly intelligent and articulate man who knows horses from the standpoint of both a successful jockey and a leading trainer, was certain there was no physical reason for Kelso's unbelievable performances. He knew Kelso as very few men in turf history have ever known a horse. It was quite obvious that Hanford thought the great horse's trouble was mainly psychological. Despite his light frame, Kelso had always been a big eater, or a "good doer," as horsemen phrase it. Now he was off his feed. He had always been a horse of remarkably equable temperament. Now he was nervous, crotchety, irritable.

Hanford simply would not accept the opinion freely expressed by the gentlemen of the press that Kelso had grown suddenly old, was past his prime and was finished as America's great champion. He knew his horse too well. He knew he was rapidly approaching the peak of his physical condition, that he was slightly heavier and more dappled than he had been even in the greatest years. Something was worrying Kelso, and Hanford was at a loss to discover the cause.

Hanford mentioned that he had not been able to give his horse enough work before his first start on the Coast. He said that a loudspeaker system on the backstretch of Hollywood Park, used to relay messages to trainers and stable hands, had bothered Kelso greatly and that he seemed to miss the sylvan quiet of his accustomed quarters at Belmont Park.

Using the hindsight we possessed after the events of that summer and autumn, we can see that Hanford had ferreted out the basic reason for Kelso's loss of form when he mentioned the strangeness of his surroundings at Hollywood and the fact that he seemed to miss the familiar scenes of the Belmont stable area. Even though he was abundantly healthy and still the toughest horse in the world physically, Kelso, at the age of seven, was an old codger as thoroughbreds go.

The horse is often damned as the most stupid of animals because he will run back into a stable that is burning down. It is true that many horses, including valuable thoroughbreds, have destroyed themselves through this lemming-like behavior. There is a reason for it, however. The horse was just about the first animal that man domesticated to any great extent and he has acquired many of the attributes of man. Even the seemingly placid Old Dobbin type of farm horse has a complex nervous system and the thoroughbred is the most neurotic of all the breeds of horses. Familiarity is of the utmost importance to all types of horses. That is why so many race horses have stable pets in the forms of dogs, goats, roosters, geese, ducks and even, in rarer cases, monkeys and more exotic playmates. They run back into the barn that is burning because in a time of emergency and panic the barn, even in flames, represents a safe haven to them.

Kelso, despite the coddling and understanding and expert care that had been given him, had always showed signs of strange misgivings and insecurity. When he suddenly found himself in a strange land with an unfamiliar climate, working over a track with an oddly fluffy surface that had been sown with tons of rice hulls to afford cushion and drainage, his reaction was much the same as that of a mature human being who is suddenly uprooted from his home and resettled in a strange country with strange customs. Certainly the sporadic bleating of the loudspeaker did little to restore his equanimity. Kelso most probably felt lost and confused and pretty damned annoyed by the whole business. It is not correct, really, to say he ran poorly in his two races at Hollywood Park. For the first time in his life, Kelso simply refused to run at all. Kelso was on strike.

"I did something wrong," Hanford kept saying to me that day when Kelso made his first start of 1964 in the East. "I don't know what it was, but maybe now he's back where he belongs, I'll find out."

That afternoon Kelso carried the enormous burden of 136 pounds in an unimportant overnight handicap against an inferior field. He had carried that weight once before and he had been one of the very few horses in history who had won under it. He packed it to victory in the Brooklyn Handicap of 1961. He carried it to victory again on that June day in 1964 at Aqueduct in the mile and an eighth event. He won, but he didn't win like Kelso. His stride was faulty. Six furlongs from home, with Valenzuela working on him, he made his move. That is the point where he nearly always begins his great runs. To me he seemed like an aging actor who knows his lines perfectly but has lost his former fire. He was following the pattern of a well-rehearsed performance. He was going through the motions, and in this case the motions were enough, but the time was slow and he was puffing after the race as I had never seen him puff before on occasions when he had run much faster.

Hanford was by no means satisfied, but he had a wry comment when I met him after the race. "Well, we ain't dead yet, anyhow," he said.

I noticed one peculiar thing that afternoon. It was a weekday and the crowd was small. But the volume of cheers that greeted the Old Man after his relatively unimportant score was greater than it had ever been after his most brilliant victories over truly great horses in the richest stakes. It was this which set me to thinking eventually about Louis XIV and the young lady with the mole on her cheek. In each start that Kelso made after that the sound of frantic cheering for him grew more and more deafening—and in four of those starts he was beaten.

Kelso's races from late June to early September of 1964 rather resembled the moods of a manic depressive. He was 'way up one day and 'way down the next. Sometimes it seemed almost as if he were learning to run all over again, that he would master the art completely in one race and forget it in the next. Or it seemed as though he were nursing a grudge against those closest to him and that his resentment was wearing off only gradually.

In the Surburban, a stakes that the famed racing official Jack Campbell once called the greatest horse race in America, the Old Man was greater in defeat than he had ever been in victory. It was one of those contests that make you wonder if there's really anything on earth worth while except a good horse race.

The race was run on July 4 and it was a Glorious Fourth indeed for the crowd of fifty thousand screaming maniacs who saw it. It was a race that had simply everything and exploited its dramatic possibilities to the ultimate limit. It had the beloved old champion who had seemed to be goggle-eyed against the ropes and about to go down at last for the slow, cruel count. It had a brash young challenger, a sensationally speedy four-year-old colt from England named Iron Peg who raced for the great turfman Captain Harry Guggenheim and who had shown the greatest speed potential of any young horse in many generations. Iron Peg was a chesty upstart who had come up the hard way, a superb physical specimen, and now he was poised impatiently on the edge of glory. The Suburban, at a mile and a quarter, lasted for a clock tick more than two minutes and those two minutes and a clock tick were packed with heartbreak, wild, surging hope, and, finally, an exaltation of the human spirit that few experiences, regardless of their duration, can inspire.

Iron Peg carried 116 pounds and Kelso had the heavy burden of 131 pounds on his back. Kelso covered 79,200 inches of ground and he lost by exactly twelve inches, the estimated length of an average horse's head. Twelve inches past the finish he was in front by three inches, the estimated length of a horse's nose.

The miracle began at the five-eighths pole where Olden Times was setting the pace, but under sufferance from Iron Peg, who quite obviously was capable of passing him and cooking him brown whenever Mannie Ycaza chose to let out a loop in the reins. Here, Kelso made his first tentative move, and there was a kind of sad and wistful groan, for while Kelso was moving, he was not moving with the commanding, absolute assurance of the fabled champion who had met and beaten all the good ones of his time. I fancied that even the thousands who had backed Iron Peg, a colt that seemed absolutely invincible at this point, were sighing sadly because it seemed there was no doubt now that the grand old horse of our generation had had it.

They came around the turn and something was happening. It was happening slowly, almost imperceptibly, yet the crowd sensed it and reacted by suddenly becoming silent, like a throng that is witnessing a miracle.

The horses were in the stretch then and Iron Peg, his destiny in his grasp, was indulging the exhausted Olden Times no longer. He had taken the lead and he was going on, fresh and determined, to increase it to an unbeatable span of dirt and daylight. Then Ycaza saw what had been happening and what was happening still. Kelso was Kelso again. There were no longer kinks in his stride or flaws in his action. The Old Man was running at last like the champion he had always been and he was gaining, no longer inch by inch but foot by foot, and Ycaza, who must have thought it was over at the quarter pole, suddenly discovered it had just begun and his whip went down on Iron Peg's dark bay hide to sting him into the realization that he was no longer playing with the boys he had beaten by six and seven and thirteen lengths, but was with the men now; specifically, with the greatest Old Man of them all.

The daffodil-yellow and smoke-gray banner of Bohemia was waving proudly again down the middle of the stretch. The dark face of Milo Valenzuela was grim at the instant it came into the focus of the binoculars I grasped with sweaty paws. And now the crowd broke its silence as they went to the eighth pole and the yards between Iron Peg and Kelso became feet, and as they passed the sixteenth pole the feet became inches.

"Kelly! Kelly! Kelly!" It was a keening, plaintive prayer. I think the ones who had backed Iron Peg into almost equal favoritism with the old champ had forgotten the tote tickets in their pockets, for they were yelling, "Kelly, Kelly, Kelly!", too.

A veteran horseman who had no vested interest in Kelso was standing beside me. I knew him as a calm and unemotional fellow. Suddenly his hand began to pound the ledge in front of him compulsively and his voice rose to the shrill hysteria of a schoolgirl's.

"Old Man! Old Man!" he shrieked. "Jesus, let the Old Man win!"

The Old Man didn't win, not quite. But the usually heedless crowd, the crowd that has sometimes hissed and sometimes booed when champions have lost, was faced with the rare thing called greatness, and for once the throng fully recognized what it saw.

Kelso never again that year quite descended to the lower depths he had known in California, but he had several bad moments between July and September. Two weeks after his great race in the Suburban he went to Monmouth Park, the pleasant oceanside course in New Jersey, and was beaten on the dirt by Mongo, who had defeated him on the grass in the International the year before. He ran a creditable enough race and was defeated by only a neck. Kelso's race might have been deemed a great one for any other horse than Kelso himself. But he simply wasn't Kelso. His stride lacked its usual rhythm, when he charged he seemed uncertain. The absolute quality of his best performances was missing. At the eighth pole he passed a horse who had not been to the races for a long while and was obviously quite short. His name was Gun Bow, and from that time on he would prove the most formidable rival for Kelso of any of the sixty thousand horses that had been foaled in America during his long reign as champion.

Kelso's behavior in his next start, the Brooklyn Handicap at Aqueduct, was the most peculiar of his entire career. It seemed old rocking chair had got him at last. In fact, he seemed to mistake his stall in the starting gate for a rocking chair, because he sat right down as soon as he entered it, like a tired old businessman throwing himself into his favorite armchair upon his return from the office. To me, Kelso's action seemed deliberate. In sitting down, he hit his head against the gate and hurt himself, although this was not discovered until later. They got him to his feet and he managed to stagger home a dazed fifth, more than fourteen lengths behind Gun Bow. That race made Gun Bow the turf's new darling. He became one of the very few horses in history to run a mile and a quarter in faster time than two minutes and broke the track record. Kelso himself was thrown out of training with a big bump on his head. Few horses who ever lived were capable of beating the Gun Bow who ran that afternoon.

With Kelso on the side lines, Gun Bow continued on his path of conquest at Saratoga in August. He broke a world's record, and a syndicate of ten men and women pooled their nickels and dimes and bought him for a million dollars. At this stage of the season—and it was growing very late indeed—it seemed that Kelso was finally finished and that Gun Bow would certainly be acclaimed Horse of the Year.

When his head stopped aching Kelso returned to the races very late in the Saratoga meeting. He ran in an unimportant race over the turf course and equaled the American record for a mile and an eighth under the light weight of 118 pounds. The race hardly served to confirm Hanford's belief that Kelso was a superior grass horse, however, for the drought had burned the turf of Saratoga to the consistency of baked clay.

On September 7, Labor Day, Kelso came back to Aqueduct and he won a stakes for the first time in 1964. Perhaps the blow on the head he suffered in the Brooklyn had been beneficial. Certainly from then on he was not the up-again, down-again horse he had been all year, and whatever trauma he had suffered from his humiliating experiences in California had ceased to affect him.

On September 7 Kelso met Gun Bow in the Aqueduct Stakes at equal weights of 128 pounds, and it was a race to remember.

That day, the small, brown-faced Mexican boy in the gaudy silk suit walked into the paddock, slapping his boot with his whip, and took the slim lady in the blue dress by the arm.

"Is all right," he said. "Is all right today. I know."

Milo Valenzuela didn't sound like a jockey talking to an owner as he addressed Mrs. duPont. He sounded, rather touchingly, like a father comforting his young daughter.

Valenzuela walked off and joined Carl Hanford and they went through the ritual of last-minute instructions about the race. It was a rather hollow ceremony. The night before Milo had had his instructions from the trainer: "If nobody else goes after Gun Bow, go after him yourself."

The man called, "Put your riders up. Put your riders up, please, gentlemen," and the small, brown-faced boy in the silk suit vaulted to the saddle, and Hanford stood there with a tense look on his face after he'd given Milo a leg up, and the lady in blue was momentarily all alone. A man walked up to her and tried to find the words that would tell her he knew how she was feeling, but he could only squeeze her arm and say, "Good luck."

"Thank you," Mrs. duPont replied. "But we'll need more than that. Gun Bow is a wonderful colt. We'll need the kind of horse that Kelso really is to beat him."

Valenzuela sensed it first, of course.

He sensed it immediately. They had straightened out on the backstretch when a million dollars' worth of horse named Gun Bow was five big lengths in front of him, and breezing. He sensed that this animal between his knees was the kind of horse that Kelso really is. He was getting into Kelso now. Nobody else was going after Gun Bow. Nobody else was capable of doing so. So Milo started going after him, more than six furlongs from home. And he felt the response, that sudden, surging, electric gathering of sinew, the lengthening of stride that he had experienced so often in the glorious years and that had been so sadly lacking during 1964's summer of despair.

In the stands Carl Hanford sensed it, too, because he saw it. The stride was Kelso's stride again, rhythmic, flowing. Carl's lips moved and he spoke aloud, although he was talking to himself.

"I told him to, I told him to," he kept repeating, as if he were absolving Milo of all blame in case the strategy failed and Milo was accused of using Kelso up too early. Mr. Hanford had been a jockey once himself and he had seen too many riders take superb speed horses like Gun Bow to the front and steal a race. He had stolen a few himself.

In her box Mrs. duPont sensed it, and hardly dared believe it. Her nails dug into her palms and she closed her eyes a moment and breathed a little prayer and when she opened her eyes again they were near the fateful turn for home and Kelso was still moving and Gun Bow was only a couple of lengths in front.

And now the crowd sensed it, too, and the great sound from sixty-five thousand throats rose, stuttering and uncertain at first, for the cheering throng was not yet quite convinced the thing was happening. But midway of the turn the sound was thunder from the hills, for Kelso was still gaining and his stride was faultless and his heart was willing. A locust plague of jets was roaring into nearby Kennedy Airport but the cheering crowd drowned out their shrieking clamor.

From somewhere, like a sharp crack in the wall of sound, a man shrieked, "Look him in the eye, Kelly! Look him in the eye!"

And now Kelly was almost looking him in the eye. As they made the curve the lean, mud-colored gelding had driven to the bulging flanks of the heavy-muscled bay and inch by inch he was still gaining.

The dagger thrust of shrill sound came again. "Look him in the eye, Kelly! Look him in the eye!"

At the quarter pole Kelly did just that.

He looked Gun Bow in the eye. He gave him the cold and calculating appraisal that a battle-scarred old veteran gives a young challenger before he delivers the knockout punch.

Old racetrackers have an inelegant but vividly descriptive expression for what happened next.

Kelso ate Gun Bow up and spit him out.

The stringy champion of so many fabled fields, whose gray and yellow banner had been dragging in the dust of late, moved on by this million dollars' worth of colt, and his flag was flying high and proud again. The noise that ensued was the loudest I've ever heard at any racetrack, and I've heard a lot of noise at a lot of racetracks in my time.

It was Kelly by a head, a neck, a half-length as they went to the eighth pole and at the eighth pole it was Kelly by three quarters of a length, but Gun Bow never quit. He had reeled off dizzying quarters and he was still running like a million dollars' worth of horse. He had a lot left when Kelso came to him. He disputed every inch, every foot, every yard, and when Kelso was three quarters of a length ahead, he could not increase his margin. For one brief second near the sixteenth pole it seemed barely possible that the stubborn colt who was running his heart out to regain the lead would get his head in front. Walter Blum, one of the best riders in America, was giving his mount everything a jockey could give a horse. And Gun Bow was giving Blum everything a horse can give a jockey.

It just wasn't enough. It wasn't enough because Kelso, at long last, was running like the horse he really is.

In the frantic seconds down that final eighth, you looked at little Milo's brown face and you wondered what he could be thinking. His expression, once he got in front, seemed to be one of sheer exaltation. "Is all right. Is all right today. I know . . ."

It was very much all right down that last furlong, from Milo's point of view, because he had Kelso—the real Kelso—between his knees again.

And down that last furlong it seemed as if the two horses, now so far in front that the others might have been running in the next event, were no longer propelled by legs, but were plummeted forward by the great engulfing wave of sound. The public announcer was rattling off his description of the battle, the sound of his voice magnified to an electronic roar, but he might as well have been chatting quietly with a friend, without benefit of microphone, for the decibels of the loudspeaker were mere murmurous crackles in the symphony of cheers.

And make no mistake about it. The heavy money was on Gun Bow, the odds-on choice, but the cheering was for Kelso, whose odds were more than 2-to-1 for one of the few times in half a dozen years of racing.

It was three quarters of a length at the eighth pole and it was still three quarters of a length when they broke the beam at the finish pole. Gun Bow wouldn't quit, but he simply couldn't gain.

Kelso had achieved something very odd indeed. When he was virtually invincible, he was accepted, admired, respected. He was there, like the Rocky Mountains or the Atlantic Ocean, formidable, impressive, yet strangely remote. Only in this season of his failures, when age had touched him and slowed him down, had he finally moved men's hearts.

I think it can be stated beyond dispute that the ovation Kelso received after his triumph on Labor Day at Aqueduct was the greatest ever given any horse in the history of the American turf.

As for the slim lady in blue—she simply forgot her dignity when her horse had won. She fairly raced to the winner's circle, her hair streaming in the breeze. She kissed Kelso. She kissed Milo. She even kissed an astonished photographer who happened to be standing there.

Kelso did not go to the post again for nearly a month. When he started he again met Gun Bow, and the race, or its finish, is likely to remain one of the most controversial turf events of all time. The two great rivals met in the Woodward at a mile and a quarter. Gun Bow and Kelso carried 126 pounds each and as the race was run they seemed to be as evenly matched as two horses can possibly be. They finished together on the same stride and virtually every observer on the finish line thought it was a dead heat. They still thought so when they saw the photo-finish pictures, but the stewards, who must have used a micrometer to measure the eyelash-breadth difference, said Gun Bow had won by a fraction of a fraction of an inch. It was probably the closest finish in history that has not been judged as a dead heat.

In this race, run over a drying-out track that was dull from recent rain, Blum did not let Gun Bow run as fast as he pleased in the early stages. He reserved him for the stretch battle with Kelso that he knew was bound to evolve. The race was of vital importance to Kelso. If he won it, he would become the greatest money-winner in the history of the turf.

The crucial point of the race came an eighth of a mile from the finish. Here, it seemed, Kelso had it won. He had drawn an inch or two in front of Gun Bow a sixteenth of a mile back. Now he went out by a foot, a foot and a half, two feet, and it seemed certain he would simply draw away from his stubborn rival as he had done in the Aqueduct.

But Kelso did something he had never done before just as

they went by the eighth pole. He had been drifting closer and closer to his rival for a sixteenth of a mile. Now he suddenly lugged toward the horse inside him and it required all the skill and strength that little Valenzuela possessed to avoid a collision that would certainly have meant disqualification. To make matters worse, Gun Bow is a shadow-jumper. This means that he is a horse who shies suddenly, often in full stride, at nonexistent objects. He chose the exact moment that Kelso lugged in to shy a bit and move out from the rail.

The ground Valenzuela lost by straightening his mount out was more than sufficient to beat Kelso. Gun Bow went ahead, but in the final breathless yards, Kelso drew alongside again.

On the testimony of the naked eye I thought Gun Bow had won by an inch or two. When I saw the photo-finish picture, I thought they had finished on an absolutely even keel. Even when the picture was blown up to enormous proportions and a hairline difference might have existed, I thought the race might well have been called a dead heat, but the stewards said the camera showed Gun Bow's nose in front. I made some measurements on the picture later. Taking the standard measure of three inches for a nose, Gun Bow's margin, if it existed at all, was less than a quarter of an inch. This is a very small margin indeed by which to lose a winner's purse of $70,330.

I couldn't account for Kelso's suddenly showing a disposition to lug in. He hadn't done it before to my knowledge. Horses usually lug in because they're hurting or because they're tired. Kelso wasn't hurting and he came on again after being headed, so he couldn't have been tired.

I sought out a very great former jockey named Conn Mc-Creary and asked him if he had a theory that would explain Kelso lugging in. He had a theory, and I found it very interesting indeed.

McCreary said, "He lugged in because of something most people don't know about great thoroughbreds unless they ride them. I don't know how many times thoroughbreds did the same thing to me that Kelso did to Milo a minute ago. Let's put it this way: You get in a fight and you land one and the other guy is groggy. You don't stand off and measure him. You crowd him. You get up close and hit him with everything you've got. It's just instinct. You couldn't help it if you tried. And it's the same way with thoroughbreds, especially the great ones. After they pass a horse, they want to crowd him if he's still around and they go in on him. That's the real reason you get so many foul claims in stakes, but nobody ever mentions it. Maybe even a lot of jocks haven't figured out why it happens."

In any event Kelso, who had been hopelessly out of the running a month ago, was now definitely a possibility for an unprecedented fifth term as America's Horse of the Year. You can't decide a championship by a rather dubious fraction of an inch. Gun Bow had to beat Kelso again before he would be accepted as the Horse of 1964. Their next meeting would come on Veteran's Day in November in the Washington, D. C., International at Laurel. The prognosis for Gun Bow was good, mainly because the prognosis for Kelso was poor. The public, along with Mrs. duPont, simply believed, on the basis of three consecutive failures, that the International was a jinx race for Kelso and something would always happen to beat him.

He had one more race before the International and in this he set about as many records as any horse in turf history has ever set in one event. The race was the Jockey Club Gold Cup, run at Aqueduct that year because Belmont was closed. Cup races are marathon events. The Gold Cup is at two miles. Kelso ran the distance in three minutes, 19⅕ seconds to break his own track record and American record. He broke the money-winning record of the world. He broke the all-time record for Cup winners in this country. It was his fifth Gold Cup. Exterminator, the great gelding of the 1920s, had won four Saratoga Cups, a record that had endured for some forty years.

The main rival Kelso faced in the race was the game, under-sized three-year-old Roman Brother, the best small horse in America. Kelso's victory was almost effortless.

The race was run on Halloween and it was a time of trick or treat and wistful autumn sadness. The trick was Kelso's, of course. The treat was the public's—the matchless experience of watching a perfect creature perform at the peak of its perfection. The wistful sadness was inherent in the lengthening shadows of an autumn afternoon, betokening the fact that sunny summer days were gone, that winter waited with frosty breath and the world was growing older. Kelso had grown older, too. Mrs. duPont had announced sadly that this would be his last appearance in New York, scene of his greatest triumphs over half a dozen seasons. He would race later in the International and retire forever. (She changed her mind, of course, the following spring.)

A startling thing happened in this Gold Cup on that autumn afternoon. Kelso had run a mile and three quarters. He was at the quarter pole and into the stretch. The doughty dwarf named Roman Brother had made his run at the champion and was beaten now and Kelso was moving on his own and the fence rails between him and the staggering three-year-old were lengthening. There was no need for cheering, no call to scream, "Come on, Kelly!" in a frenzied crescendo as there had been when Kelso waged his stretch battles with Iron Peg in the Suburban and with Gun Bow in the Aqueduct and the Woodward. Kelso had won the race at the quarter pole beyond all possible dispute.

And then it happened.

First there was a sudden, almost absolute silence among the thousands. Then, as if they were acting on cue, 102,000 hands belonging to 51,000 persons began to clap. It was an awesome sound, one I had never heard before in the United States. It was applause in unison, hands beating rhythmically to Kelso's rhythmic stride. I had heard that sound in Europe, at great concert halls and opera houses, but never at a racetrack. This cadenced clapping is the ultimate accolade that European audiences bestow upon great performances. That this form of acclaim should arise suddenly and unrehearsed from the horse players of Aqueduct was a small and very lovely miracle. It lasted from the quarter pole to the finish line, and when you recognized the depth of human emotion that engendered it, it was as beautiful as music.

I like to get down to Washington for the International a few days early, for the preliminaries are often as interesting as the race itself. The International is one of the great sporting events of the American turf. It was established in 1952 after it was proved that horses could be shipped across the ocean by plane and that the experience did not upset them as much as a long voyage by ship. International matches had been tried over the years. In 1923 Zev beat the great English horse Papyrus in the International Race at Belmont Park. The following year the French champion Epinard came here for a series of three International Specials. He was beaten by Wise Counsellor at Belmont, by Ladkin at Aqueduct and by Sarazen at Latonia, Kentucky. Foreigners quite obviously took the worst of it when they shipped here and the same was true of American horses when they went to Europe. The plane changed that.

John D. Schapiro, president of the Laurel track, just over the Maryland line from Washington, offered numerous inducements to foreign horses. Laurel pays all the traveling expenses of entrants and their handlers. The International is run over a European-type turf course. Up to 1965, it was started from a web barrier, although this is a dubious advantage to any but English horses, since the electric starting gate is used widely throughout Europe, South America, and Japan. And the mile and a half event has a prize of $150,000.

In 1964 the score was even. Foreigners had won six of the twelve runnings.

In 1964, however, the foreign invaders were little more than a Greek chorus background for the two great Americans. The International appeared to be a match race between Kelso and Gun Bow—and it turned out to be exactly that.

The International is surrounded by many social activities. There is a white tie and tails ball. There is a pre-race dinner at which ambassadors of the foreign countries represented by horses in the race are guests. The horses themselves are housed in a segregated part of the stable area called International Village. State-owned Russian horses always try for the International and they are handled by their State-appointed trainer Nikolaevich Dolmatov, a heavily made, square-faced man with bushy black eyebrows who might well play the role of a spy from an Eric Ambler novel. He had Aniline in the race and he would run third, the only Russian ever to receive an official placing. A horse that attracted special attention in 1964 was the Japanese Ryu Forel. Neither his owner Teizo Miyoshi nor his trainer Masaharu Hashimoto spoke a word of English but a Japanese jockey from Canada named "Spud" Uyeyema acted as interpreter. He had little to interpret. Once Miyoshi confided that the "Ryu" in his horse's name meant "a very virile dragon." When anyone asked Miyoshi about his horse, Spud would grin and shake his head when he translated the answer. It was always, "All he say is Ryu hard as rock."

I felt very optimistic as a partisan of Kelso. Hanford had brought him to the most superb condition of his life. That was evident not only in his appearance, but in every move he made. The Old Man was busting out all over with good health and good spirits. And I was encouraged, too, by the sun-parched condition of the turf course. It was harder than the main track.

Two days before the race, Kelso had his final trial and he went in sensational time. I watched it from the backstretch with several European correspondents who had come on for the race. Hanford galloped up to us on his stable pony. He reined his horse and looked down at me, shaking his stopwatch in my face and grinning broadly.

"Now do you think Kelso can run on grass?" he asked.

I didn't have to answer. Colonel Tom Nickalls of London's *Sporting Life* answered for me. "But, Mr. Hanford, it isn't rahlly grahss, is it?" he said.

It wasn't. It was green-dyed dirt with some dry sprigs sticking out of it like porcupine quills.

Mrs. duPont was not encouraged. She was absolutely convinced that this race was a jinx and that something would happen to prevent Kelso from winning. After the race, for a few awful moments, it seemed she might have been right. She was extremely discouraged when Gun Bow drew No. 1 post, absolutely perfect for him. She had wanted Kelso inside of Gun Bow. Kelso drew No. 5 on the dice.

In the race Gun Bow went out at once to make the pace as expected, and Kelso stayed closest to him, as expected. Six furlongs from home, Kelso began to move. Half a mile from home, Kelso collared Gun Bow. They went around the turn locked together, far, far in front of the foreigners. A quarter of a mile from home, Kelso took the lead. From that point to the finish he drew off and off from his rival.

Seldom has one great horse ever asserted his absolute superiority over another great horse as convincingly as Kelso asserted his superiority over Gun Bow in that final quarter-mile.

But it wasn't over. The jinx was still around.

Mrs. duPont and Valenzuela were standing in the winner's circle when Gun Bow's jockey, Walter Blum, claimed a foul. He later admitted frankly that Gun Bow could never have beaten Kelso that day and that he had no hope of his claim being allowed. But when all that money and all that prestige and Horse of the Year honors are at stake, a jockey will clutch at any straw, as Valenzuela himself had done the year before when he claimed foul against Chambers and Mongo. Kelso had moved to the rail when he was well clear of Gun Bow and at that stage Gun Bow, dead tired and beaten, began to jump at shadows. Blum based his faint hope on these facts.

Little Milo again played his paternal role. Mrs. duPont stood there waiting, a smile frozen on her face, a tear coursing down her check, and Milo kept squeezing her arm and saying over and over again, "Our number won't come down. I tell you for sure, our number won't come down."

It didn't.

Kelso was for the fifth time the Horse of the Year and the cheers were heard as far away as Baltimore and Washington.

Kelso returned in 1965, raced six times, won half his races, increased his earnings to $1,977,366 and was finally retired to the farm after being hit in the eye by a clod of dirt in the Stymie Handicap at Aqueduct, which he won by eight lengths. His greatest performance came in the Whitney at Saratoga when he virtually hurled himself under the wire to beat Malicious by a nose. He seemed to be reaching the peak of his form in September when a speck of dirt achieved what neither weight nor age nor prowess of his foemen could accomplish. As 1966 dawned, it seemed possible he might come back again as a nine-year-old.

Carl Hanford says Kelso is the greatest horse in his experience, hastening to add that he never saw Exterminator and Man o' War. Tommy Trotter, secretary and handicapper of the New York Racing Association and official handicapper for the Jockey Club, did not see Exterminator or Man o' War, either, but thinks Kelso is the greatest horse he has known on every count.

I saw both Man o' War and Exterminator race (the latter many times), but I saw Man o' War when I was a child and Exterminator when I was an adolescent, and admittedly I was incapable of mature judgment. Still, I did not think I saw a better horse than either in the long, long post parade between the 1920s and the 1960s when Kelso reached his prime. I am convinced that Kelso is the greatest thoroughbred race horse we have ever known.

Such a judgment cannot be proved, of course. It is entirely subjective and varies with the qualities you seek in a horse. If we could base it on money, Kelso is the richest, but that means nothing, for purses and stakes have doubled, trebled and quadrupled in comparatively recent years. If we could base it on the flat figures of time, Kelso would win hands down because he has run all distances from six furlongs to two miles in faster time than either Man o' War or Exterminator, but tracks today are at least two seconds faster for a mile than they were in the 1920s, and Man o' War's comparative speed figures are the best. The ability to carry weight over a distance of ground may afford a better comparison. Man o' War raced so briefly that he can hardly stand up here. He won under 130 or more (the weight that separates the men from the boys) five times as a two-year-old, but in those races the distance was no more than six furlongs and he was racing under Walter Vosburgh's high weight scale for young horses, which meant others in the field were carrying relatively as much. As a three-year-old he took up 130 or more only three times. His greatest performance was at a mile and a sixteenth under 138 pounds. He carried 135 to victory at a mile and 131 at a mile and three sixteenths.

In eight years of racing and one hundred starts Exterminator won under 130 or more at a mile or more sixteen times. He won once at a mile and a quarter under 138.

In seven years of racing and sixty-two starts Kelso has won over distances of a mile or more under 130 or more twelve times. He has won at a mile under 136 and at a mile and an eighth under the same weight.

Both Man o' War and Exterminator often frightened their most formidable rivals out of races. Today second and third money is so large in the big stakes that the best horses will try for it despite the presence of great conquerors like Kelso. Also, about ten times the number of horses are being foaled today as in the days of Man o' War and Exterminator. That means that you are bound to get more good horses along with more worthless ones. And every one of the best horses of half a dozen racing years have had a try at Kelso—the very best of sixty thousand horses. Some have beaten him, as Gun Bow, Mongo, Carry Back, and Beau Purple did, but in almost every case he has come right back to beat them.

If I were asked to state my reasons for thinking Kelso is the greatest of them all, I wouldn't throw statistics at you, however. I'd simply tell you that I think he's done more things better on more occasions over a longer period of time than any other horse in history.

Or maybe, I'd just say it's because I love him. For after all, it's not the pedigrees and performances of thoroughbreds that have been most important since the little foal arrived during a total eclipse of the sun two centuries ago. It's the effect that horses have had on human beings.

On Gold Cup Day in 1964 when Kelso was supposed to have made his last appearance at Aqueduct, I encountered a stranger as I left the track. He was a fat and wheezy fellow clad in a gaudy South Seas sports shirt, and although the day was cool, he was sweating and he reeked of whiskey.

"You think they're really going to retire him?" he asked. "Hell, they can't do that to me. Hell, it just won't seem like Saturday if Kelso's not around."

He reminded me of somebody, but I was sure I'd never seen him before.

Then I knew.

He made me think of another fat and boozy fellow who had loved a mare named Spiletta two hundred years before.

His name was William Augustus and he was Duke of Cumberland.

Bread and Butter Letter

The *Thoroughbred Record,* the N. Y. *Herald Tribune* and the *Blood Horse* have kindly granted their permission to reprint, in considerably altered form, portions of articles I have written for them over the years. I am especially grateful to the *Thoroughbred Record* for permission to use many rare photographs from their invaluable files, and to Roger Williams III of the *Record* staff, for his help in searching out photographs I required.

William H. P. Robertson, president of the *Thoroughbred Record* Corporation, grew footsore conducting me over broad acres of Kentucky's horse farms during the preparation of this book and patiently answered hundreds of queries regarding forgotten dates and obscure facts. I am more deeply grateful to him, however, for writing *The History of Thoroughbred Racing in America,* which is the classic and definitive study of the turf of the United States and the only one-volume standard reference work on the subject in existence.

I was aided and abetted greatly in my task by the charming and hospitable Mrs. Amelia Buckley, librarian of the great Keeneland collection of racing literature and photographs. Reproductions of many Keeneland photographs appear in these pages.

J. A. Estes, director of the Jockey Club's project at Spindletop Research Center and one of the world's recognized authorities on the thoroughbred, put his five-gaited computers through a trial run for my special benefit.

I was merciless in plucking the long memory of John I. Day, Jr., director of the Service Bureau of the Thoroughbred Racing Associations of America, and I borrowed many of the rare volumes from his fine private library of turf literature.

Betty Moore, a talented turf writer and librarian of the N. Y. *Morning Telegraph,* searched the yellowing files of that ancient sporting sheet time and again for data I required.

Calvin Rainey, formerly a great jockey, now steward for the Jockey Club, supplied me with valuable information about racing in Japan. The New York Racing Association's Pat O'Brien, director of racing, and Sam Kanchuger, press director, were graciously cooperative in obtaining material and pictures that I needed. Lou Weintraub of Photo Communications Service made many photographs especially for this book, as did the brilliant horse photographer, "Skeets" Meadors of Lexington, Ky. Henry Chafetz and Sidney Solomon of the Pageant Book Shop and Cooper Square Publishers spent long hours searching out and purchasing rare books I required.

Robert F. Kelley, of Thomas Deegan Associates and the National Museum of Racing, a distinguished turf journalist, was extremely helpful in many areas of my research. My life-long friends Judge Charles Hatton, columnist Bob Horwood and editor Saul Rosen, all of the *Morning Telegraph,* were always available to confirm or correct my memories of racing events of the recent past.

Most of all, I owe a debt of gratitude to the hundreds of horsemen and thousands of horses I have known since that day in 1915 when I perched on my father's shoulder to watch Regret win the Kentucky Derby. They have added greatly to the sum of my existence.

Index

California Racing Board, 228-29
Calumet Farms, 130, 151-52, 234
Camel, 262-63
Campbell, Jack, 282
Canfield, Richard, 250
Carlaris, 87
Carleton, Sir John, 196
Carrus, André, 219
Carry Back, 3, 131, 246, 300
Cartout, Jacques, 213, 215
Cassidy, Mars, 8
Cavanaugh, John, 63
Chambers, Wayne, 277
Chance, 42
Changeling's Dam, 24
Chantilly, Forest of, 215-18
Chaplin, Charlie, 77
Charles I, King of England, 195-96
Charles II, King of England, 4, 23, 101-
    102, 194, 199
  as jockey, 163, 176
Charles Town Racetrack, 15
Charteris, Sir Evan, 32
Chateaugay, 3
Cheney, Christopher T., 154
Chesapeake, 157
Cheveley Park, 196-99
Chicken-Fry Ben, 248-49
Chinn, Colonel Phil, 223
Chronicle, San Francisco, 56
Church, Norman, 59, 64-66
Churchill, Sir Winston, 206
Churchill Downs, 142, 153
Citation, 129-36, 145, 152, 261, 284
Claiborne Farm, 235, 264
Clark, Ambrose, 139
Clore, Charles, 252
Clydesdale horse, the, 22
Cob horse, the, 22-23, 196
Coffroth Handicap, 90
Coffroth, Sunny Jim, 87
Cohn, Harry, 82
Cole, Ashley Trimble, 242
Colin, 131

Conductor, 124
Connolly, Walter, 69
Conway, Jack, 97
Coogan, Jackie, 77
Cook, Theodore Andrea, 45
Corsican, 199
Corum, Bill, 153
Cow pony, the, 112
Cowell, W., 197-98
Craft's Partner, 21
Crash, 136
Cream de Barble, 202
Cripple, 107
Crosby, Bing, 69, 76, 186
Crozer, Allaire. *See* du Pont, Mrs.
    Richard C.
Culchett, Benjamin, 202
Cumberland, William Augustus, Duke
    of, biography, 16-21, 31-34
  and Eclipse, 5, 11-13, 35, 49
  and horse racing, 14, 192, 196, 202, 300
  and thoroughbred horse, 19-20, 26-30,
    33, 45, 52-53
Curran, Bobby, 94
Curwen's Bay Barb, 25
Cypron, 20-21, 23

Daly, Father Bill, 170-172
Damask, 126
D'Arcy Grey Royal Mare, 102
D'Arcy Yellow Turk, the, 25
D'Arcy's Royal Mare, 102
Darley, American. *See* Lexington
Darley Arabian, the, 13, 20-21, 25-28, 45
  and Eclipse, 35, 36
  and Kelso, 262-64
  and Lexington, 114
  at Narragansett, 99
  and thoroughbred horse, 106-108
Davison, Emily, 6
Day, John I., 249
De Bloch, Henri, 225
Decidedly, 162

New York Turf Writers' Association, 84
Newmarket Challenge Whip, 48, 90
Newmarket Heath, 4-5, 28, 192-201
    races, 4, 21
Newminster, 262
Niccols, Richard, 101-102, 104
Nickalls, Colonel Tom, 297
No Robbery, 8-9, 37
Noble, Heather, 135, 260-61
Norfolk, 117-18, 210-11
Northern Dancer, 154, 161-62

Oakley, John, 37
Obert, Uncle Bill, 169
O'Brien, Chicago, 8, 57, 139, 146, 249
O'Brien, Pat, 69, 76
O'Connor, Winnie, 167-68, 171-72
Oglethorpe Arabian, the, 25
O'Hara, Cle, 93, 98, 99
O'Hara, Walter, 91-99, 232
O'Kelly, Dennis, 29, 37-49
Old Bones. *See* Exterminator
Old Mets, the, 138
Olden Times, 283
One Bold Bid, 238
Options, 58
Oral system, 62-63
Oriental horse. *See* Arabs, Turks, Barbs
Orléans, Duc d', 217

Pageboy, 9
Palmer, Joe H., 255
Palmer, Mrs. Mary Cole, 255
Papyrus, 295
Pardal, 198
Pari-mutuel system, 58, 63
Park Jefferson, 119
Parr, Major Ral, 146-47
Parrish, J. W., 122
Parsons, Louella, 77-78
Patchen Wilkes Farm, 251-52
Paul Jones, 146-47

Payson, Mrs. Charles Shipman, 246
Pensive, 152
Percy-Gray laws, 105
Pettingill, Judge C. H., 125
Phil, Pittsburgh, 57, 139
Pimlico Futurity, 261
Pimlico Racetrack, 179
Pimlico Special, 131
Pitt, William, 19, 32-33
Place's White Turk, 24-25
Plesh, Mme. Arpad, 198
Politicians and horse racing, 14-16, 21,
    137, 240
Pollard, Agnes, 168, 181-83, 186
Pollard, Johnny (Red), 168, 177-190
Ponder, 152
Porter, Dr. Robert A., 255
Poseidon, 104
Pot-8-0's, 31, 262
Preakness, 161
Press, New York, 248
Price, Jack, 3, 131
Prix du Jockey Club, 177, 218
Prudery, 148
Psidium, 198
Purner, Fred, 67-68, 73
Putnam, George, 56

Quarter horse, the, 112
Quickly, 263
Quicksilver, 107
Quinn, Robert, 6-7, 95-97

Rabelais, 218
Races: Canadian: Hendrie Memorial,
    134
    Kenilworth Gold Cup, 126
  English: Ascot Gold Cup, 174, 208-13
    Epsom Derby, 5, 6, 47, 107, 192, 198
    Grand National, 104-105
    King's Plate, 43
    Newmarket Heath, 4, 21

Racetracks: United States *(cont.)*
    Saratoga, 125, 239, 286
    Sheepshead Bay, 110
    Tanforan, 58-59, 62, 65
    Tropical Park, 2
    Union Course, 110, 115, 121-23
    Woodward, 274-75
Racing silks, 30
Raft, George, 77
Randolph, John, 122
Ranger, 103-104, 195
Ras el Fedowa. *See* Darley Arabian, the
Redd, Colonel Dick, 237
Reel, 118
Regret, 147, 156-57
Regulus, 22, 27, 44
Rey El Rio, 120
Rey El Santa Anita, 71
Rey El Tierra, 120
Ribot, 135-36
Rice, Grantland, 153
Rich, Bernie, 77
Richards, Keene, 118
Riddle, Sam, 127, 134
Rienzi, 113
Roach, Hal, 65-68
Rockingham Park, 75
Rolled Stocking, 122
Roman Brother, 294
Romanet, Jean, 213
Rooney, Mickey, 78-79
Roosevelt, Franklin Delano, 95
Rosemont, 179
Rothschild, Baron, 214-15
Rothstein, Arnold, 9-10, 45-46, 138-39
Rotz, Johnny, 37
Round Course Racetrack, 101-102, 192, 199
Round Table, 268, 274
Rowlandson, 37, 45
Royal Ascot. *See* Ascot
Royal Flush, 249
Royal Hunt Cup, 206, 208
Royal Mares, 4, 24, 27, 102

Rubio, 105
Runyon, Damon, 153, 248-249
Russell, Lillian, 138, 172
Rysdyk's Hambletonian, 112
Ryu Forel, 296

Saggy, 3, 131
Sahri II, 175
Saint-Martin, Yves, 170, 214, 218, 277
St. Simon, 218
St. Victor's Barb, 25
Saliva test, 222-27
Sande, Earl, 164, 166-67
Sande, Handy Guy, 138
Sanford family, 246, 248
Sanford race, 247
Santa Anita Handicap, 86, 166, 179, 186
Santa Anita Racetrack, 53, 61, 66-69, 75-84, 231
    and Ascot, 203, 242
    and Doc Strub, 52, 59-60, 69-75
    See also Turf Club
Saracen horse, the, 22
Saratoga Cup, 294
Saratoga Racetrack, 125, 243-44, 286
Sarazen, 295
Sartorius, 81, 265
Saxon Chronicles, 194
Scott, General Winfield, 119
Seabiscuit, 83, 84, 166, 168, 178-81, 183, 185-90
Sedbury Royal Mare, 102
Sefar ha-Razim, 101
Seminole Handicap, 132
Shakespeare, 44-45
Shapiro, John D., 295-96
Shark, 107-109
Shaw, Tom, 139, 249
Sheridan, General Phil, 113
Shipman, Evan, 135, 228
Shire, 22
Shock, 28
Shockley, Clarence, 175
Shoemaker, Willie, 154, 161, 166

Silverspur, Jack, 48-49
Singleton, John, 37
Sir Archie, 115, 121-22
Sir Barton, 126
Sir Gaylord, 154-55
Sir Henry, 121
Sir Mostyn's Jigg, 21
Sister to Miss Partner, 24
Sister to Old Country Wench, 5, 27
Skouras, Nick, 81
Sloan, Cash, 174
Sloan, Ted, 167, 172-74
Sloane, Isabel Dodge, 259
Smith, Red, 153
Smith, Richard Stafford, 197
Smith, Tom, 185
Smith's Son of Snake, 27, 108
Société d' Encouragement pour l' Amé-
    lioration des Races de Chevaux
    en France, 177, 213, 217
Somerset, Charles, Duke of, 202
Son-in-Law, 80
Spendthrift, 124
Spiletta, 5, 27, 31, 33, 44, 262
Sporting Life, 297
Squirt, 5, 27, 29, 45, 262, 264
Stagehand, 166, 179
Standardbreds. *See* Trotters
Stanford, Leland, 58
Star, Pawtucket, 94
Star-Tribune, Pawtucket, 94, 96-97
Stefan the Great, 263
Stephanie, 263
Strickling, Howard, 79
Strub, Bob, 72
Strub, Doc, 50-58, 69-73, 81-82, 84
    and Santa Anita, 64-68, 91, 92, 231
Stuart, Prince Charles Edward, 18, 30
Stubbs, George, 34
Stud Books, 106-108
Stuyvesant Handicap, 249
Stymie Handicap, 298
Suburban, 138, 270, 282-85
Suffolk Punch, 22

Sullivan, Frank, 245
Sullivan, Yankee, 250
Sultan, 118
Sun Beau, 127
Sun Briar, 128
Swaps, 3, 117
Sweepstakes, 107
Swift, Jonathan, 202
Swope, Herbert Bayard, 10, 138

Tanforan, 58, 62
Tarol, Fred, 171
Tartar, 20-21
Tattersall, 109
Teizo Miyoshi, 296
Ten Broeck, 115, 157
Ten Broeck, Richard, 115-17
Tenney Meshach, 3, 162
Tetrarch, the, 263
Thoroughbred Racing Associations, 85
Thoroughbred Record, 254
Thoroughbreds, 6, 13-14, 23-30, 52-53,
    70, 162-63
    definition of, 106-107
    and humans, 261
Thorp, Tom, 170
Tia Juana Racetrack, 87-88, 183
Tim Tam, 152
Time, 178
Timoleon, 115
Tom Fool, 235-36
Tompkins, Daniel, 123
Toney, Black, 150
Touchstone, 31, 262-63
Toulouse-Lautrec, 6
Tout, derivation of, 40-41
Tra. *See* Thoroughbred Racing Associ-
    ation
Tranel, 218
Traveller, 103
Travers, 247, 251
Trentham, 107
Tribune, Providence, 94